NOV   2007

HUGO CHÁVEZ

HUGO
CHÁVEZ

Cristina Marcano and
Alberto Barrera Tyszka

TRANSLATED BY KRISTINA CORDERO

INTRODUCTION BY MOISÉS NAÍM

 RANDOM HOUSE NEW YORK

Published in the United States by Random House,
an imprint of The Random House Publishing Group,
a division of Random House, Inc., New York.

RANDOM HOUSE and colophon are registered
trademarks of Random House, Inc.

This work was originally published in Spanish by Debate,
an imprint of Editorial Sudamerican, a division of
Random House Mondadori, Argentina, in 2004 as *Hugo
Chávez sin uniforme*. An updated edition, also in Spanish,
was published by Random House Mondadori, Spain, in
2006. The English translation published herein is based
on the 2006 edition.

LIBRARY OF CONGRESS CATALOGING-IN-PUBLICATION DATA

Marcano, Cristina.
　　[Hugo Chávez sin uniforme. English]
　　Hugo Chávez: the definitive biography of Venezuela's
controversial president / by Cristina Marcano and
Alberto Barrera Tyszka; translated by Kristina Cordero.
　　　　p.　cm.
　　Includes bibliographical references and index.
　　ISBN 978-0-679-45666-7
　1. Chávez Frías, Hugo.　2. Venezuela—History—
1974–1999.　3. Venezuela—History—1999–　4. Presidents—
Venezuela—Biography.　I. Tyszka, Alberto Barrera.
II. Cordero, Kristina.　III. Title.

　　F2328.52.C48M3713　2007
　　987.06'42092—dc22　　　2007010041
　　[B]

Printed in the United States of America on acid-free paper

www.atrandom.com

9 8 7 6 5 4 3 2 1

FIRST U.S. EDITION

Title page photo by Jesús Castillo
Book design by Barbara M. Bachman

I put for a general inclination of all mankind a perpetual and restless desire of power after power, that ceaseth only in death. And the cause of this is not always that a man hopes for a more intensive delight than he has already attained to, or that he cannot be content with a moderate power, but because he cannot assure the power and means to live well, which he hath present, without the acquisition of more.

—*Thomas Hobbes*

CONTENTS

I**T IS ALWAYS A BIT OF A GAMBLE TO ATTEMPT A BIOGRAPHICAL ACCOUNT** of someone who is still alive and who, moreover, plays an active and prominent role in current affairs. The task is even trickier when your objective is neither to sing praise nor issue judgments, when you wish neither to sanctify nor condemn—when you are not trying to turn your subject into the victim of your own premeditated, malicious intentions.

At the other end of the spectrum lies the illusion of objectivity. Thanks to Georg Lichtenberg, ever since the end of the eighteenth century, we have known that "even impartiality is partial." It would be foolish of us to try to deceive our readers into thinking that as the authors of this book we have no opinion, that we feel an academic indifference for the character that has inspired these pages.

Our biography of Hugo Chávez represents an effort to contribute a certain amount of complexity to a process that many people seem determined to simplify. The polarization that the president of Venezuela generates, both in and out of Venezuela, reflects the complex and very broad range of feelings he tends to inspire in people. It is almost impossible to observe him without being affected by the strong sentiments of those who alternately idolize and demonize him.

We chose to assess this reality by writing the story of a man's life in the manner of journalists, basing our research on the testimonies of a number of people who have been at his side during different periods in his life. Some of these people have stood by him, whereas others have distanced themselves and now count themselves among the opposition. Through a labyrinth of different paths, this work also led us to a great deal of written material, including the president's own personal diaries and a small sliver of correspondence from his early years. However, more than a linear narrative, this book offers something of a choral dynamic, a collective construction of the experience of Hugo Chávez Frías.

We would like express our gratitude to all the people we interviewed and who agreed to work with us, people who offered us both their time and their trust. We would like to thank the journalist Fabiola Zerpa, our assistant in this endeavor, whose contributions were invaluable. And Gloria Majella Bastidas and Ricardo Cayuela, always precise and lucid in their reading and comments.

Cristina Marcano
Alberto Barrera Tyszka

J ANETTA MORTON LIVES ABOUT A HALF HOUR AWAY FROM THE WHITE House. Not that she has ever been there. The unemployed single mother of two girls shares a small house with her sister in one of the poorest neighborhoods in Washington, D.C. Morton does not know much about Hugo Chávez. But for her, the Venezuelan president is a hero. "I wish George W. Bush was like him," she says. Morton is one of the 1.2 million poor Americans who get discounted heating fuel for their homes from CITGO, an Oklahoma-based oil company owned by the Venezuelan government. She also got a glossy brochure explaining that this was just an act of basic human solidarity from a president that cares for the poor everywhere, not just in his native Venezuela. "This is not about politics," the brochure said.

In South Africa, President Chávez also has admirers. In Soweto, a poor neighborhood in Johannesburg, political activists enthusiastically follow Chávez's Bolivarian Revolution, and some of them were invited to Venezuela to see it firsthand and even to meet with the president. They too say that they would like a leader like Hugo Chávez for their country. In Lebanon, some Hezbollah supporters have named their newborn sons Hugo.

Andres Oppenheimer, a syndicated columnist for *The Miami Herald,* traveled to India in January 2007 to interview business leaders, politicians, and others about that nation's profound transformation. One of his stops offered quite a surprise. Reporting from New Delhi, Oppenheimer writes:

I happened to be giving a talk at the Jawaharlal Nehru University here the day that Venezuelan President Hugo Chávez announced the nationalization of key industries. I thought the news would help me make the case that Chávez is destroying Venezuela's economy. How wrong I was!

Far from applauding, the professors and students at the School of International Studies—a major recruiting ground for foreign service officials—were looking at me with a mixture of anthropological curiosity and disbelief. It was obvious that, for most of them, Chávez was a hero. . . .

"How many of you think Chávez is doing a lot of good for Venezuela?" I asked my audience. Most of the students raised their hands.

"Why do you think that?" I asked. A doctoral student named Jagpal, who is doing his thesis on Venezuela, said that Chávez had put an end to a corrupt economic and political elite, and had focused the government's attention on the poor.

Janetta Morton, the Soweto activists, the Lebanese parents, and the Indian university students are only four examples of a rare and far wider phenomenon: a Latin American political leader who becomes a household name and a global icon.

It is a rare phenomenon because Hugo Chávez is the only Latin American politician in the past half century who has been able to acquire the type of worldwide name recognition and star power enjoyed by Ernesto "Che" Guevara and Fidel Castro.

How did this happen? How did a poor boy, born and raised in Sabaneta, a small city deep inside Los Llanos ("the plains") of a country mostly known to the rest of the world for its oil and beauty queens, grow up to become almost as well known as—and far more admired than—the president of the United States? What does Hugo Chávez have that other leaders in Latin America or any other poor region in the world don't have?

The answers to these questions provide interesting clues not just about Chávez the man; they also reveal interesting trends in the politics and economics of the world in the early years of the twenty-first century.

Of course, Hugo Chávez's personal history is the earliest source of hints about his surprising performance. And herein lies the importance of this biography by Cristina Marcano and Alberto Barrera Tyszka, two of Venezuela's best journalists, who produced this carefully reported and objective narrative of Chávez's life as he approached his fiftieth birthday. Marcano and Barrera eschew easy generalizations and facile conclusions about the nature of the man and his motives. They are careful not to rely on psychological speculations or pass political judgments about a man whose personal charisma and polarizing decisions have made it so hard for most commentators to retain objectivity and balance. But their dogged reporting and interviews with crucial individuals in Chávez's life do yield interesting insights about this perplexing, contradictory leader. Readers will find interesting links between his past and his present and perhaps even his future and that of his political career.

Personal histories, as we know, are shaped by the places and times in which they occur. In an increasingly connected and interdependent world, they are also shaped by what is going on elsewhere. And sometimes "elsewhere" can be very far away. Afghanistan, for example, is very far from Venezuela. So is Iraq. Yet Hugo Chávez's performance and possibilities are closely intertwined with events in these places located at Venezuela's antipodes or to the events in lower Manhattan on September 11, 2001. For many reasons unrelated to Chávez, he turned out to be one of the main beneficiaries of the terrorist attacks of 9/11 against the United States. Not that he had anything to do with the attacks. But partly as a consequence of 9/11, oil prices more than doubled—and sent a tsunami of petrodollars to the coffers of the Venezuelan government.

Moreover, 9/11 also focused the American superpower almost exclusively on Islamic terrorism and on waging wars in faraway places. Leaders in the United States had no time to pay much attention to what was going on in their traditional geopolitical backyard, Latin America. Chávez deftly exploited this distraction. In addition, President George W. Bush's decisions, rhetoric, and demeanor boosted anti-American sentiments worldwide to levels that may well be unprecedented. The Venezuelan president was ready, even eager, to seize the moment and become the world's most strident critic of the U.S. president.

Chávez was not just well positioned—financially and politically— to take advantage of these global trends; he was also ready to boldly act on his instincts. He understood very quickly that the emperor had no clothes and that challenging the American "empire" and its internationally unpopular leader was a sure bet. He could afford the gamble thanks to the oil money that had made Venezuela less reliant on foreign investors, U.S. credits, or aid. President Chávez calculated that insulting the American president carried low risks and would yield huge political benefits at home and abroad. Not even Osama bin Laden or Saddam Hussein had said in front of the cameras—or the United Nations—what the Venezuelan president says about George W. Bush. "Drunkard," "asshole," "coward," "thug," "assassin," "baby killer," and "genocidal war-criminal" are just some of the names that President Chávez regularly calls his American counterpart. Most of the world smiles and privately (and often not that privately) shares the negative feelings about one of the most disdained U.S. presidents in recent history. From Moscow to Malawi, the anti-Bush antics of Hugo Chávez are part of the regular fare of the evening news.

But Hugo Chávez has not just been bold abroad; he has also been daring at home. There he detected another emperor who had no clothes: the traditional Venezuelan power elite. And, once again, he boldly acted on that instinct. He gambled on the possibility that the political parties, business conglomerates, media tycoons, oil-industry executives, and labor oligarchs that had called the shots for half a century in Venezuela were weak and vulnerable. He realized that the country's power structure was ready for a hostile takeover. Further, he discovered that this takeover could be based on ballots, not bullets.

And that in the twenty-first century in a country like Venezuela, democracy could be used to acquire enormous powers not afforded to democratically elected presidents elsewhere.

In the opinion of some, the almost dictatorial powers acquired by Hugo Chávez are being put to good use. He needs the power to redress the injustices wrought by centuries of abuse against the poor and the powerless. To others, this is not different from any other authoritarian episode in a region where they have been all too common.

So, is Hugo Chávez a democrat committed to helping the poor, or just an old-school, power-grabbing populist? Once again, in the answers to these questions lie interesting clues about larger trends in Latin America and elsewhere. But the answers, of course, depend not only on political and economic circumstances. They also depend on Chávez, the man.

As Marcano and Barrera's reporting shows, Hugo Chávez has harbored grand, enduring ambitions since he was a very young man. "One day I will be the president of this country," he told an incredulous friend during a road trip when they were both in their early twenties. ("I told him he was drunk," the friend recalls.) This book also documents how from a very young age, crude Communist ideas, plotting against "the system," and becoming "someone that really matters in this country" were permanent drivers of Chávez's behavior. These thoughts have not gone away. In fact, they have grown larger. For example, the now middle-aged president is obviously no longer satisfied to be someone who matters in Venezuela. He is already living that dream. Now he clearly hopes to be "someone who matters in the world." And that dream too is becoming a reality.

Unchecked access to a rich national treasury and the ability to spend it at his own discretion anywhere in the world have certainly helped President Chávez become an influential international figure. But his influence is not only driven by the money. It is also fed by the allure of his personal story and his irreverent, made-for-TV style. And, very important, his political message has also hit a global nerve that makes him internationally relevant.

Chávez identifies themes that have political resonance beyond Venezuela. His denunciations of corruption, economic inequality, and social exclusion have been constant fixtures of his rhetoric. He was early in detecting that these perennial themes had acquired renewed political potency in the 1990s, and he very effectively made them the pillars of his political message at home. He soon realized that his themes had strong echoes elsewhere and that political leaders in other countries who adopted them made great strides in popularity. In many countries, fighting for equality became more important than promoting prosperity, fighting corruption became a larger goal than defending democracy, and fighting social exclusion became far more important than boosting economic efficiency.

The messages that helped propel Hamas to electoral victory in Palestine or Mahmoud Ahmadinejad in Iran, for example, bear a striking resemblance to those that Chávez had been stridently hammering for a decade. The same ideas are fueling the popularity of countless politicians in Central and Eastern Europe, parts of Asia, and all of Latin America. Of course, they differ in context and nuance; religion, for example, weighs far more heavily in local politics in the Middle East than in Latin America. But despite their differences, what these successful politicians have in common is the ability to persuade the electorate that they are better than their rivals at listening to the poor, fighting public corruption, correcting longstanding inequities, or delivering food subsidies and social services, especially health and education. Their more concrete promises are far more powerful drivers of electoral support than the allure of the larger geopolitical struggles in which these politicians are also engaged. President Ahmadinejad in Iran was elected because he was seen as the honest and competent mayor of Tehran, not because Iranian voters were looking for a president who would wipe out Israel or build a nuclear bomb. Voters care more about getting a job or a cash subsidy, or ousting thieving politicians, than about the latest real or imagined threat coming from the devilish American superpower.

Such similarities and their lessons, however, become invisible if the political dominance achieved by Hugo Chávez in Venezuela is written off as the inevitable—and probably fleeting—outcome of a flamboyant strongman with too much oil money. To critics, what happened in Venezuela is as obvious as it was predictable: Chávez's popularity is the inevitable product of a population won over with oil money and mesmerized by the siren songs of a populist. Much of this is, of course, true. In the last election Chávez won, in December 2006, his campaign showed no compunction about freely tapping into government coffers or using public assets. The violations of electoral laws, tolerated by a compliant electoral arbiter whose members could never have gotten their jobs without Chávez's personal approval, were myriad. Indeed some were even televised, as when the head of PDVSA, the state-owned oil company, was caught on video announcing to PDVSA workers that those who did not support the "maximum leader" and the "revolution" risked losing their jobs. The next day President Chávez reiterated the threat, saying that he hoped the oil company's boss would repeat it "not once, but a thousand times a day."

Prior to the election an Associated Press survey showed that 57 percent of Venezuelans were concerned about facing reprisals for the way they would vote. Soon after being elected, Chávez named the former head of the electoral authority as his vice president, explaining that his new cabinet needed to reflect the even more radical orientation that his revolution would take in the new term. This appointment—and the revolutionary zeal exhibited by the new vice president—confirmed widespread suspicions that the electoral arbiter in Venezuela's hotly contested elections was not exactly a paradigm of impartiality. After appointing his new cabinet, the reelected President Chávez announced sweeping changes to the Constitution, including no limits to his future reelection; forced the compliant National Assembly to grant him the power to enact laws by decree; and instituted the nationalization of oil, telecommunications, and electricity.

But it would be a mistake to conclude that Chávez's victory in 2006 was solely driven by unfair play and abuse. He would have probably won even without resorting to dirty tricks, albeit with a far smaller margin. And why not? Thanks to booming oil revenues and an equally booming public debt, Venezuela, with a population of only 26 million, has received revenues estimated at $175 billion. And President Chávez has not been shy in spending this windfall, especially on social programs targeting the poor. But this is hardly a first for Venezuela, and cannot by itself explain Chávez's popularity.

Indeed, an oil boom that boosts government revenues, which in turn are spent on social programs that alleviate poverty, is not an unprecedented event in Venezuela—nor in other oil-producing countries. According to the Wesleyan University professor Francisco Rodriguez, the last time this happened in Venezuela was between 1996 and 1998, just before Chávez took power, when, thanks to higher oil prices and government spending, poverty dropped from 64.3 percent to 43.9 percent. Professor Rodriguez, writing in *Foreign Policy* online magazine in 2006, concluded that, on the basis of the data available at the time, "there is little or no evidence that Chávez is finally sharing Venezuela's oil wealth with the poor. Most existing statistics do not show significant improvements in either the well-being or the share of resources directed at Venezuela's most disadvantaged citizens." This surprising finding contradicts not only Chávez's propaganda but also the claims of critics who argue that his popularity has been simply bought with oil money. Indeed, if all it takes to buy political support is to spend oil money, why were Chávez's predecessors so inept at capitalizing on their own populist policies that they are now political pariahs? Why were the political effects of their social spending so meager and fleeting? In contrast, one of Chávez's main political achievements is the level of support he still enjoys despite the fact that, after all his years in power, dire social problems persist and some, like crime, have only gotten worse. Obviously there is more at work sustaining Chávez's popularity among Venezuelans than government spending.

For starters, it is important to recognize that Hugo Chávez is one of the most astute politicians in power today in Latin America. In the long run his economic policies will surely hurt the material well-being of most Venezuelans, and his authoritarian behavior is clearly eroding the basic political freedoms that the country enjoyed for decades. The damages inflicted by the cult of personality, institutional devastation, and militarization of Venezuela's political life will take years to repair. But to a majority of poor Venezuelans, none of this matters. For them, Hugo Chávez is the leader who provides what no other before him gave them: a sense that he cares deeply, almost personally, for each one of them. A large number of Venezuelans voted for Chávez not as the lesser of several evils but as their leader, one who speaks to their wants and needs. "He cares about people like me." "He represents me." "Even if my situation has not gotten better, at least I know he is trying." These are the phrases one hears in the barrios across Venezuela.

But Chávez is reinforced by his clever exploitation of the three themes that drive the political behavior of most Venezuelans: the need to wage war against corruption, inequality, and injustice.

These are far from new problems for Venezuela or Latin America. Indeed, they have been the fodder of many electoral campaigns, revolutions, and political movements. But during the 1990s Latin Americans' historic tolerance for dramatic economic inequities and the thievery by their elites began to abate thanks to the heightened awareness brought about by political and economic globalization. People's impatience was also fueled by the disappointments with the pro-business, market-oriented reforms known as "the Washington Consensus" (trade and foreign investment liberalization, privatization, deregulation, etc). The promise at the time was that these economic reforms, while initially painful, were the ticket to imminent prosperity. Instead, what most Latin Americans got for more than a decade were financial crashes, higher unemployment, mediocre economic growth, and, thanks to freer, more ubiquitous media, a daily window into how the rich lived and the politicians stole. Corruption—widespread, persistent, and cruelly damaging to the poor—became an obsession everywhere. And the war on corruption was corrupted by politicians who used it as a weapon to sink rivals. In this they were joined by media owners and journalists who found in the war against corruption a never-ending source of profits, power, and personal advancement. Becoming a corruption fighter was—and still often is—a tool more effective for making money and gaining political influence than for ridding society of the conditions that make corruption endemic.

Chávez rode to power in 1998 on an anticorruption, antiestablishment platform. Far from eliminating corruption, he succeeded in bringing down the old corrupt order only to put in place a new one, the so-called *boliburguesia,* short for "Bolivarian bourgeoisie." This was formed by a coterie of family and friends of the Chávez regime known for their conspicuous consumption, luxurious homes, private jets, and megayachts. (During Chávez's reign Venezuela has become once again one of the world's top markets for business jets, and eighty new Rolls-Royces have been sold in the last couple of years alone.) Surprisingly, this has hardly alienated Chávez's core supporters. The poor who support him believe that "their" president cares not about money or power, but only about helping them. Chávez is more preacher than politician, and the hallmarks of his approach to corruption and the twin ills of social exclusion and economic inequality are his almost religious, missionary zeal and moralistic discourse. By his own account, Chávez is Jean Valjean fighting the evil Javert in a twenty-first-century version of *Les Misérables.* The social welfare programs he never ceases to tout are aptly called "missions." The multiple *misiones*—all of which have colorful names derived from Venezuelan history and folklore—offer everything from subsidized groceries to stipends for those who enroll in the incipient Bolivarian universities. In typical populist fashion, Chávez eschews political parties and intermediary institutions, taking his message directly to "the people" through his weekly TV talk show, *Aló, Presidente.*

The Venezuelan president has also been an early and enthusiastic adopter of GoNgos (Governmental-Nongovernmental Organizations). The government funds and controls these "nongovernmental organizations," a powerful new political tool that the Venezuelan president has effectively deployed at home and in other countries where he is trying to build support for his agenda. In this, President Chávez was again early in taking advantage of two global trends of the 1990s: the disrepute of political parties and the popularity of "civil society" and nongovernmental organizations. Throughout the hemisphere, nongovernmental organizations that are aligned with Chávez's politics or that explicitly support him and his Bolivarian revolution are direct or indirect beneficiaries of his cunning largesse. The Zapatistas in Mexico, the *piqueteros* in Argentina, Sem Terra in Brazil, the *cocaleros* in Bolivia, indigenous groups in the Andes, and myriad other "social movements" that are formally unrelated to political parties have received the president's enthusiastic support. Even in the United States, Bolivarian Circles patterned after those operating in the Venezuelan barrios are sprouting on college campuses and in inner cities. Well-subsidized opportunities to travel to Venezuela to attend short "experiential" courses offered by the new "Bolivarian University" that give Americans a chance to learn about the revolution's progress are promoted by nongovernmental organizations, churches, and YMCA branches in the United States. Meanwhile, in Venezuela the Chávez-controlled National Assembly has been actively considering a law whereby officials and members of local nongovernmental organizations that receive funding from any foreign organization will face criminal charges and long prison sentences.

While some of these practices are offensive to a substantial segment of Venezuela's society, they are applauded by the majority, which has given Hugo Chávez a political blank check. Through a variety of means—from his TV shows to the *misiones* and a well-funded, world-class propaganda machine with access to the best international talent money can buy—Chávez puts a name and a face on the anonymity of poverty. He makes virtues out of misfortune and inequality while demonizing wealth and its pursuit. The net effect is the perception among many that Chávez has brought "dignity" to the poor and the excluded, who constitute the majority of Venezuelans. Therein lies the key to understanding Chávez's popularity. It helps that oil prices have allowed his spending to keep apace with many of his programs. It also helps that all Venezuelans learn early in school and through the media that theirs is a very rich country and that therefore the only possible explanation for the widespread poverty is not bad policies but the bad morals and corruption of the political and business classes. Put an honest man in power and the country's wealth will almost effortlessly enrich everyone, goes the deeply rooted thinking that Chávez so brilliantly exploits. It helps that the political opposition in Venezuela is inchoate and leaderless and that the United States is unpopular, clumsy, and distracted. But none of these trends in Venezuela and abroad can really explain Chávez's political ascendancy. For that one needs to look at the man himself and his almost incredible life history—a history that the pages ahead tell very well.

PART ONE

CHAPTER 1

The Revolution Has Arrived

O N THE NIGHT OF DECEMBER 6, 1998, A LARGE CROWD GATHERED IN front of the Teatro Teresa Carreño, close to the center of Caracas. The atmosphere was festive. Moments earlier, the National Electoral Council had read the first official bulletin of the day's election results. With 64 percent of the votes counted, there was no longer room for doubt. Fifty-six percent of the Venezuelan electorate had voted for Hugo Chávez, while his principal opponent, Henrique Salas Römer, a coalition candidate representing the traditional political parties, had garnered only 39 percent of the vote. Venezuela now had a new president, a man who had tried to reach the presidency scarcely six years earlier by attempting to overthrow the government. What had been unattainable by military uprising in 1992 became reality via the democratic process. He was not a career politician, nor did he have any experience in the public sector. And he was barely forty-four years old, much younger than the average age of the presidents who had preceded him. Invoking the memory of the Latin American liberator Simón Bolívar, Chávez vowed to end corruption and democratize the oil business, and he expressed his dream of a country free of poverty. And from deep within the shadows, he dragged out one of Latin America's mustiest ghosts: revolution.

Though on the surface it may have seemed otherwise, December 6, 1998, marked the fulfillment of a deeply rooted obsession of the newly elected president. As his childhood friend Federico Ruiz recalls, on December 31 of 1982 or 1983, Hugo Chávez decided to take a day trip from the city of Maracay to Barinas, some 525 kilometers from Caracas, to visit their mothers and give their families a surprise New Year's hug. Five hours there and five hours back, at least.

"It was just the two of us, in a Dodge Dart he had, passing a bottle of rum back and forth," Ruiz recalls. Of their very lengthy conversations, one moment remains crystal clear in Ruiz's memory. "He said, 'You know something? One day I'm going to be president of the republic.' And I said, 'Damn! Well, you can name me minister of, of . . . I don't know!' And then we joked around about it." Clarifying that this was not an idle comment made during a lull in the conversation nor due to an alcohol-infused bravado, Ruiz adds, "Hugo was very serious when he said that."

Of course he was serious. He was dead serious. This wasn't the first time the idea had popped into his friend's head. As a nineteen-year-old cadet in the military academy, Chávez had marched in a procession shortly after Carlos Andrés Pérez had been elected to his first term as president of the republic (1974–79). The moment established an unforeseen link between the two men, though it is entirely probable that Pérez walked past the young Chávez without giving him a second thought. Why on earth would Pérez have bothered to think that this cadet, who hadn't even graduated from the military academy, would one day conspire against him during his second term as president by staging a violent military coup against his government? How on earth could Pérez have ever imagined that this young soldier would become president of Venezuela one day? Young Hugo, on the other hand, had a very different experience of this moment. On March 13, 1974, he wrote in his diary, "After waiting a long time, the new president finally arrived. When I see him I hope that one day I will be the one to bear the responsibility of an entire Nation, the Nation of the great Bolívar."[1]

Twenty-four years later, he had finally done it. Most Venezuelans, however, were probably not aware of the fervent determination that had driven him for so long. Chávez had taken care not to publicize these aspirations. In a 1999 interview, Mempo Giardinelli and Carlos

Monsiváis, two renowned Latin American writers, asked him, "Did you ever imagine that you would be sitting here today, in the presidency and in the seat of power?" Chávez's simple response: "No, never. Never."[2]

Perhaps, on this December 6, the deeply personal meaning of this achievement was something he would celebrate on his own, for Venezuela was celebrating something else entirely: the triumph of antipolitics. The people of Venezuela had brought an outsider to the presidency, delivering a severe blow to the traditional political machine. A substantial sector of the middle class, fed up with the incompetence and corruption of the previous administrations, had fashioned a kind of revenge through the figure of this former military officer and coup leader. The media, dedicated as always to criticizing anything and everything in politics, were satisfied. The poor also identified with this message of "getting even," with this man who spoke of Venezuela's age-old debt to those who had always been excluded from the system. Chávez's victory, in this sense, was a new version of an old product, wrapped up in a bright, shiny package: Great Venezuela, the kingdom of magical liquid wealth; the paradise from which so many Venezuelans had felt themselves marginalized; the fantasy of instant success.

The candidate representing an alliance known as the Patriotic Pole won the election with an unprecedented majority. According to the final count, he earned 56.44 percent of the vote. But who was Hugo Chávez, really? Where did he come from? Where was he going? How would his dreams and those of his country merge into one? On that victorious night in Caracas, after his rivals and the official institutions had formally acknowledged him as the new president-elect of Venezuela, this is what he had to say: "My dear friends: very simply, what happened today *had* to happen. As Jesus said, 'It is accomplished. What had to be accomplished was accomplished.' " And beneath the long shadow of the early dawn hour in Caracas, Chávez began to sing the national anthem.

——

SCARCELY SIX YEARS EARLIER, when Hugo Chávez had appeared on television to claim responsibility for attempting to overthrow the government, all his family could possibly feel were shock and embarrassment. At that time, nobody thought that Hugo Chávez was on his way to a meteoric political career. One of his friends from secondary school said, "It's something very difficult to digest. You have to take into account the significance of never having been a councilman, a congressman, a [political] leader, never having been a goddamn thing in politics . . . and then suddenly ending up president."

Indeed, nothing indicated that this would be Hugo's destiny. Many people probably would have said that simply being born in Sabaneta was a great disadvantage. On the other hand, it was also the ideal beginning of a grand myth, that of the humble man who rises to achieve untold powers—a potent, emotional dream for anyone with a melodramatic vision of history. There may have been presidents before Chávez who had risen to the pinnacle of power from simple, humble beginnings—in fact, none of the presidents from Venezuela's democratic age had come from Caracas. Just like Chávez, all of them had come from the provinces—the majority from poor families, as well. Yet Hugo Chávez, the first one from Barinas, in the far reaches of the Venezuelan plain, was the first president to transform his geographic circumstances into a symbol.

Regionalism is a tricky thing. The simple recipes that use geographic ingredients to define cultural traits are so very easy to believe and are repeated over and over again: people who live near the ocean or sea are open, honest, spontaneous people, whereas those who hail from the Andes, who live in the cold, vertical silence of the mountains, are taciturn, withdrawn. These kinds of classifications are hard to avoid. According to the Venezuelan stereotype, the *llanero,* the man from the plains, is a reserved, skeptical type who, once you break the ice, reveals himself to be a loyal, talkative person who loves to tell a good story. They say that there is something about the plains, with their converging horizons and interminable, flat terrain, that produces an odd combination of silences and long musical *corridos*, filled with protracted screams and counterpoints. It is a territory that is also a climate of the interior, a place where cattle, ghosts, horses, and apparitions coexist.

Manuel Díaz, also known as "Venenito"—Little Poison—worked for some thirty years as a chemistry teacher at the Daniel Florencio O'Leary secondary school in Barinas, where Hugo Chávez was his student. According to Díaz, the *llaneros* "are hard to understand. They are very suspicious people. Always thinking about what people want from them. But once they know you, they are genuine. . . . They offer their friendship when they see that it is reciprocal." He also adds another bit of insight: "They are marked by machismo. The man is the one who does everything." According to a common maxim that the people of the plains often use to describe themselves, "The *llanero* is as great as the task he sees in front of him." Obviously, there is nothing terribly specific about this refrain: a multitude of regional identities could easily jibe with this definition.

Of all Venezuelan presidents, however, Chávez has most consistently invoked the spirit of the region from which he comes, frequently peppering his speeches with personal anecdotes, cultural references, and songs relating to the plains and its inhabitants. He loves to regale his public with childhood memories, and when he speaks of his retirement, he talks about going back to his roots and spending his golden years on the banks of a river, in some faraway outpost of those vast plains.

Efrén Jiménez, Hugo's childhood playmate and next-door neighbor, says of those days, "Sabaneta was made up of about four streets. At that time I think there must have been about a thousand people, maybe a little more. We all knew each other, we were all like one big family." There was no regular electric light, but the village had a generator that delivered electricity every day from 6:30 P.M. to 10:30 P.M. Hugo's father, Hugo de los Reyes Chávez, taught at the Julián Pino school, the only one in the village. Another childhood friend recalls the elder Chávez as a good educator, "strict, demanding, and disciplined, but not arbitrary."

HUGO RAFAEL CHÁVEZ FRÍAS was born in Sabaneta, in the state of Barinas, on July 28, 1954, the second of six brothers. His mother, Elena, has admitted that during those years "my work was all family. I couldn't do anything else." They lived in a house with a roof made of palm leaves. That was where all her boys were born: "With a midwife. Like a pig, because back then there was no hospital, no doctor, nothing. It was just you in childbirth. And the pain was the same with all of them. All of them."

The Chávez family finances were very precarious; the money disappeared as fast as the children appeared. Perhaps for that reason, Rosa Inés Chávez, Hugo's paternal grandmother, would become an important figure in his life. Because of the family's strained budget, she was the one who raised young Hugo, and Chávez has openly acknowledged the tremendous role his grandmother has played in his life. When his second wife bore him a daughter, she was baptized Rosa Inés. Those close to Chávez's grandmother confirm that she influenced Chávez in a way that would have been all but impossible in his parents' home.

Elena Frías de Chávez was eighteen years old when she gave birth to Adán, her first son. A year and three months later, she gave birth again, to Hugo. Another year and three months later, she gave birth to yet another baby. At that point, her mother-in-law offered to lend a hand, and it was agreed that Adán and Hugo would move to their grandmother's house. Economically, it was probably not much of an improvement, but at least the responsibilities were spread around. In her kitchen, Rosa Inés would prepare *arañitas,* papaya sweets, and Hugo would go out and sell them in the street. In a diary entry dated June 12, 1974, Hugo recalled, "Around here, in the area nearby, there was lots of mountain broom and just looking at it brings back the distant but indelible image of my life as a child, in the fields of Sabaneta, with Adán and my grandmother, gathering handfuls of that plant to sweep our modest house with the dirt floor."[3] Chávez's many fond references to his grandmother clearly reveal that her affection and love were and are of paramount importance to him. As far as anyone knows, she was a quiet, good-humored woman. Her death, in 1982, was a terrible blow to the two brothers whom she raised.

Elena eventually decided she wanted her children to return home, but by then it was already too late.

"Afterward, when I wanted to get my children back, my husband said to me, 'Elena, if you take those little boys away from her, my mother will have a heart attack. And if my mother dies it will be your fault.' And so I didn't say anything, because if she died, they were going to blame it on me. . . . After a while I brought it up again, I said, 'Hugo, I want my sons to come back here with me.' " The verb "take away" may sound harsh, but that is precisely what they would have been doing. The years went by, and the two little boys would never return to live in the home of Hugo and Elena. They would often spend much of the day at their parents' house, but at night they always went back to sleep at their grandmother's. According to Elena, her house was home for the two boys "until Hugo went to the Academy and Adán left for college."

The influence of his grandmother and the early separation from his mother have served as fodder for many hypotheses regarding the evolution of Hugo Chávez's personality and character. Some people feel there is a connection between the circumstances of his early life and the incendiary tone of his political rhetoric. Some people sense in him a perpetual aggression that they believe stems from a deep-seated resentment regarding his early childhood experiences. This would be supported by a related theory suggesting that Chávez harbors muted feelings of ill will toward his mother.

Herma Marksman, the history professor who was Chávez's lover for nine years, says, "I felt that he loved his father more than his mother. I think that he really missed the warmth of his mother during those early years. That is my personal perception." Marksman also recalls a heated discussion they once had as a couple, which ended with the following exchange. " 'So you don't love your mother?' I asked him. And he said, 'No. I respect her.' On two separate occasions," she says, "he brought up this distance from his mother. It was so extreme that, for a time, if the two of them crossed paths on the street, they would avoid each other so they wouldn't have to say hello. That's what he told me." According to Marksman, there was a period of two years when Chávez did not speak to his mother at all.

In an interview with the magazine *Primicia*, in 1999, a confession from Elena added more fuel to the fire: "I didn't want to have children . . . I don't know, I didn't like them, it didn't seem appealing, but since God told me, 'That is what you are going to do,' I got married and a month later I was pregnant."[4] She also admits that she was very strict, and would often hit her sons to keep them in line, a common practice in Venezuela in those years.

When Chávez entered the military academy in 1971, the very first letter he wrote was to his grandmother Rosa Inés, and she was the person he would write to again and again after that, his letters filled with expressions that confirmed their closeness: "Dear *Mamá*," he often wrote to her, and he also referred to her on occasion as "*mamita*." His words reflect genuine warmth and affection, a strong, profound emotional bond. At the end of one of these letters, dated August 31, 1971, he said as much: "Finally, I want you to know that I have always felt proud to have been raised by you and to be able to call you *Mamá*. And I ask you to bless me, your loving son." This deep-seated devotion contrasts a bit with the feelings he expressed in letters to his birth mother. The correspondence with Elena de Chávez was also loving and affectionate but far more sporadic, which does seem to suggest that young Hugo's maternal bond was with his grandmother. That, at least, is how he put it on the eve of his graduation from the military academy: "I have been alive for twenty years, sixteen of which I spent with you. I have learned so many things from you: to be humble but proud, and the most important thing, which I

THE REVOLUTION HAS ARRIVED | 11

inherited from you, was that spirit of sacrifice that I hope will take me far, although perhaps, if I am unlucky, it will cut my illusions short."

While some believe that the circumstances of his childhood were extremely traumatic, others feel the exact opposite is true: one childhood friend remembers Hugo as a happy child and points out that this type of family arrangement, in which grandparents or uncles and aunts raised grandchildren or nieces and nephews, was quite normal in the rural Venezuela of those years. In general, Chávez himself has also tended to recall his childhood as a happy time in his life; he has never spoken of his early years as a hell from which he needed to escape. On his Sunday radio show of October 17, 2004, he remarked that his early years had been "poor but happy," and he has often delighted in telling stories about his two great childhood passions: painting and baseball. Elena also remembers the talent and skill her son demonstrated: "He liked to draw a lot. He painted everything. He would sit down right here and look at a little dog, and in a flash he'd paint it. He would make drawings of his brothers, his friends . . . anyone who came his way would say, 'Huguito, make me a drawing.' And right away he would draw a little something. Just like that."

His other great passion was *el juego de pelota:* baseball. Almost all little boys in Venezuela, at one time or another, dream of being baseball players, and around that time, a Venezuelan pitcher whose last name also happened to be Chávez had made it to the American big leagues with a promising future. His first name was Isaías, though thanks to his superlative pitching skills, he became known as "Látigo"—the Whip. Huguito took an immediate shine to the Whip, who was ultimately more than just an idol—he was a model, a dream that Hugo could aspire to. Whenever Hugo played in the streets or in one of the empty lots in his village, he would daydream about one day becoming a real-life baseball player, a celebrity who could command ovations from the crowds in a massive stadium somewhere.

Others from Sabaneta who were close to the family during those years also agree that Hugo Chávez's childhood was not a wretched experience that warped his personality and made him resentful, aggressive, and vengeful. Aside from speculations about what went on inside the family nucleus, there seems to be only one distant story offering any suggestion of a childhood marked by humiliation. His aunt Joaquina Frías describes it: "The first day Hugo went to school they wouldn't let him inside. He was wearing an old pair of canvas slippers, the only ones he had. His grandmother Rosa Inés cried and cried because she couldn't afford to buy him shoes. It was heart-wrenching to watch that woman, so strong-willed in general, break down like that. I don't know how she managed to buy another pair of slippers, but the boy was able to go back to school."[5] This scene hardly seems like something that could define the totality of a man's character, but yet again it does underscore the importance of his grandmother: after all, it was Rosa Inés who accompanied him on his first day of school, and it was Rosa Inés who confronted even the tiniest of everyday mishaps and troubles.

Edmundo Chirinos is a nationally renowned psychiatrist. Associated with leftist politics, he is the former rector of Venezuela's Central University and was once a candidate for the presidency. After the 1992 coup attempt, he became acquainted with Hugo Chávez.

When he was imprisoned in Yare, he didn't know many people in the civilian world. He called some of us who had a certain prestige or were known by people. That's how he called the current vice president [at that time, José Vicente Rangel], his mentor, Luis Miquilena, and many others that have come into his government. He called me because I had been a presidential candidate and had political experience; second, he had family problems, and required my services as psychiatric counselor. He was not perturbed; he only had common problems anybody could have had with wives or children. That's how I became his friend and counselor.[6]

When Chirinos describes Hugo Chávez, he does not single out the president's relationship with his grandmother, but he does highlight some notable personality traits that are clearly linked to his life experience, including his childhood: "Chávez feels genuine scorn for oligarchic people, not only in the sense of possessing money but of affectation, through gestures, language . . . and so in that respect, he exhibits an evident bipolarity, of an affinity for the humble and a rejection of the all-powerful."

As time goes by, it will become more and more difficult to study the facts of Hugo Chávez's journey through life. His story already has an "official version," a party line that has been reconstructed and retold from his position of power. Any anecdote about his childhood, any distant event, is now seen in a different light, either magnified or diminished, reinvented or dropped. This is almost part of the natural process by which power invents a new kind of memory. When Elena was asked if she had ever known of her son's intentions of becoming president, she replied, "We hadn't planned anything, anything at all. Look, all this has come to us by the work and the grace of the Holy Spirit. Nothing more."

BUT IT WAS MORE than the Holy Spirit that shook the country on December 6, 1998. It is no coincidence that the person running Venezuela today came of age in the army. Nor is it anything new: between 1830 and 1958 the country was governed by civilians for a scant nine years. In 1958, the demise of General Marcos Pérez Jiménez's dictatorship marked the beginning of the longest period of democracy Venezuela has ever known. During this era the main parties opposing the military regime came together and, with the exception of the Communist Party, drafted an agreement of governance, later known as the Punto Fijo Pact. Ultimately, Democratic Action (the Social Democratic party) and the Christian Democrats' Independent Political Electoral Organizing Committee (known as COPEI, from its initials in Spanish) took control of the public sector in Venezuela. During four decades, the two parties took turns in the presidency. The *adecos,* as the Social Democrats are called, governed for five terms, and the *copeyanos,* as the Christian Democrats are known, led the government on three occasions. By 1998, this model was so deeply in crisis that Hugo Chávez's main promise to the country was to end "forty years of corrupt democracy." This was the central theme of his campaign: to do away with the past.[7]

On December 7, 1998, the editorial page of the newspaper *El Nacional* neatly summarized the sentiments of the majority of the voting public:

> The results of this Sunday's election speak very clearly about Venezuelan society, not just about the great hopes for change that have been evolving at its core, but also about the tremendous levels of frustration that have turned the majority against the old political leadership. It is absolutely clear that the entire country has chosen an option that is different from that which the traditional ruling class was trying to impose.[8]

It was clear that the punishment vote had worked, and that democracy—at least the kind that the Venezuelan elite had engendered—was no longer a promise that people felt they could believe in. In 1998, everyone in Venezuela, even those who did not vote for Hugo Chávez, wanted a change.

This evaluation of the immediate past, however, may be unfair. It may also be influenced by the way Venezuelans relate to their own reality, to the culture of a country that has never quite figured out how to assimilate its oil wealth. There is little doubt as to how or why, in scarcely forty years, Venezuela's civilian-democratic project became so warped and so corrupt, dissolving in a debilitating crisis that touched every area of society and its institutions, from the economy to political representation to the delivery of justice and beyond. On the other hand, it is also important to recognize that, at least in the beginning, the democratic experience modernized the country and served to interrupt the militarist tradition—and temptation—of Venezuelan history, introducing educational reform, agrarian reform, the decentralization process, the nationalization of the oil business, the creation of scholarships and specialized study programs abroad. No legitimate assessment can overlook the country's very deep complexities during this period. Even in economic terms, the verdict always requires a good deal of qualification.

In 1997, a group of academics and researchers decided to undertake a serious and exhaustive analysis of poverty in Venezuela. In 2004, they published the results of their study:

> By the middle of the twentieth century, there was already a deeply rooted conviction that Venezuela was rich because of oil, because of that natural gift that does not depend on productivity or the enterprising spirit of the Venezuelan people. Political activity revolved around the struggle to distribute the wealth, rather than the creation of a sustainable source of wealth that would depend upon the commercial initiatives and the productivity of the majority of the Venezuelan people. Under democracy (starting in 1958), the income from oil (which represented almost 90 percent of exports and 60 percent of the national budget) was distributed more broadly, but this distortion in the mentality and the economic dynamic became a permanent factor in the country. Politicians rested on their promises—as well as some successful initiatives to expand public services—of distributing the wealth that was in the hands of the state.
>
> More and more, the country harbored the illusion that it could advance toward modern consumer habits (through imports purchased with its petrodollars) without having to develop a diversified production through a modern culture of productivity. To a certain degree, this was possible for 10 percent of the population in a Venezuela of less than 5 million inhabitants, but there is no way that in Venezuela today, with 25 million inhabitants, 11 million workers will enjoy decent, steady jobs while clinging to the oil dynamic and the culture of

easy money. Twenty-five years ago, after sixty years of growth from 1918 to 1978, a period in which the gross national product grew more than 6 percent annually and Venezuelans experienced the sensation of social mobility, the country fell into decline, and poverty began to grow at an alarming and sustained rate.[9]

Hugo Chávez was born in that Venezuela of less than 5 million inhabitants. He benefited from the advantages of that first democratic, modernizing impulse of the governments that succeeded the Pérez Jiménez dictatorship. But he also witnessed and lived through the decline. In this sense, he was a link between these two countries: one captivated by the quest to build a fairer, more evolved society with solid institutions and enterprises, the other in thrall to the great national illusion, a utopia in which the state is the providential benefactor, all structure and rules are dispensable, effort is a distraction, and destiny is not a future to build but a heaven that already exists, a treasure already won that needs only to be meted out properly.

Those who worked on Chávez's presidential campaign took brilliant advantage of the widespread desire for a clean break with the system. "The country had expectations for Chávez," says Juan Barreto, a journalist close to the president. "[This was] because he was the person who, in the most frontal way imaginable, had stood up to the symbolic forms of political power: the central government and Carlos Andrés Pérez, who at that moment was the living incarnation of corruption."[10] Though the people who designed his electoral campaign say that Chávez did not let people advise him and "created his own image," it is clear that they did have to fix certain things along the way. For example, Chávez often sounded extremely aggressive when he made speeches. He also had a tendency to use a confrontational, macabre vocabulary—the word "death" frequently popped into his speeches, which led people to think of his candidacy as something frightening. In addition, the many groups that supported him, which were lumped together in an alliance called the Patriotic Pole, included the Communist Party and other leftist organizations with extremely radical postures. His campaign strategists soon realized that the real debate and the real issues were more than just a repudiation of the past and of the country's traditional parties and their corrupt practices. Nobody, they realized, could win an election without offering hope.

Rafael Céspedes, who served as an adviser to Dominican president Leonel Fernández on two occasions, played a key role in fine-tuning Chávez's public image. One of his principal strategies was to use Marisabel Rodríguez, the candidate's second wife, in the campaign. Marisabel was part of an elaborate plan intended to soothe the Venezuelan populace by softening the candidate's image. Marisabel is well educated, kind, attractive, and spontaneous. Her type of beauty was especially useful to the campaign because there is something about her that recalls the stereotype that so many people seem to adore: she is white, she has blue eyes, and in fact, she had even participated in a competition sponsored by Revlon to find the most beautiful face in Venezuela. At the side of the unpredictable, aggressive soldier, suddenly there was a real-life Barbie doll who even made sense when she talked.

All through 1998, Chávez and his team plugged away, and his campaign went from strength to strength. The statistics are overwhelming: in January the polls reported a 9 percent approval rating, whereas by October, just two months away from the elections, the same polls revealed that 48 percent of the electorate was on his side. It hadn't always been smooth sailing. In June, Bandera Roja (Red Flag), one of the leftist groups that had supported his candidacy, dissociated itself from the campaign and accused Chávez of working a "double discourse": "In front of the nation he acts like an avenger who wants to sweep the decks and start with a clean slate, turn the country upside-down, but when he is among the powerful he shows his true colors and confesses his true intentions, which are to carry out nothing but superficial changes."[11] Also that month, Teodoro Petkoff, the leader of the Venezuelan leftist opposition and founder of MAS (Movimiento al Socialismo, the Movement Toward Socialism party)[12] and an internationally renowned activist, called him a populist and compared his demagogy to that of Carlos Andrés Pérez. Chávez did not even flinch.

On July 24, the date on which Simón Bolívar's birthday is celebrated, Hugo Chávez registered his presidential candidacy with the National Electoral Council and declared, "Let the whole world know that in Venezuela, a true social revolution is now under way. Nothing and nobody will be able to stand in the way of the triumph of the democratic revolution."[13] The parties that made up the Patriotic Pole and supported his candidacy were the Movimiento V República (Fifth Republic Movement), an entity founded by Chávez himself; Movement Toward Socialism; PPT (Patria para Todos, or Homeland for All); the Venezuelan Communist Party; and the Movimiento Electoral del Pueblo (People's Electoral Movement). This was not a massively organized machine by any stretch of the imagination—quite the opposite, in fact. It was a collection of relatively small leftist parties, united behind the personal figure of the candidate. With his unusual talent for communication, Chávez capitalized on the collective desire for change by cultivating and promoting the idea that his election, in and of itself, already represented a rupture in the historical continuum, a transformation. Jimmy Carter, who attended the elections that Sunday, December 6, 1998, as an observer, confirmed this by stating that he had witnessed a democratic and peaceful revolution.

Chávez's campaign chief, the retired general Alberto Müller Rojas, suggests a less heroic version of that election day: "The campaign won pretty easily. The victory had more to do with his adversaries' political errors than the quality of our own electoral campaign, which was relatively disorganized because that was the only way it could be. The elections were won more because of what the opposition didn't achieve than because of what *chavismo* [the Chávez movement] actively achieved. I am absolutely convinced of that." Anyone who studies the performance of Chávez's opponents will undoubtedly discover a number of grave miscalculations. First, his opponents seemed unaware of the fact that the country was changing. They never seemed capable of reading the reality of what was going on—neither in the very beginning, when Irene Sáez, a former Miss Universe without much substance, enjoyed tremendous popular support, nor at the end, when a number of parties and organizations, in desperation over Chávez's imminent triumph, came together far too late in support of Henrique Salas Römer, the only candidate with a chance of beating Chávez, according to the polls. The opposition simply had not offered any coherent political alternative for the Venezuelan voters—not even in their electoral demagogy was there the glimmer of a serious proposal. Their only objective was to avert a Patriotic Pole victory. Quite aptly, the press labeled the movement the "anti-Chávez front."

Nedo Paniz, another close Chávez collaborator during this period, clarifies that the campaign was not all improvisation and guesswork. It was very expensive, and Chávez doggedly pursued the strategy of nothing but ferocious, constant criticism of those in power. He also refused to take part in a broadcast debate with his main opponent, and it was this aloof, fierce attitude that ultimately brought the traditional political parties and the entire political class to their knees.

The rest of the country, however, was jubilant. It had been years since so many Venezuelans had come together to celebrate a victory like this. When he assumed the presidency, Hugo Chávez enjoyed 80 percent of the population's support. Müller himself confirms that Gustavo Cisneros, the wealthiest man in the country, supported the Chávez cause with cash donations and free airtime on Venevisión, his television channel. This gesture of confidence is an interesting example of the enigmatic and ambiguous relationship that has always existed between the president and the magnate. Cisneros has long since been the emblematic enemy of the Venezuelan left as well as the living image of the reactionary far right. Some years later, Chávez would say Cisneros was conspiring against his government. On a radio program in May 2004, Chávez bristled when he spoke of Cisneros: "The day will come, and hopefully it is not far off, when we will have a body of judges and prosecutors who are afraid of nothing and who will act according to what the Constitution says, and send capos like this Gustavo Cisneros to prison." Shortly thereafter, however, a private meeting was held between Chávez and Cisneros under the stewardship of Jimmy Carter. The Chávez camp claimed that Cisneros was involved in drug trafficking and had been one of the masterminds behind the April 2002 coup to remove Chávez from the presidency. Apparently, things have always been like this between the two men. Müller recalls that at one dinner together, both men were surrounded the entire time by their respective aides, who acted as intermediaries because the two refused to speak to each other directly.

"The compromise that Chávez reached with Cisneros was that he would give [Cisneros] a monopoly on educational television in Venezuela," says Müller Rojas. If that was the case, Chávez never made good on his promise.

With respect to support and alliances, this was far from the only bit of unexplained business on the path to electoral victory. In 2002, the Spanish newspaper *El Mundo* reported that Banco Bilbao Vizcaya had donated $1.52 million to Chávez's electoral campaign. Luis Miquilena, the head of finances for the Patriotic Pole, was involved in this relationship. One of Venezuela's veteran leftist leaders, Miquilena was Chávez's mentor and his first interior minister. He and his business partner Tobías Carrero were rumored to have accepted money from a foreign institution for an electoral campaign, which is a crime in Venezuela. This revelation led to another bit of information that raised even more eyebrows: on January 11, 1999, during his first trip to Spain as president-elect of Venezuela, Hugo Chávez met with Emilio Ybarra, president of Banco Bilbao Vizcaya, and then with Emilio Botín and his daughter Ana Patricia Botín, of Banco Santander. At first, the new administration denied everything, but the situation soon became unmanageable: according to the Spanish daily *El País,* the central bank of Spain reported that BBV (which has since merged and is now Banco Bilbao Vizcaya Argentaria) had diverted funds of "more than $1.5 million through two payments to the Chávez campaign with the intention of protecting itself in the event of a possible nationalization of the finance industry in this Latin American country." On April 6, 2002, General Müller acknowledged the BBV donations, adding that the majority of international banks operating in Venezuela had also contributed to the Chávez campaign.

A few days later, however, on April 25, Hugo Chávez said on the Spanish TV station Telecinco, "I have not received one dollar from these people, this bank . . . what is it called? . . . Bilbao Vizcaya." It is also rumored that the campaign had received $1.8 million from Banco Santander. In Spain, on June 20, Emilio Ybarra, the former co-president of Banco Santander, admitted to Spanish magistrate Baltasar Garzón that in fact he had donated money to finance the Chávez campaign in 1998. Müller has said that "Luis Miquilena handled these resources in a secret manner. Nobody—neither the parties that comprised the Patriotic Pole, nor the apparatus I had in place at campaign headquarters—knew how much money was there, what it was spent on, or how much was spent on each individual item." Venezuelan justice sank into these shadows. The charge against Chávez of illegal campaign financing, which was filed with the attorney general of the Republic, never went anywhere.

On the night of December 6, 1998, however, the country was in the throes of euphoria and had little interest in such details. In the gathering in front of the Teresa Carreño Theater, Hugo Chávez began to speak. The cameras of every media organization in the country were firmly fixed on the new president's face, and the entire country anxiously awaited his words. William Izarra, a retired military officer and the secret protagonist of many a military conspiracy, watched as if he couldn't believe it was really happening. As he walked past Izarra, Hugo Chávez stopped to embrace him. And in the middle of this emotion-filled moment, the president-elect whispered, "We did it, brother. After all those years, the revolution can finally begin."[14]

CHAPTER 2

"Me, a Communist?"

"I, HUGO CHÁVEZ, AM NOT A MARXIST, BUT I AM ALSO NOT AN ANTI-Marxist. I am not a Communist, but I am not an anti-Communist, either."[1] With vague contradictions, the brand-new president of Venezuela evaded his political adversaries whenever they tried to pin a label on him. Ever since emerging from political anonymity, Chávez has always used ambiguity when asked to explain how his political pendulum swings. During his long battle for the presidency, he clung to the expression "I am neither left-wing nor right-wing," and every effort to get him to identify his position on the ideological spectrum was fruitless. A great admirer of vernacular history, he has always preferred to situate himself two centuries in the past. "I am Bolivarian," he has often said, referring to the ideas of Simón Bolívar, liberator of half of Latin America, including Venezuela, Colombia (which at the time included Panama), Peru, Ecuador, and Bolivia. He has consistently operated within the realm of the same enigma. Is he a left-wing Bolivarian? A right-wing Bolivarian? Publicly, the furthest he has ever gone in this sense was his open appreciation of British prime minister Tony Blair's Third Way, but that was back when Chávez was at the door to Miraflores, the Venezuelan presidential palace.

Was he simply being sincere and never really saw himself as a left-wing politician, even when many people from all ends of the political spectrum saw him as such?

"As far as I see it," says Luis Miquilena, "he is a left-winger. Obviously. But he has gotten into bed with the failed left." Miquilena, a veteran ex-Communist, is widely considered to have been the architect behind the creation of Hugo Chávez the presidential candidate. And though on the one hand, it is entirely possible that Chávez's ambiguity was just part of his campaign strategy, given that his opponents constantly accused him of being a veiled Communist who would wipe out private property in Venezuela, it is still astonishing that for so many years he consistently refused to reveal his true political inclinations. "Me, a Communist?" he would say. He would deny it every time—that is, until 2005. That was the year he decided to declare himself a socialist and set out to invent twenty-first-century socialism.

This did not take anyone by surprise. Despite his ambiguity, his rhetoric has always been dominated by a rudimentary amalgam of leftist ideas. "So what if they call me a radical, a revolutionary? That's exactly what I am, and I believe that's exactly what I have to be," he retorted in early 1995, when his popularity was nil and he agreed to participate in a series of talks with the Venezuelan historian Agustín Blanco Muñoz, which culminated in the publication of the confessional book *Habla el comandante* (The Commander Speaks)[2] three years later. At the time he was the self-proclaimed leader of "an anti-exploitation, anti-imperialist movement" and prescribed the following rather obvious solution: "For a movement to be revolutionary, it has to be transformative, it has to take a swing at the powerful."

Where does Chávez's revolutionary fervor come from? When did he become inspired to subvert the Venezuelan system? When did he become so drawn to power?

Chávez was around twelve or thirteen when he first met José Esteban Ruiz Guevara at the Ruiz family home in the city of Barinas. Hugo was a slender teenager who had befriended Guevara's sons Vladimir (named after Lenin) and Federico (named after Engels) while playing baseball. In honor of their new friend's big, ungainly feet, the two young boys took to calling Chávez "Tribilín," the Spanish name for Goofy, the Disney character. Young Hugo had just arrived in Barinas with his grandmother and older brother Adán from the village of Sabaneta, where education ended with primary school.

The boy's father, a schoolteacher, had managed to secure a house for them in Barinas, the state capital, so that the boys could study at the large secondary school there.

An old-school Communist, Ruiz Guevara openly acknowledges his political orientation: "I have always been a Communist Party militant," he says. Chávez, along with Vladimir and Federico, would sit on the rug of the Ruiz family library in the afternoons and listen to the stories and lessons imparted by the impassioned Communist with the long beard.

"Listen kids, this is the book you have to read," he would say, and their eyes would follow him up to the shelves upon which Jean-Jacques Rousseau's *The Social Contract* and Machiavelli's *The Prince* sat. Ruiz also introduced the boys to eighteenth-century Venezuelan political theory, "so that they might familiarize themselves with our own socioeconomic issues." Ruiz recalls that Chávez "was not much of a talker in those days, he spoke very little. And so, basically, the boys would usually just listen to me talk and every so often utter an 'Uh, umm' along the way."

The rest of the Chávez family relocated to Barinas shortly afterward, settling down in a house on Carabobo Avenue, across the street from the Ruiz family and just a few yards away from the home of Hugo's grandmother. At the time, the state capital was a large town of sixty thousand inhabitants, but for the Chávez family it was the big city.

Vladimir, Federico, and Jesús Pérez (who would later become Chávez's foreign minister and currently serves as the Venezuelan ambassador to UNESCO in Paris) were young Hugo's closest friends in those days. Their tight-knit foursome served as a kind of social nucleus for the other teenagers in town, and they would gather together in a small plaza between the Chávez and Ruiz homes every weekend. This is where Chávez spent his adolescence, often organizing baseball games, a childhood passion he inherited from his father.

In the plaza, sometimes the young men would talk about current events. They would also play *cuatro* music, and they would sing, too—almost always the *llanera* music of the Venezuelan plains. Upon hearing himself sing, Hugo became fascinated with the sound of his own voice. Together, the teenagers crooned their first serenades, organized parties, and went down to the river to go fishing. More than anything, however, the four young friends cultivated one of the qualities that is most often associated with *llaneros:* they talked. They talked and they talked and they talked. For hours. About everything. Sports, movies, politics, girls. Everything.

Sometimes on Sundays they would go to see westerns or kung fu movies, or to the Derby Theater, where they might be able to grab hold of a pretty girl's hand. On those evenings out, Chávez was the ugly duckling alongside the Ruiz brothers. He was friendly and likable, but he wasn't the kind of boy that the girls fought over. "He had one or two girlfriends that everyone knew, but they were ugly—boy, were they ugly. He was pretty ugly himself," recalls his secondary school classmate Rafael Simón Jiménez, a former Chávez party congressman who was vice president of the National Assembly during the early years of the Chávez administration.

ON WEEKDAYS, HUGO AND ADÁN, who lived with their grandmother, would walk to the O'Leary secondary school with Ruiz Guevara's wife, Carmen Tirado, and the couple's three oldest children, Vladimir, Federico, and Tania. At O'Leary, Hugo passed the time with other Barinas teenagers, including Rafael Simón, a chubby, rebellious kid who was the coordinator of the local Communist Youth groups. Hugo never exhibited any interest in this particular organization, but "he did participate in some activities. Just as he himself said, 'When Rafael Simón said we had to throw stones, we threw stones,' " according to Jiménez.

Throwing stones, however, was not part of Hugo's agenda. The only activity that interested him was the kind that took place on the baseball field. But then one Sunday in March 1969, when Chávez was fourteen, the *llanera* music playing on Radio Barinas was interrupted by a breaking news bulletin. Chávez later described it:

My grandmother Rosa was preparing my breakfast, and turned on the radio to listen to some music. Then, suddenly, we heard a news flash, and for a moment, I felt as if death had struck me, right then and there. An airplane had gone down shortly after taking off from the Maracaibo airfield, and there were no survivors. Látigo Chávez was on that plane. Terrible. I stayed out of school that Monday and Tuesday. I fell apart: I even came up with a little prayer that I said every night, vowing that I would grow up to be like him, a big-league pitcher. From that point on, my dream of being a painter was completely eclipsed by the desire to be a baseball player.[3]

Chávez worshipped his fallen idol so fervently that five years after the incident, he continued to record the anniversary of the pitcher's death in his diary.

At school, Hugo Chávez was just another kid in the crowd, but he did possess one special characteristic: he read anything and everything that was given to him—especially if it was given to him by Ruiz Guevara, his first political mentor.

"Another thing I was pretty insistent about," notes Ruiz Guevara, "was the importance of reading Karl Marx, and Marxism in general. In the end, I said to them, it isn't political science we're talking about, it's economic science, but you still have to deal with both things. You can't practice politics without economics. There's no way around it. And so I told them, listen, you better get Marxism into your brains, and good. Of course, they [the books] are a little dense."

Ruiz also walked them through Venezuelan history. "I focused a lot on two figures in particular: Napoleón Sebastián Arteaga, a native of Barinas who was one of the ideologues behind the federal revolution (1840–50), and, of course, Ezequiel Zamora," the latter being the foremost figure of Venezuelan federalism, an icon and recurring figure in President Chávez's discourse. And naturally, Chávez's impromptu instructor taught his pupil about Simón Bolívar, drawing him into the "religion" of that exclusively Venezuelan god. As

Federico Ruiz recalls, "My father's library was always the source from which Hugo Chávez drew his knowledge and understanding of Bolivarian thought. . . . Hugo always had this combined interest—and I mean long before he went off to the [military] academy, maybe it was just starting back then—in baseball and political thought, and in that area he already had begun to take an interest in Bolívar. And our house, most specifically my father, was where he found the most important repository of all this information. They would spend hours and hours just talking. I was a Marxist, a Communist, I didn't understand. I thought it was a waste of time to sit around talking about Bolívar."

Young Hugo stuck like glue to that library. The Ruiz house became the magnetic center and intellectual reference point of his adolescence. He devoured all kinds of books, from westerns to things like *Los conceptos elementales del materialismo histórico* (The Elemental Concepts of Historical Materialism).[4]

"I practically grew up with his [Ruiz Guevara's] children," Chávez once remarked, noting more specifically that the older of the two brothers was "something of a political guide for me."[5] The brother in question, Vladimir, an oddly affable yet terse man, recalls that "a kind of political empathy" sprung up between them.

Despite his bond with Vladimir and the friendly lessons imparted by the elder Ruiz, Chávez did not become active in the Communist Party, or any kind of political endeavor, for that matter. He may have had certain social concerns, he had read some books, but nothing more. He was not committed to any kind of revolutionary enterprise, and when he decided to join the army, he did so without any pretensions of infiltration.

"He didn't go into the army under any kind of influence, the Communist Party had nothing to do with that. There is no question that by then he had a certain level of political education, no question at all, and that he had an understanding of the constructive function of the Red Army," Ruiz Guevara acknowledges, but the veteran Communist does believe that in some sense, the young Chávez must have been somewhat inoculated by "that contact he had with us, with me and my sons, while he was in secondary school."

The path toward the army barracks might have been otherwise. Once he became president, Hugo Chávez offered two versions of his academic inclinations. In a documentary about his life, broadcast by the state-run television station in August 2004, Chávez stated that when his father asked him what he wanted to study when he finished secondary school, he replied, "I'd like to study engineering." He also discussed the topic in an interview, saying, "I told my father that I wanted to study the same thing as my brother: physics and mathematics."[6] In any event, his father brought up the possibility of securing Hugo a spot at the University of Mérida, where one of his uncles taught. "But I thought to myself, 'Mérida? They don't play baseball in Mérida! They play soccer there. No, for God's sake, I'm not going to Mérida.' And so you know what I did? I'll never forget it. One day an officer from the military academy came to my school to give a lecture, it was mandatory attendance for all of us. I didn't really want to go." He knew, however, that the army had good coaches, and as he listened to the officer's speech, an idea began to take shape.

"That's it: that's my future. I'm going to go to the military academy in Caracas, I'm going to get to know Caracas, and then I'll quit the military academy and stay there."[7] His idea was to remain in the capital and focus all his energies on baseball. Hugo Chávez's big dream was not the military life. The military was a shortcut; a picaresque South American solution, not a political utopia.

In 1998, Chávez declared that "social justice, equity, liberty, democracy, democratic revolution" were "the patriotic declarations I heard when I was a boy, in secondary school, back in Barinas right around the time MAS [Movement Toward Socialism] came about. That was right around the same year that I entered the army, in 1971."[8] He heard the call. But he wasn't proclaiming it himself, at least not yet.

After he finished secondary school and moved on to the military academy, Hugo was hardly a Communist agent, as some have insinuated. Just seventeen years old in late 1971, he had never set foot in the Venezuelan capital, nor had he ever seen the sea. He was just a boy from the countryside who, like so many others, saw the armed forces as a way to make a living of some sort. That, at least, is the version offered by a close neighbor. "Hugo was one of three boys from our group who went to the military academy, and they all went for the same reason: because they were broke. In big families, that was one way of solving the situation for a boy like him." His athletic prowess was what allowed him to enroll in the military academy with one failure on his record: chemistry. Manuel Díaz has frequently been referred to on Chávez's weekly TV shows as the man who failed him in chemistry. Looking back on his former student, Díaz says that Chávez "would sit in the back of the class, at the back of the classroom. He was just another kid in the group."

At the O'Leary secondary school he was just another face in the crowd. Average. Nothing about him back then could have foreshadowed what he would become. He was a happy, polite young man with a normal amount of self-confidence. In the eyes of his friend Federico, he was a kid with a strong character and a talent for organizing, someone who possessed a kind of intellectual compass that drew him toward certain authors and certain heroes and away from others. "The idea that someone laid a magic wand on him that turned him into the man he is today when he got his first uniform and pair of boots, that's just not the way it was." True enough: there was no magic wand. But there were most definitely several elements at play, not just the dreams of becoming a big baseball player. There were other things that young Hugo brought with him to the military academy. The book with which he started his new life, for one thing: *The Diary of Che Guevara*. That was the volume tucked under Chávez's arm when he entered the military academy.

ON SUNDAY, AUGUST 8, 1971, a group of almost eighty young men lined up, with serious, anxious faces, in the courtyard of the military academy. Among them was a thin boy dressed in gray twill pants and a white khaki shirt, the cadet-in-training Hugo Rafael Chávez Frías.

"From those first six months, what I most remember about him was that he was an excellent baseball player, and he had a real way with words. He was always cracking jokes," recalls his former classmate General Alcides Rondón. Their 1975 graduating class was the first in the history of the Venezuelan armed forces to graduate with degrees in military sciences and arts, a fact that would leave its mark on them as a group, and which would also incur some resentment from their predecessors, who would contemptuously refer to them as "the doctors." Until then, the military academy had simply turned out high school graduates with military degrees. The new program, inaugurated during the first term of President Rafael Caldera, a Christian Democrat, was an attempt to professionalize the armed forces. The Venezuelan Army has always been made up of a strong working- and lower-class component, its barracks filled with men from humble backgrounds drawn by the real possibility of ascending to the highest ranks.

Hugo Chávez studied political theory from the very first year. Recalling his days in the military academy, Chávez once said:

> We studied Political Science, and I began to feel motivated when we started studying military theory. I liked Mao a lot, and so I started reading a little more by him. . . . With that topic, I would read everything I could get my hands on. . . . I remember the book: *The Military as an Agent of Social Change,* by Claude Heller. I also read a lot about military strategy, Clausewitz on the history of war, and I also read Bolívar, the work of [José Antonio] Páez, Napoleon, Hannibal.[9]

This new program, called the Plan Andrés Bello, was considered quite demanding by the students, but Hugo didn't have too much trouble keeping up with things. He got along well with everyone in his class and made friends quite easily. On his first trip outside the academy as a cadet, Hugo was joined by his classmate Rafael

Martínez Morales. A year older than Hugo and also a baseball fan, Rafael offered to act as Hugo's guide around the capital of Venezuela, at the time a city of some 2.7 million inhabitants.[10] But Caracas intimidated Hugo; it was a place where he would never quite feel at home.

At the military academy, Chávez was a competitive and, on occasion, rebellious student. He liked to make his opinion known, recalls Rondón, who says his classmates most definitely noticed Chávez's "tremendous social calling."

He also seems to have been rather apolitical: Rondón, at least, never heard him talk about the Central American guerrilla or spout left-wing opinions.

During his vacations, Hugo would return to the home of his grandmother, who would light candles and pray to the saints in the hopes of getting her grandson to leave the academy. "She didn't like it one bit that I was in the military."[11] He would also visit his parents and his younger brothers, Narciso, Argenis, Aníbal, and Adelis, and every so often he would see his older brother, Adán, who had gone to study in Mérida. And he continued to visit the Ruiz family home.

"Whenever he came back home on vacation," recalls Carmen Tirado, the ex-wife of José Esteban Ruiz Guevara, "he would come over here before he did anything else. The minute he arrived he would give me a big hug, because that's the way he is, that's how he's always been. Then he would hug my mother and say to her, 'Make me some coffee, your coffee, will you? Because the kind you make is the kind I like the best.' And that's the way he was with everyone in the house. Very affectionate. A man with his heart in the right place. All his life he was like that. José Esteban loved Hugo a great deal, gave him lessons in Marxism right in my house in Barinas, and Vladimir sat in, too, he studied history and was always ahead of things." By this time the boys would hole up in Ruiz Guevara's library, where there were three typewriters: one for the patriarch Ruiz Guevara, one for Vladimir, and one for Hugo. When she would return home from teaching school, Carmen would bring them coffee. Often, she would say to them, "Don't you get tired of talking about communism? Good

God, I have had it up to here with communism! I don't want to hear another word about it." According to Carmen, the three men would spend entire days like that, locked up in Ruiz Guevara's library.

With his own family, however, Chávez seems to have been quite different from the young man he was at the Ruiz Guevara home. His mother, Elena, for example, swears that Hugo "didn't like politics." He didn't even like talking "about those things" with his father, Hugo de los Reyes, an activist with the Christian Democrat party COPEI and director of education for the state of Barinas during the presidency of Luis Herrera Campins (1979–84). "He always said that you had to be neutral, not tie yourself down to anyone. He never got mixed up in things that involved his father or mother." Elena does not believe that her son talked politics with the Ruiz family, nor does she acknowledge that they influenced him at all. "No, this thing grew inside of him, it was sent down to him by the power of our blessed God. My son did not inherit or learn anything from anyone. He cooked all this up himself, as they say, with the hand of God."

As far as his mother is concerned, Hugo was just a typical boy who misbehaved every so often, nothing out of the ordinary—for example, stealing a chicken to make a stew along the riverside with his friends. Just a boy who sought approval from others and who occasionally overreacted when he felt rejected, as his friend Vladimir's anecdote suggests: "One night we were out having a few drinks and we saw this girl. She was very pretty but she wouldn't give us the time of day. Back then we drove around in an old jeep that belonged to Hugo's father. Iván Mendoza, another friend of ours, was with us that night. Well, out in some bushes there was a dead donkey, and I don't remember who came up with the idea, but we took that donkey's head, which smelled like hell—can you even imagine it?—and left it for the girl at her doorstep, at around four in the morning. We woke up the entire block with that, and then we spent three whole days cleaning out the jeep."

CHAPTER 3

An Existential Conflict

THE CHANGE FROM THE RURAL WORLD OF BARINAS TO CARACAS WAS an abrupt one for Chávez. In the capital, he no longer had the kind of time he had once had for drinking all night with his friends. At the academy, he had to get up at the crack of dawn. There he searched for definitions that would eventually bring him closer than ever to the Ruiz family, and once he graduated he began to make contacts with recalcitrant members of the military and prominent figures of the Venezuelan left, the most radical of whom maintained clandestine ties with the governments of Libya, Iraq, North Korea, and Algeria.

His first two years in the academy, however, went by without much drama. "I worked hard there, but it never felt like a burden to me,"[1] he has said. Listening closely to his personal passions, Hugo Chávez combined his classes in military strategy and political theory with lessons in Venezuelan history, memorizing the long-winded proclamations of the South American Liberator Simón Bolívar that José Esteban Ruiz Guevara had taught him. Thanks to Ruiz Guevara, Chávez also fell under the spell of Ezequiel Zamora, a seminal figure in the history of the Venezuelan left whose motto was the unforgettable battle cry of "Popular elections, free land, and free men. Horror in the face of the oligarchy."

Chávez rapidly acquired a taste for life in the military. "By the time I dressed in blue for the first time, I already felt like a soldier,"[2] he once said. Once a goal, baseball was now a mere pastime. According to his own account, this was true from his very first year in the military academy, when he was given "a uniform, a gun, an area, close-order formation, marches, morning runs, studies in military science, and science in general . . . in short, I liked it. The courtyard. Bolívar in the background. . . . I was like a fish in water. It was as if I had discovered the essence or at least part of the essence of life, my true vocation."[3] This same enthusiasm bubbled forth in one of the letters he wrote to his grandmother, in which he described the military life as a great adventure:

> Grandma, if you had only seen me firing away like a maniac in our maneuvers. First we worked on instinctive shooting— immediate action, daytime attack, infiltration, etc. Then we went on a march—120 kilometers—and at the end we performed a simulation of war. The enemy was attacking us at dawn, and we would have ended up soaking wet if we couldn't pitch the mountain tents. We walked through little villages where the girls stared at us in awe and the little kids cried, they were so scared.[4]

In 1971, after being promoted to full-fledged cadet, Chávez was given two days' leave. In his blue uniform and white gloves, he went alone to the old cemetery, the Cementerio General del Sur, in southern Caracas. "I had read that Látigo Chávez was buried there. And I went because I had a knot inside of me, a kind of debt that came out of that oath, that prayer. . . . I was letting go of it, and now I wanted to be a soldier. . . . I felt bad about it." Locating the spot where his old idol had been laid to rest, he prayed and asked him for forgiveness. "I started talking to the gravestone, with the spirit that penetrated everything there, talking to myself. It was as if I was saying to him, 'Isaías, I'm not going down that path anymore. I'm a soldier now.' And as I left the cemetery, I was free."[5]

Why would Chávez, a young soldier, feel the need to explain his decisions to a dead idol? Beyond the possible psychoanalytic interpretations, events like this may suggest a way of viewing history as a series of hidden meanings, plans, and oaths that suggest the certainty that one has been tapped for a very great destiny.

Hugo Chávez continued playing baseball, and often, but as a diversion, not a vocation. He still painted occasionally, too, and would get up and sing every chance he got. A *corrido llanero* that begins *"Furia se llamó el caballo"* (Fury was the name of the horse) became a personal leitmotif of sorts. His fellow cadets, who considered him the best pitcher of the lot, baptized him "El Zurdo Furia"—the Left-handed Fury. Yet, despite all this, the decision had already been made. That, at least, is how Hugo Chávez, president, has processed his memories. "It wasn't just that I felt like a soldier; at the academy my political motivation flourished, as well. I couldn't pinpoint one specific moment, it was a process that began to replace everything that, until then, had been my dreams and my daily routine: baseball, painting, girls."[6]

Judging by Chávez's own words, expressed much later on,[7] it was at the academy that he began to feel drawn to the leftist military regimes of Latin America. These were years during which the United States, consumed by the Vietnam War, began to suffer the decline of its traditional economic hegemony in the region. As a wave of nationalizations and reforms took place in various countries, the United States became more and more determined to pull political strings all over Latin America, supporting right-wing regimes and sabotaging those of the left. In Venezuela, the government of Christian Democrat Rafael Caldera (1969–74) invoked the thesis of ideological pluralism and "international social justice," aligning itself with those who were calling for a new international order that would diminish the inequalities between North and South. His successor, Social Democrat Carlos Andrés Pérez, nationalized the iron and steel industries, as well as the mammoth oil industry at a time when Venezuela was the world's third largest producer of crude oil. Until then these sectors had been dominated by North American, British, and Dutch interests.

Between 1971 and 1973, the Venezuelan Army was visited by a group of Panamanian cadets, among them the son of General Omar

Torrijos, who had taken control of Panama through a coup d'état, staged when he was still a lieutenant colonel. As the head of the nationalist government from 1968 to 1978, Torrijos put an end to the predominance of the economic elite in Panamanian politics.[8]

"Hearing those kids talk about General Torrijos and the Panamanian Revolution, about how they reclaimed the canal . . . the impact was tremendous."[9] Chávez also felt the blow of September 11, 1973, when Chilean president Salvador Allende was overthrown: "Since I felt a certain affinity for those left-wing tendencies, I was very affected by that coup."[10]

The model that left the deepest mark on Chávez, however, was the nationalist revolution led by Peruvian general Juan Velasco Alvarado (president 1968–75). In 1974, Chávez traveled to Lima with a group of fellow cadets to join the celebrations in commemoration of the 150-year anniversary of the Battle of Ayacucho, which had sealed the independence of Peru. "I was twenty-one years old, in my last year at the academy, and I already had very clear political motivations. For me, as a young soldier, it was extremely moving to witness the Peruvian national revolution in that way. I met Juan Velasco Alvarado personally; one night he received us at the Palace . . . the revolutionary manifesto, the man's speeches, the Inca Plan—I read all those things for years."[11] Velasco, whose government was toppled eight months later by a right-wing coup, gave each of the cadets a gift that night: a little blue paperback entitled *La revolución nacional peruana* (The Peruvian National Revolution), which became a seminal text and a kind of amulet for Chávez, who would carry it in his briefcase everywhere he went, from that point on, up until the day he was arrested during the 1992 coup attempt. That day, the book was lost. Some twenty-five years later, Chávez would order the reprinting of millions of copies of his own *Constitución bolivariana* (Bolivarian Constitution) of 1999, very possibly with that book in mind. But Velasco's book was hardly the only volume to become a touchstone for Chávez.

"With Torrijos, I became a Torrijist. With Velasco, I became a

Velasquist. And with Pinochet, I became an anti-Pinochetist." This was what he declared in 2002, almost three decades after the facts, in an amiable conversation with the Chilean journalist Marta Harnecker. Perhaps it shouldn't come as too much of a surprise that, in the reference game, Chávez omitted the name of Salvador Allende when he made this comment. In other words: he did not become an Allendist. This detail may very well have been an element of the personal profile that Chávez was honing at the time, a reflection of his belief that the military order should always prevail over the civil experience.

Every time he got the chance to return to Barinas, Hugo would spend a great deal of time with his Communist buddies. "By now, our conversations were on a whole different level, politically speaking, both on his side and ours. At this point, both of us, Vladimir and I, were active in the Causa R [Radical Cause], with Vladimir in Barquisimeto and me in Guayana, and we started talking and talking. . . . And in the middle of his life at the academy, putting up with things there, Chávez was a great observer of this process," his friend Federico has stated.

In 1971, Chávez's friends Vladimir and Federico were indeed participating in the creation of the left-wing party known as Causa Radical, the Radical Cause, which was associated with the labor struggle. At the beginning, the group was so small that Federico likens the experience to an old joke, saying that "the Cause was founded inside a Volkswagen." The engine behind the party was Alfredo Maneiro, a philosopher and former Communist guerrilla whom Chávez met a bit later on.

In 1975, the first graduating class of "doctors" in military arts and sciences received their degrees in a solemn ceremony at the academy. President Carlos Andrés Pérez himself placed the saber in the hands of Hugo Chávez, a second lieutenant at the time. At that brief moment, neither could have possibly imagined that their paths would cross again. For the president, Chávez was just another cadet. Chávez had graduated number eight among a group of seventy-five students, with a concentration in engineering, a minor in land expertise, and a specialty in communications. As such he was attached to the radio communication service. The yearbook of his graduating class offers brief profiles of all the cadets, complete with individual caricatures—many of them drawn by Chávez. In this book, Chávez's classmates praise his "camaraderie," his pitching ability, and the "colorful, descriptive, and not least of all entertaining lyrics of his *joropos, corridos,* and *pasajes* [folkloric music from the region of Los Llanos], which he shared with us so that we might truly understand and feel the meaning of his *llanero* homeland."

LUCK WAS ON HIS SIDE. After a month, he was sent to Los Llanos, his homeland, as head of a communications unit, one of the thirteen battalions that the army had established as part of its antiguerrilla efforts in the early 1960s, a decade known in Venezuela as "the violent years." By this time, however, in the state of Barinas and almost everywhere else in Venezuela, there was little or no sign left of the guerrilla. The majority of the country's subversive elements had laid down their weapons in deference to the country's peace-building policies, which made Chávez's work somewhat routine. Drawn to the microphones and the sound of his own voice, he began to host a radio show, and every week his writing would appear in a column in the newspaper *El Espacio.* It was around this time that he began to consider other goals, his big goal: power. At twenty-one years of age, Hugo Chávez was no longer satisfied by the prospect of becoming just another military officer and began to flirt with the idea of staging a coup, according to a friend from Los Llanos, Rafael Simón Jiménez. "Every time he saw me, on any street in Barinas, he would get out of the car to say hello. 'What's up, brother?' I would ask him, and he would answer, 'I'm good, man, because 2000 is around the corner.' And then he would add, 'Before 2000 I'm going to be a general, and I'm going to do something major in this country.' "

A lover of history, he may have felt that Venezuela's history was on his side. In the nineteenth century, the country endured "166 armed confrontations with political intentions, of which 39 were relatively important revolutions expressly aimed at overthrowing the government."[12] During the twentieth century, until that date at least, only five successful coups and some eight unsuccessful ones had been carried out.

The decisive year, however, would be not 1975 but 1977, which was when he began to conspire in earnest. Still a communications officer, he was transferred to a tactical operations center in San Mateo, in the eastern state of Anzoátegui.

Over and over again his personal diary reveals the evolution of his political aspirations and his incipient vision of himself as someone predestined, a man with a historical mission. The entry dated October 25, for example, harks back to Che Guevara's now-legendary 1967 declaration: "Vietnam. One and two Vietnams in Latin America." A few lines away, he did the same with Simón Bolívar: "Come. Return. Here. It is possible." A bit further along he actually inserted himself directly into this saga: "This war is going to take years. . . . I have to do it. Even if it costs me my life. It doesn't matter. This is what I was born to do. How long can I last like this? I feel impotent. Unproductive. I have to get ready. To act." Two days later he would write, "My people are stoic. Passive. Who is going to fan the flames? We could create a great blaze. But the wood is all wet. The conditions aren't there. We don't have the conditions. Goddamn it! When will we have them? Why can't we create them? We don't have the conditions. Subjectively, we do. Objectively, we don't. Tremendous excuse. That's where we are."

The conditions weren't there because Venezuela, right then, was enjoying an period of political stability after four consecutive democratic elections, as well as an economic boom. The country was reveling in the riches generated by its oil industry, the currency was strong, dollars were cheap, and the solid middle class was living quite well indeed. There was even a certain amount of social mobility, and people at the lowest rungs on the social ladder had actually begun to view the future with some measure of optimism. Carlos Andrés Pérez's first term as president was marked by its ostensibly populist policies and an administration in which corruption did not seem especially easy to hide, especially in its last months, according to press archives. In the so-called Saudi Venezuela, where the nouveau riche would jet off for shopping sprees in Miami, a coup was simply not possible.

During this time, Hugo Chávez filled his diary with expressions of frustration and irritation. This is where his nationalism and anti-Americanism began to emerge. At one point, he mentioned that his favorite baseball team, Los Navegantes de Magallanes, had lost a game, and suddenly he confessed, "I let go of that fanaticism. This baseball, it isn't ours. It's theirs, it belongs to the North Americans. Out there, I hear the sound of a *joropo*. That's our music. And that, too, has been trampled by foreign music." He went on to bemoan the fact that "we have no identity" and to question the consumer culture that had invaded Venezuelan society. From there, he went on to surmise that the only salvation for his country was to "cling tight" to its heroic past. Hugo Chávez was scarcely twenty-three years old at the time and married to Nancy Colmenares, also from Barinas. They were awaiting the birth of their first daughter. In his diary, however, none of this is described with the same energy that characterizes his political ruminations.

The pages of his diary also neglect to tell the story of a guerrilla raid[13] that seems to offer another perspective on the president. In the city of Barcelona, the capital of the state of Anzoátegui, Chávez was "looking for combat rations" when some wounded soldiers found their way over to him and he helped carry one of them to safety, though the man would later die in the hospital. As he later confessed to Gabriel García Márquez in 1999, that night he experienced his "first existential conflict" and asked himself some tough questions: "What am I doing here? On one side we have country peasants dressed in military fatigues torturing peasant guerrillas, and on the other side we have peasant guerrillas killing other peasants dressed in green. At this stage, with the war over, there was no point in firing a gun at anyone."[14]

Shortly afterward, Chávez created his first nucleus of conspirators with three other soldiers from Los Llanos. "We gave it a name: The Liberation Army of the People of Venezuela."[15] Around that time he was transferred to Maturín, also in eastern Venezuela. There, he re-connected with his former classmate Jesús Urdaneta Hernández and invited him to join the new initiative. According to Chávez, Urdaneta promised to talk to two other former classmates, Jesús Miguel Ortiz Contreras and Felipe Acosta Carles, who would go on to aid in the creation of the Bolivarian Revolutionary Army two years later. "Those were the first steps we took,"[16] Chávez has stated.

One month before this "first existential conflict," however, the cards had already been dealt. His official account may describe the guerrilla raid and the torture of peasants as a critical moment that changed his way of thinking, but by that time Second Lieutenant Hugo Chávez had, in fact, already made his decision to conspire against the government. On September 18, 1977, his friend Federico Ruiz engineered a meeting with Alfredo Maneiro and Pablo Medina, general secretary and leader, respectively, of the Radical Cause. That night the men held a secret meeting in an apartment that Chávez had been renting across from a military base in the city of Maracay. And as their spaghetti with cheese and fried plantains began to simmer, so did their alliance. "Alfredo was intent on convincing Hugo that the idea right then was to build the organization and start a revolutionary movement that was totally different from the traditional model. Instead of doing it from the top down, he thought it should be carried out from the bottom up."

As Pablo Medina remembers, the meeting with that "skinny guy, straight out of the military, was very short—among other things be-cause Chávez spoke very little. The one who spoke almost the entire time was Alfredo, who told Chávez that he ought to do his best to survive inside the armed forces, not to make mistakes, and, most of all, to do what he could to keep from getting desperate because we were in for a long period of political stability, since the two-party system in Venezuela was by then quite solid." This is what Chávez had to say about this same meeting: "I remember, very clearly, when Maneiro said to me, 'I'm only going to ask you for one thing: I need you to commit yourself and to promise me that whatever we plan together isn't something we're going to do right now but down the line, ten years from now.'"[17]

As they said their good-byes, Maneiro grabbed Federico by the shoulder, pulled him aside, and whispered, "I think we can make something happen with this second lieutenant, what do you say?" Federico simply responded, "Well, we already made some spaghetti with him, didn't we?"

CHAPTER 4

The Man, the Conspirator

A̲s FAR AS ANYONE KNOWS, HUGO CHÁVEZ BEGAN TO LEAD A DOUBLE life when he was around twenty-three. In the presence of military superiors, he would feign obedience and discipline. With his family he pretended to be "neutral," as his mother put it, exhibiting no interest in politics. In his clandestine life, however, he was another person entirely, forging ties with left-wing activists, debating Venezuela's political future with the Ruiz men, refining his powers of observation, so that he could sniff out possible recruits within the military. He was aided by his intuition, eloquence, passion, and innate histrionic streak, which emerged whenever someone pushed a microphone in front of him during armed forces cultural events. But he watched his step at every turn. Nobody inside the institution had any idea what he was up to.

THE LIEUTENANT FROM Sabaneta was far from the only person determined to conspire against the government. In the course of a few months, Chávez made contact with several other army officers who were thinking along the same lines, among them Francisco Arias Cárdenas and air force major William Izarra. While studying for a master's degree at Harvard, Izarra had developed "a revolutionary thesis for the armed forces," and when he returned to Venezuela in 1979, he organized a conspiracy cell with four army officers. R-83, as the cell was named, shorthand for "Revolution 1983," was inspired by the idea of working toward "the implantation of a serious socialist system."[1]

The Cuban Revolution left a deep impression upon Venezuela. Fidel Castro had lent a helping hand to the Venezuelan guerrillas. Toward the end of 1961, Caracas cut off diplomatic relations with Havana in response to Cuba's open support of Venezuelan radical left-wing groups,[2] and in 1963, a shipment of weapons sent by Fidel was intercepted upon arrival, causing a spark that quickly set off a diplomatic meltdown. As a result of this discovery, the Organization of American States (OAS) imposed a series of draconian economic and diplomatic sanctions on Cuba that definitively isolated the island nation.[3] Cuba supported the local guerrillas for almost a decade; it wasn't until August 1969 that Castro decided to withdraw his Sierra Madre commanders. During those years, Chávez was just entering adolescence. In 2004, he recalled those days: "I was thirteen, and I heard over the radio that Che was in Bolivia, that they had him surrounded. I was just a boy, and I remember asking, 'Why doesn't Fidel send some helicopters to rescue him? . . . Fidel has to save him.'"[4]

Chávez also admitted to having been affected by the battles that raged in those days. "I think that the struggles of the 1960s left behind such a strong level of fragmentation and such venom that we ended up contaminated by the product, as well."[5]

The Marxist rebels and the left-wing military officers who allied themselves with the guerrillas to stage the 1962 coup attempts known as El Carúpañazo and El Porteñazo (in reference to the towns where the action was most intense)[6] electrified the country for some time, but they were defeated in the end. By the end of the 1970s, they were nothing but dim memories of "the violent years," little more than footnotes from the past that a handful of people insisted on dredging up over and over again. Among these diehards was the unflinching guerrilla commander Douglas Bravo, the man who founded the Armed Forces of National Liberation after being expelled from the Venezuelan Communist Party in 1966 for straying from the Soviet hard line.

Following the tactic of liaising with the armed forces, Bravo began feeding William Izarra names of officers in the armed forces whom he wanted to draw into the conspiracy. He also connected Izarra with both national and international political groups. International support for the Venezuelan guerrillas came primarily from Cuba and Algeria, and to a lesser and more sporadic degree from Libya, Vietnam, North Korea, and Iraq, according to the testimony of acknowledged former guerrilla leaders. Between 1980 and 1985, Izarra made clandestine trips to Havana, Baghdad, and Tripoli, the governments of which he admired, saying, "Their experiences could serve as lessons that might be applicable for us in our quest for power, as well as later on in the exercise of government."[7] In Tripoli, the air force officer met with Muammar Gaddafi, and the two men met on several subsequent occasions as well. He also claimed to have made contacts in Mexico with Cuban government officials, as well as in London and Barbados.[8]

Toward 1980, Izarra's group, which after 1983 would be renamed the Revolutionary Alliance of Active Military Personnel, made contact with the then lieutenant and antigovernment conspirator Francisco Arias, who was busy identifying potential recruits from within the military academy, where he was an instructor. "More than once they even suggested I travel to Libya, in connection with some Latin American military officers who were going there, to get a sense of Gaddafi's experience," states Arias, who would go on to become a mastermind, along with Chávez, of the 1992 coup attempt. In this way, the conspiring officers made contact with one another, often through Douglas Bravo and his people, slowly building their network. One of their basic texts was Gaddafi's *Green Book*.

William Izarra and Hugo Chávez met for the first time in 1981, but it remains unclear whether during those years Chávez received the same invitations to join the external training trips that Arias made. Soon enough, Arias and Chávez would be linked; as Arias recalls it, their first contact was made via one of Douglas Bravo's men.[9]

"We agreed that there was a need for an organization that could stimulate the process of structural change within the armed forces and in the country in general, and that was when we decided to join the Bolivarian Revolutionary Army,"[10] Arias notes. Bravo and Chávez had still not yet met personally, but the veteran guerrilla, a key influence behind the military movement, would soon enter into contact with the restless officer from the plains.

Hugo Chávez has acknowledged that his older brother, Adán, a physics professor, was one of his greatest political influences: "He was very important in my political education. My brother was in Mérida and was an activist in the MIR [Movimiento de Izquierda Revolucionaria, Movement of the Revolutionary Left].[11] I didn't know it, all I ever noticed was that he and his friends went around with their long hair, some of them with beards. Apparently, I didn't fit in with my short hair, my uniform. [But] I felt very good in that group."[12] Later on, the officer would learn about the activities undertaken by his brother, who was in fact associated with the Party for the Venezuelan Revolution. Douglas Bravo indicated that "in 1982, Chávez joined the rebel officers who were already working with the FAN [Fuerzas Armadas Nacionales, National Armed Forces]."[13] He did this through Adán, who had alerted the party that he had a brother in the army. At that point, through a professor at the University of the Andes, also an activist in the outlawed group, a meeting between Chávez and Bravo was engineered.

"We met on the basis of structuring a civilian-military movement that would make long-term plans for a revolutionary insurrection,"[14] says the former guerrilla leader. Hugo Chávez would meet with Bravo often over the course of several years. And he would make Bravo's ideas his own.

THE FINAL MONTHS of the government of Carlos Andrés Pérez (1974–79) went by amid a flurry of corruption scandals, which paved the way for the opposition. In the 1978 elections, the Venezuelan electorate awarded the presidency to Christian Democrat Luis Herrera Campins, who announced at his inauguration that the country had been "mortgaged" by its foreign debt. Following the oil bonanza of the Pérez administration—the period of the so-called Saudi Venezuela—the inevitable lean years rolled around. The price of crude oil took a sharp nosedive: from $19.3 million in 1981, Venezuelan oil exports fell to $13.5 million in 1983. During this period, foreign investment plummeted and the state coffers were literally drained. Venezuela's foreign debt ballooned to more than $30 billion.

The year 1983 was a turning point of sorts, not just for the conspiring military officers but for Venezuela as a whole. With the economy teetering on the edge of insolvency, the government was forced to devalue its currency for the first time in decades and set restrictions on the sale of dollars to the general public. That day, February 18, 1983, went down in Venezuelan history as "Black Friday." Herrera Campins's administration, dogged by constant economic crises and occasional corruption scandals, gave way to the return of the Social Democrats. It was a time of crisis across the continent, and Venezuela was one more recession-plagued country during the "lost decade" of Latin America.

Hugo Chávez had also entered a kind of crisis around this time: he was seriously thinking about retiring from the military. On a trip to Barinas, he confided this to his old friend José Esteban Ruiz Guevara, who recalls, "I told him, 'No, stay. You say it's a load of shit. Well, stay in and get rid of all that shit you see in the army!' " A captain at the time, Hugo Chávez heeded the advice of his first mentor and stayed in the army, where he began working with the younger men, still on the inside, in the very classrooms of the military academy where he worked as site officer and instructor in Venezuelan military history, from 1981 to 1984.

"There, he took advantage of the opportunity to persuade potential followers from among the group of cadets and second lieutenants—the men who, much later on, would execute his plans. Apparently some of the students' guardians registered complaints with the director of the academy after they heard their sons talking about coups and other related topics,"[15] says General Iván Darío Jiménez. It was during that year at the academy that Chávez created the group that would later become the Bolivarian movement.

December 17, 1983, was no ordinary December day—at least not for the four officers who met at 1 P.M. in the La Placera barracks in Maracay to commemorate the death of Simón Bolívar. The day before, they had chosen an orator by drawing straws: Hugo Chávez was to speak before an audience of a thousand. He began by quoting the Cuban José Martí: "There is Bolívar in the sky of the Americas, watchful and frowning . . . because what he left undone remains undone to this very day." For half an hour he spoke about the Liberator's life, asking himself and his audience: If Bolívar were alive today, what would he think of the way the country was being handled? Would he chastise them for failing to achieve his dream? A jumble of words fell from his lips, prompting one major to say, "Chávez, you sound like a politician." As the event came to a close, the head of the regiment announced that, in memory of Bolívar, everyone had the afternoon off.

Chávez took off with Jesús Urdaneta, Felipe Acosta, and Raúl Baduel. Acosta suggested they run a race. The four men, all from Los Llanos, began sprinting and didn't stop until they reached the remains of the Samán de Güere, a tree immortalized by Bolívar, who had often rested in its shade. "We plucked some leaves, it was all very symbolic, very ritualistic—that's the way we are, us soldiers. Inspired by the president, we paraphrased the Monte Sacro oath and swore that we would never be party, through either omission or action, to the state of things as we saw them in our country,"[16] recalls Baduel, now defense minister and one of Chávez's closest allies.

"I swear to the God of my fathers," they recited in unison, "I swear on my homeland, I swear on my honor, that I will not let my soul feel repose, nor my arm rest until my eyes have seen broken the chains that oppress us and our people by the order of the powerful." Guided by Chávez's solemn voice, the men replaced "the powerful Spanish" whom Bolívar had invoked in his 1805 declaration with "the powerful."

It is difficult to pin down the exact year of the creation of the military group known as the EBR (Ejército Bolivariano Revolucionario,

Bolivarian Revolutionary Army) and then rebaptized EBR-200 in honor of the bicentennial of Bolívar's birth in July 1783. Chávez and Baduel maintain that it came about in 1982. At first, Urdaneta said 1983, and then he said that perhaps it was 1982. The fourth member of the group, Acosta, died in 1989 without ever having spoken publicly about the initiation rite. Chávez himself, however, in a letter dated November 1, 1992, stated, "I have a proposal for you—which, to me, is already a decision: to reorganize the Bolivarian Revolutionary Army 200; the one that was born on December 17, 1983."[17] In the magazine *Quinto Día,* he spoke of the oath and recalled, "that was the year of Black Friday."[18]

The 1983 ritual at Samán de Güere reveals Chávez's affinity for drawing parallels between landmark moments in his life and certain historical events. This unusual act was a point of departure in many ways. Until then, Chávez had been a militant working on his own. Now he had a team. As he has remarked on occasion, "more than a lodge, it was a cell." And it was a cell that soon started reproducing. In three years, the conspirators would hold "five national conferences" for their cause. The first one boasted a public of some fifteen people. The second one took place inside the Maracay central command. By then, Hugo Chávez was using his position as a military academy instructor to raise awareness among the cadets and spur them into action.

Pedro Carreño, one of Chávez's students from the 1985 graduating class, eventually became one of the disciples Chávez attracted to his cause. Today a Chávez party congressman, Carreño recalls the experience: "There, no less than thirty second lieutenants had taken the oath. We were to graduate that year, and we knew we would be scattered among all the military units in the country. Before graduating, each one of us had committed to making contact with at least two cadets before leaving [the academy], to keep the movement from dying out. That was when it began to multiply . . . we knew that the enemies of Venezuela were hunger, corruption, indigence, unemployment, and the misuse of our nation's immense riches. At military school they talked about this, given the overwhelming importance of the topics of security and defense. The ceremony during which we recited our oaths was held during the day. If it was at night, as was often the case during the days of Captain Chávez, it was carried out in the academy's parade ground, where there is a monument called 'The Bust of the Cadet' and, next to it, a votive candle that symbolizes the light that illuminates us all. There are also an oak tree, which represents fortitude, and a *samán* [rain tree], which represents endurance over time. There, we were all sworn in by Chávez himself."

In July 1984, when General Carlos Julio Peñaloza arrived as the military academy's new director, some of the cadets' parents complained to him that the school "was the center of the conspiracy." He duly informed his superiors, and the officers under suspicion were removed from the military academy. Chávez was sent to the town of Elorza in the state of Apure, close to the Colombian border and far from Caracas. The transfer, however, did not discourage him. The most active of all the conspirators, according to Douglas Bravo, "was Hugo Chávez, in both the theoretical and the practical sense. He was tireless, moving around from Táchira to Guayana, to Falcón, to Zulia, organizing officers."[19]

A few months earlier, Social Democrat Jaime Lusinchi had assumed the presidency (1984–89); his administration would go down in the history books as one of Venezuela's most corrupt.

Bravo does not remember the exact date, but sometime in 1984 representatives from the conspiracies within the army, navy, and air force met in the city of Maracay. It was a year of frenetic activity, and Hugo Chávez had his eyes fixed on his goal: to storm the bastion of power. To this end, he worked tirelessly, making contacts and organizing meetings nonstop. Those present at this particular meeting included Chávez, on behalf of the Bolivarian Revolutionary Army; William Izarra, for the Revolutionary Alliance of Active Military Personnel; and an unidentified officer representing the navy.

The men were meeting in a fifth-floor apartment where the windows were outfitted with ropes for escape. The men were tense because they were afraid that agents from the Directorate for Intelligence and Prevention Services might burst in at any moment. There were nine of them: six military officers and three civilians. Hugo Chávez called the meeting to order. According to Arias, he proposed they "search for a 'breaking point' by generating anarchy within the military realm." He wanted to light the flame. He then suggested that they act as a guerrilla group inside the armed forces. "Chávez was proposing that we undertake violent actions. Blowing up electricity posts, for example," said Francisco Arias, who was against it. "That was our first disagreement. I said to him, 'Now? Just as we're building steam, as we're growing stronger, consolidating our territory? . . . We can't think about blowing up electricity posts, drawing our weapons. We have to strengthen our ranks, grow, and politicize the people inside the military so that they can analyze their function critically, and then when we're strong, in a few more years, we'll be able to come out with a political plan.' "

Chávez, however, was impatient and argued with Arias. "The problem is, you get to a point in the revolution, but there's a Social Christian inside of you," he said, referring to Arias's connection to the Jesuits. The meeting went on for hours, and the balance eventually tipped in favor of Arias's proposal: to grow, build strength, and arm themselves with patience. The path of the classic conspiracy. There would be two figureheads: Chávez and Arias, aka Che María and Gabriel. That dawn, they gathered in a circle and held hands to swear in Arias, transporting themselves back to the nineteenth century. To Bolívar's oath, they added the motto of the rebel leader Ezequiel Zamora: "Popular elections, free land, and free men. Horror in the face of the oligarchy." The civilians committed to the cause included Narciso Chávez Suárez, an uncle of Hugo Chávez; a militant from the Party for the Venezuelan Revolution; and one woman, who was given the pseudonym of Anabela, and whose real name was Herma Marksman. In addition to being the most enthusiastic of the civilian activists, she was also Chávez's lover and had been for two years.

—

PROFESSOR MARKSMAN HAD arrived in Caracas in 1984 to work on a postgraduate degree in history and was living with a friend in Prado de María, a neighborhood at the southern end of the city. The apartment of her friend Elizabeth Sánchez served as a meeting point for Hugo Chávez and Douglas Bravo. Elizabeth's cousin, a professor at the University of the Andes, had organized the very first meeting between the two men. Though Herma was unaware of the nature of their meetings, she sensed something mysterious about them. Every time a certain "Martín" came over, her friend would ask her not to leave her room, because she didn't want Herma to recognize Bravo. Hugo would turn up in civilian clothes. After five months of this, Herma knew they were up to something, but her friend still said nothing. Finally, Hugo himself told her everything. "Listen, Herma," he said, "I like you a lot, more than I should, and I have to confess to you, first, that I'm married, but my relationship is traumatic because she [my wife] is someone who doesn't really understand me, I drive in the car with her for hours on end and I have nothing to say to her. . . . But that's nothing. I have a double life: during the day I'm a career military officer who does his job, but at night I work on achieving the transformations this country needs."

That September night in 1984, when Marksman turned thirty-two years old, Hugo proposed a double adventure of sorts: "The one thing I want is for you to help me in this struggle, and to stay at my side until the end of my days. I want you to think about it, reflect on it, and we can decide as we go along." Herma neither thought nor reflected on it; she felt it. At that moment she decided to become a part of Hugo's life, not just as a woman but as a member of his conspiracy. She would go on to work tirelessly on behalf of the movement, becoming well known among her comrades in the Bolivarian Revolutionary Army under the pseudonym of Commander Pedro Luis, among others.

According to Marksman, "Hugo was the head, the one who worked round the clock for that cause, every day, all year long. I saw it all up close: he was the one who scheduled the meetings, organized the agenda, and together we would contact everyone. . . . During those years he worked nonstop." Of the Chávez family, only Hugo's brother Adán participated in some of the meetings. According to Marksman, the others were not aware of what was going on. Around that time Bravo, well seasoned in the art of clandestine activity, served as a kind of adviser to Chávez, offering him guidance on some issues and urging him to be more careful. "Douglas told him that there were already too many people involved with and aware of the conspiracy, and he advised him to close the circle," recalls Marksman. By the time this decision was made, in 1986, it was too late: one lieutenant who had attended an earlier meeting had "talked too much." And though eyebrows had been raised before at the military academy, this was the first real accusation. "He is either a man with very good luck, or else Maisanta really and truly protects him," says Herma, referring to Chávez's great-grandfather, a controversial figure who participated in the rural uprisings at the turn of the twentieth century. In response to a particularly idiosyncratic need that might well etch him into the Latin American tradition of magical realism, Chávez would go on to venerate Maisanta when he became president, invoking him as one of the gods sitting atop his self-styled Mount Olympus.

"A young man whom Hugo had tried to bring into the group found out about the accusation in the army command headquarters because he saw the report and informed them in time." With the Bolivarian Revolutionary Army on high alert, Marksman ran off like mad with a box of documents under her arm; at dawn, she burned them on a beach at Macuto, half an hour from Caracas. Hugo was not always discreet and circumspect. He would hide what he had to hide, but every so often he did something rash, like ordering his subordinates to sing Zamora's federalist anthem, the chorus of which is "Tremble, oligarchs, long live freedom," or spouting impassioned speeches in plazas everywhere. In those days, Herma says, the security agencies left much to be desired: "I can't believe they didn't discover what he was doing."

CHAPTER 5

Preparing the Uprising

Toward the end of the 1980s, the indisputable leaders of the Bolivarian Revolutionary Army were Hugo Chávez and Francisco Arias, making decisions and planning their long-term strategy for their big day. Between 1986 and 1987, based on the "hammock thesis," they decided to wait until the midway point of the next administration, which would begin in February 1989, before attempting a coup. According to this thesis, government administrations generally enjoy higher popularity ratings at the beginning and end of their terms, whereas the middle period tends to register a lull. This movement is visually represented by the curve of the hammock. Far more relevant, however, was the second reason that led them to hedge their bets on the long term: the fact that they, as officers, would have troops under their command by that time. Sometime between 1991 and 1992 the moment would be ripe for action.

In 1987, Hugo Chávez, having been promoted to the rank of major, was transferred to Caracas—specifically, to Miraflores Palace, as an aide to General Arnoldo Rodríguez Ochoa, secretary-general of the National Security and Defense Council. Once again, historical happenstance had a hand in his life story. There he was, at the epicenter of Venezuelan power, when, in December 1988, Carlos Andrés Pérez was reelected president, commanding 52.9 percent of the vote. CAP, as he is called by Venezuelans, was back, but the "Saudi Venezuela" of his first term was now in dire economic straits. Scarcely three weeks after an inauguration ceremony so extravagant that the press nicknamed it "the coronation," the new head of state issued a package of economic adjustments that sparked massive social unrest. On February 27, 1989, public transportation fares went up, causing riots in Guarenas, half an hour away from Caracas. Suddenly the protest extended to the lower middle classes, who took to the streets in droves and vandalized storefronts. The flurry of rioting spread like wildfire, and in a few hours the capital of Venezuela was sacked and looted. A massive swarm of Caracas's poorest residents pounced on the city, taking food, appliances, furniture, records, frying pans, and even cash registers. Pérez sent in the army to control the rioting and imposed a curfew the following day, but by then the death toll was already in the hundreds. Felipe Acosta, one of the four founding officers of the Bolivarian Revolutionary Army, was among the victims.

Hugo Chávez was lucky: he didn't have to use his rifle during those dark days. He had left Caracas the day before the riots, having been diagnosed with chicken pox, and later stated that he had been at his home in Maracay with his wife, Nancy. According to Herma Marksman, however, she had been with Chávez that day in the country's capital. No matter where he was, Chávez became convinced that *el caracazo,* as the incident came to be called, "sensitized many people in the military, especially the youngest ones, who experienced the horror up close," and it served to "accelerate things considerably." In the aftermath of the incident, a number of officers in the presidential guard who had been confidants of Pérez joined the conspiracy.

In some way this popular uprising led Chávez to believe that the time had come to take action. The firewood was no longer wet. Finally the conditions were there, as he might have written in his diary. Later on it became clear that neither military nor civil intelligence had been working very hard to infiltrate conspiracies, that the executive branch had not paid much attention to the matter.

An odd episode toward the end of 1988 served as a wake-up call: on "the night of the tanks," as the incident came to be called, a column of armored vehicles emerged from Fort Tiuna, bound for the Ministry of the Interior. With the president out of the country, the stewardship of Venezuela had fallen to Interior Minister Simón

Alberto Consalvi, who was sitting in his office at 7 P.M. when he received word that ten tanks had surrounded the city block and a squadron of soldiers had occupied the doors to the building. Consalvi was then told that the soldiers were under orders to guard him. Consalvi recalls, "I called Minister of Defense Italo del Valle Alliegro to tell him what was going on, and he told me, 'Oh, Minister, you and your black comedy—for the first time in weeks I'm sitting here [at home] in my pajamas watching television.' " Consalvi convinced him that this was no joke and asked him to order the military officers to "withdraw and allow me to leave." The defense minister obliged, and when the acting president met with the high command later on, the military officers offered no explanation for what had happened.

"Nothing was investigated . . . that republic was paradise on earth for conspirators," Consalvi says. "No serious investigation was ever launched. Nothing serious and nothing not serious, either. As far as I understand it, Hugo Chávez was not involved in that affair. I never heard that. Maybe it served him in some way, as an example of how far you could take a conspiracy without suffering major consequences." Chávez himself stated that he was interrogated about the incident but had had nothing to do with it. From that point on, however, the conspirators were under much closer watch.

By December 1989, the suspicions of certain generals were confirmed, and they duly identified the leaders of the former Bolivarian Revolutionary Army, which by then had been renamed the Bolivarian Revolutionary Movement to reflect the civilian elements that had been incorporated into the organization. On December 6, the day of the regional elections, Hugo Chávez was removed from Miraflores Palace, taken into custody, and delivered to the Defense Ministry at Fort Tiuna, where he was greeted by his co-conspirators, Majors Jesús Urdaneta, Jesús M. Ortiz, and Yoel Acosta, among others. They were accused of conspiring to assassinate President Carlos Andrés Pérez and the entire military high command during their Christmas dinner. "Some fifteen of us, all majors, got arrested that day," Chávez said.

An investigative council was subsequently convened to handle the case, but no charges were ever made due to lack of evidence. General Carlos Julio Peñaloza, commander general of the army, and Manuel Heinz Azpúrua, chief of the Directorate for Intelligence and Prevention Services, who were the bloodhounds behind the detentions and the investigation, did manage to have the officers in question transferred to various remote locations far away from one another. According to Chávez, General Fernando Ochoa Antich, the defense minister at the time, invited him to dinner on the very same day he was interrogated. For the three hours they were together, the general calmed Chávez down, reiterating that he believed in his innocence. "Ochoa said good-bye to me there and told me, 'You can count on me, I told Peñaloza to send you to me, under my command.' And that was what happened: they transferred me to the combat brigade in Maturín, which reported to Ochoa, who was the commander of all the brigades in the east."

WHILE HUGO CHÁVEZ was in Maturín, he began to take the General Staff course via long distance, though he had a bit of a hard time with it.

"Commander Chávez failed military intelligence, a technical subject. He almost passed when he took the exam a second time, but he was not removed from the course, because that might have been perceived as a form of retaliation against him and a suspicion that he was conspiring [against the government],"[1] Minister Ochoa commented on one occasion. Chávez, in fact, has declared in no uncertain terms that there was a conscious effort to fail him and thus thwart his military career. "They tried to kick me out of the General Staff course, hiding exams from me so that I would flunk out of the classes. . . . I passed, but just barely, at the bottom."[2] During those years Chávez also registered for a postgraduate course in political science at Simón Bolívar University, and following his sudden departure from Caracas he relocated to the university's satellite branch in Maturín. One of his professors, Federico Welsch, remembers him as "just another student, one of the students in the top quarter, who maintained a good average in the courses he took. A student with a low profile, with no desire to dominate the discussions. Not at all . . . he had a hard time attending class because he was stationed in Maturín, but still he managed to get himself the education. . . . He was a hard worker, quiet." Or so he pretended. He himself has acknowledged that the postgraduate course "was very difficult because it was a matter of hiding my reading and my work through the classes I took; [we had to] pretend that we were working toward improving the armed forces."[3]

According to his postgraduate thesis proposals, which he sent via Herma, Chávez said that he "was thinking about working on a thesis regarding political transitions, inspired by the Spanish transition, from an authoritarian regime to a democratic one," according to Federico Welsch, whom the army major had selected as his tutor. His average hovered at around 4.5 out of a possible 5. In the end, however, Chávez did not go on to earn his postgraduate political science degree.

It was around the middle of 1991 when the Bolivarian Revolutionary Movement began counting the days until the coup. During this time, Chávez began to put distance between himself and the civilians, in particular those from the Party for the Venezuelan Revolution. For several years he had continued to cultivate a very intense relationship with Douglas Bravo, unbeknownst to the majority of the conspiring officers, who did not wish to be connected in any way to the radical left. In fact, according to Herma Marksman, back in 1986 Francisco Arias had stated very clearly that he would join the movement only if they were kept out of the picture. "Douglas would come to my house, but I never told anyone because Hugo had asked me to keep quiet about it. I never told a single one of the officers, it was a kind of secret between me and Hugo. He said to me, 'This cannot leave this room' . . . and when I moved to my apartment in El Paraíso, he [Douglas] would turn up in some kind of disguise. . . . Hugo was very worried that the other officers would find out."

Chávez began to distance himself from the ex-guerrilla a few months before the insurrection. Bravo sensed that Chávez did not trust civilians and felt that this was why the coup, originally intended to be a civilian-military operative, turned out to be a purely military endeavor.

In 1991, Hugo Chávez was promoted to the rank of commander. "As we continued to receive our troop units, the Plan Ezequiel Zamora [for the coup] was put into action, with military and political missions, the project of the constitutional [assembly] as well as economic projects, and we were constantly thinking about who among us would be the ones to govern, etc." According to the "hammock thesis," the moment was ripe. The temperature had risen elsewhere, as well: Hugo Chávez was very, very angry. After finishing his General Staff course, he was given a second-rate administrative job at a supply post in the city of Cumaná in eastern Venezuela. As Chávez recalled, the news was like "a slap in the face." But it wouldn't last for long. The wheel of fortune spun, once again, in his favor. Two weeks later, as August 1991 neared, another commander who had been stationed in Maracay to head up a battalion of paratroopers asked to be relieved from duty. According to Chávez, Minister Ochoa decided to have Chávez fill the vacancy—despite the fact that as a commander with a specialty in armored vehicles, Chávez should have been leading a tank battalion, not a group of paratroopers. Chávez assumed the position, despite the fact that in June, just after being sworn in as defense minister, Ochoa had received a detailed report with names, places, and dates of Chávez's conspiratorial undertakings. According to Iván Darío Jiménez, head of the armed forces' Unified Command at the time, the major who drew up the report "was disregarded. And then, on top of it, he was forced to undergo a psychiatric exam."[4]

The die had been cast. Hugo Chávez was now a commander. Starting August 28, he would be heading up a key battalion. The preparations gained momentum.

It wasn't until the end of the year, however, that the chief conspirators gave some thought to the day after, to the Venezuela that would be theirs following the coup. In November, they turned to an intellec-

tual who had been active in the Communist Youth, one of the founding members of the Party for the Venezuelan Revolution, and asked
him to create a document that would outline the legal framework and
the administrative structure of their regime. The intellectual in question was Kléber Ramírez Rojas, a civil engineer who had retired to a
small plot of land in Los Andes when Francisco Arias persuaded him
to join the movement in the middle of 1990. Later on, with Kléber
Ramírez's theses in mind, Chávez renamed his party the Movimiento
V República—the Fifth Republic Movement—and whenever he
would speak of the inaugural phase of his own administration he
would refer to it as "the fifth republic."

December was a feverish month of many a fruitless effort. A
group of impatient captains threatened to stage an uprising of their
own, with the support of the left-leaning Bandera Roja (Red Flag)
party, if the commanders didn't take action soon. This, in turn,
prompted them to set dates and establish plans that they would end
up scrapping at the last minute. First they thought they might take advantage of the annual parade on December 10 held in honor of the
air force, to stop CAP in his tracks. Then they postponed it until the
sixteenth and then, finally, they set Christmas as the target date. The
situation was unbearably tense.

"I had to threaten several captains that I would tie them to a tree if
they tried anything, and, of course, then I had to come to Caracas and
get myself into Miraflores to speak with the battalions and to tell our
officers that until they received a written order signed by me, along
with a security code word, no action was to be taken," recalls Chávez.
"That December was a black one for us. We had the enemy right behind us, and serious internal problems that were threatening to split
us apart. Rumors were flying everywhere, and people were saying
that those of us at the top had backed out, that we had made a deal
with the defense minister."[5]

In addition to all this, Chávez had had a serious disagreement with
someone who was to be a key figure in the uprising: his friend Jesús
Urdaneta, an army commander who had participated relatively little

in the preparatory meetings "because I just couldn't stand those meetings, they went on for hours and hours, for so many years." Urdaneta had told them, however, that when the moment arrived, he would tell them what he thought of the operative.

"When we were discussing the general plan of action, in November 1991, he had a serious problem with me because the two of us would be coming to Caracas, where there were fourteen objectives. He had assigned me twelve and given himself only two. I got annoyed and said I didn't agree with the plan: 'If there are twelve, then it should be six for you and six for me.' He got very irritated and said to me, 'How dare you come here, at this stage in the game, and tell me that you don't agree with the plan?' And I said, 'Just because I did not help map out this plan does not mean that I don't have the right to tell you that I disagree with something I think is poorly distributed. Plus, it is completely crazy, and I'm not going in with you. I won't support you in that game. I'm not going!' And I left, furious."

Things went ahead as planned. On December 31, meetings were held in Caracas and Maracay. On January 1, Hugo Chávez met with Francisco Arias and Kléber Ramírez in Barquisimeto to talk details. Then he returned to Maracay to patch things up with Urdaneta. "He creeps up behind me and says, '*Compañero,* you were right,' because when Chávez needs to swallow his pride, he does. 'My plan was all wrong, I reformulated it. I'm leaving for Caracas with Chivito [Yoel Acosta]. I did a better job of distributing the work. Since you know Maracay, you stay here,' " Urdaneta recalls him saying. "He knew me very well, he knew that he would achieve more by behaving himself."

During this period, Venezuela was not a happy country, nor did Carlos Andrés Pérez seem a particularly happy president. By November, his approval rating had sunk to 35 percent.[6] The year ended with an inflation rate of 31 percent. And as the new one began, public transportation fares and telephone rates went up; the dwindling water supply sparked massive protests; the doctors' and teachers' strikes went on; and students staged riots at the Central University of Venezuela. *The New York Times* stated that the Venezuelan government was clearly not in the business of punishing corruption. Labor groups were demanding a 50 percent increase in the minimum wage, but the only publicly announced raise was for military personnel, who received a 33 percent raise in salary.

January came to an end. There was no time to lose. Chávez knew that his superiors were planning to have him transferred far away, to the western town of El Guayabo, on the Colombian border, by February 15. "For that reason, I spoke to Arias and Urdaneta and laid it out for them: if we didn't take action in the next fifteen days, it was over . . . Pérez was away. The Thursday before the week of February 4, we met one last time in Caracas, and they left it up to me to pick a date. That decision would depend on the day Pérez returned. We remained on alert from Thursday the thirtieth."[7]

On Sunday, February 2, close to midnight, Chávez received a phone call from the palace. A contact informed him, in code, of the date and time that President Carlos Andrés Pérez would touch down in Caracas after his trip to Europe. The commander glanced at his watch. The countdown began.

CHAPTER 6

Stroke of Luck

I N REALITY, IT COULD HAVE HAPPENED TO ANYONE. UNWITTINGLY, HOW-
ever, the Venezuelan voters had decided that it would happen to
Carlos Andrés Pérez, when they elected him president in December
1988. Seventeen years had gone by since the president had placed the
saber in the hands of the young official everyone called Goofy. Pérez
was returning from the Davos Economic Forum in Switzerland. Sixty-
nine at the time, he was bone tired: two sleepless days followed by a
grueling twelve-hour flight. As the aircraft taxied down the runway at
the Simón Bolívar International Airport at Maiquetía, thirty minutes
from Caracas, the one thing on his mind was getting home to La
Casona and resting his head on his pillow.

It was 10:10 in the evening on Monday, February 3, 1992. As the
plane touched down, Pérez was jolted out of his bleary-eyed haze
when he saw General Fernando Ochoa waiting for him. "I always told
Interior Minister Virgilio Ávila Vivas to be there [at the airport].
Whenever I returned from a trip, he was the one person I would see,
so that he could update me on things. I was taken aback when I saw
the defense minister. So I asked him, 'What are you doing here?' and
he replied, 'Well, I was in Maracaibo and I heard that you were on
your way home, so I decided to stay and wait for you.' For the moment, they didn't say anything. Then, as I was getting into my car,
Ochoa said to me, 'President Pérez, around here people were saying
that they weren't going to let you land.' But that it was just a rumor,
you know. That was all they said to me."

Considered an old fox in the world of Venezuelan politics, Pérez was annoyed. Not alarmed. So he gave Ochoa an order: "I don't like rumors involving the armed forces. Tomorrow at eight a.m. I will be waiting for you and the military commanders in Miraflores so that we can open an investigation." That meeting never happened, nor did they need to intercept any rumors. Once he arrived home, the president dismissed the patrol cars with his bodyguards, dragged his feet up to his bedroom, put on his pajamas, and collapsed onto his bed.

At that very moment, in Maracay, Hugo Chávez was wide awake, more awake than ever. And he was smoking. Chain-smoking. It was time to activate Operation Zamora. He himself had made the decision early that Monday morning. Zero hour would be midnight. His great night had only just begun. He had already issued the order for some 460 men,[1] of the paratroopers' battalion under his command, to board twenty rented buses that would take them to the state of Cojedes in the region of Los Llanos, where they were to embark on a training session—that, at least, was what the drivers and 440 recruits believed. Chávez acknowledged, "Of those men, only a very small group of officers knew what we were going to do that night, the troops didn't know a thing."[2] In other words, their superiors had decided that these men would risk their lives for a political enterprise about which they knew nothing. The conspirators and their unwitting recruits left the Libertador Air Base at approximately eleven in the evening. Several minutes went by, and then, in a flash, Commander Chávez, riding in a vehicle ahead of the buses, surprised his driver by suddenly ordering him to take a detour toward Caracas. The driver objected, stating that it was not the route they had agreed upon. Chávez, firm and unblinking, told him that there were riots in the capital and that what he had just said was an order. They were to go to Caracas.

His explanation was not terrifically far-fetched. According to the newspaper El Universal, a total of 120 protests and 46 strikes had taken place during the first three years of Pérez's government. And only three days earlier, the police had threatened to intervene in response to the student riots at the Central University of Venezuela. President

Pérez was sailing in choppy waters: 81 percent of the Venezuelan populace no longer had faith in him, and though 50 percent of all Venezuelans claimed to respect their president, 57 percent stated that they wanted a new government. Half of the population would repudiate a coup d'état, but a significant third would support one. Something was brewing. The possibility of a coup had, in fact, already been examined in a study conducted by the survey firm Mercanálisis, the results of which had been published on January 27. When asked, "Do you think that military officers would or would not participate in a coup?" 31 percent said yes, and 59 percent got it very wrong with a resounding "no." Ten percent didn't know what to think. Carlos Andrés Pérez likely fell into this last group.

The president snored away in his bedroom inside La Casona. Then, ten minutes before midnight, he was jolted awake by a ringing phone, which he answered testily. Between yawns, he heard the word "coup" at the other end of the line, and he jumped with a start, instantly recognizing the sharp voice of Minister Ochoa: "There's been an uprising at the Zulia garrison!" The president dressed so quickly that he didn't even remove his pajamas before putting on his suit. Never a man to take refuge by fleeing, he was on his way to Miraflores in a matter of minutes, without bodyguards. On the way there, his car crossed paths with military vehicles being driven by conspirators, who never would have guessed that the man behind the wheel of the car hurtling down the highway was the president. It was 12:05 A.M. by the time Pérez made it through the palace gates. Right behind him was the chief of his personal security detail, Vice Admiral Iván Carratú. Inside Miraflores, Interior Minister Ávila Vivas and several aides-de-camp were already waiting for him. Minutes later, as he absorbed the first few reports, the siege began. Pérez's pulse would not flicker if he had to use a machine gun, but his hands were ice cold.

In the meantime, Hugo Chávez was just arriving at his destination: the Military History Museum at La Planicie, about a mile from Miraflores. Chávez claims he entered the museum at around 12:30 A.M.

to lead the insurrection that would take place in Caracas. By that hour, the insurgents had already taken their positions at the following locations: Maracaibo, the capital of the oil-rich state of Zulia and the second largest city in the country; Valencia, the third largest city; and Maracay, a key location because of its military installations. Commander Chávez was unaware that CAP was already at Miraflores. According to the plan, by that hour, the coup's most important human target was already to have been arrested at the Maiquetía airport or captured at La Casona. According to Chávez, "the operational plan Ezequiel Zamora was conceived on the basis of several principles of war. One of them was the element of surprise. . . . Surprise, tactics, mobility and a concentration of troops at nerve centers. That was the strategic plan."[3] The element of surprise, however, often works both ways. Chávez and the five men who stepped out of the car with him were received "with a spray of machine-gun fire that almost wiped us out right then and there," he says. The leader of the coup then summoned his histrionic talents, assuring the military officers guarding the museum that they were reinforcements who had just been alerted of a possible riot. According to Chávez, his performance was convincing.

At La Casona, a fierce battle raged with misinformed insurgents on one side, and agents from the Directorate for Intelligence and Prevention Services on the other. The president, by now, was long gone. The first lady, Blanca Rodríguez de Pérez, and one of her daughters, joined the forces attempting to repel the onslaught of the insurgents.[4] At La Carlota airport, shots were fired in both directions. The air base, east of Caracas, had been taken by Commander Yoel Acosta Chirinos. The sound of cocked guns thundered in the ears of the people living in the vicinity, who slowly woke up to the realization that this was not just another night of garden-variety delinquency. Chávez then ordered two of his captains to launch the frontal attack on Miraflores, and one of them clumsily steered a Dragon tank up the palace stairs, intending to knock down the front door. The moment was captured on television, offering the Venezuelan people a truly absurd image to ponder. Was there really no other way to take down the palace? The insurgents had twelve tanks on their side. Inside the palace, Pérez knew he had to get out as soon as possible. But where would he go? That was when he said to himself: "I have to get on television to take control of this." He and his advisers decided to broadcast on Venevisión, owned by the magnate Gustavo Cisneros.

BY NOW BOTH THE insurgents and those loyal to the government had begun to count their first casualties of dead and wounded. Shortly before one in the morning, they reached the television station, in the neighborhood of Las Palmas.

By 12:50 A.M., Chávez had telephoned Marksman. "All he said was 'I'm nearby,' and then he hung up." Ten minutes later, he received a phone call from Acosta, who informed him that La Carlota was under control. At the museum in La Planicie, someone had turned on a television. Chávez, who had yet to unveil his plot to the world, sat waiting to see his face appear on the tiny screen, exhorting the people of Venezuela to join the uprising. That was part of the plan. A dozen or so troops had been ordered to take control of the television station and broadcast his proclamation, which he had recorded on videotape. As it turned out, his men had indeed commandeered the station but had been unable to transfer the video to U Matic format, a simple process they were not familiar with. In light of this glitch, they had no choice but to settle for the explanation of the station's technical staff: it couldn't be done. And so, just when Chávez least expected it, the face of Carlos Andrés Pérez, not his own, suddenly appeared on the screen. Overwrought, his hair a mess, the president of the nation announced that a group of "rogues" had attempted to overthrow the government and that the coup was doomed to fail.

At the museum, all eyes turned to the commander. "That's right. This is a coup and we have you surrounded," Chávez said, raising his voice several notches to intimidate the officers stationed at the museum. "Surrender your weapons, because if you don't the massacre will start right here between you and us."[5] According to Chávez, a group of reinforcements arrived, allowing him to maintain control over the museum until almost 2 A.M. By then, however, the assault on Miraflores was already a disaster. President Pérez had made it to safety, and the government's forces had effectively subdued the insurgents. Failure hung in the night air.

By the time Pérez took to the airwaves, Commander Francisco Arias had already gained control of the military garrison at Maracaibo and had the governor of the state of Zulia in custody. Commanders Jesús Urdaneta and Jesús M. Ortiz were still fighting away in the Maracay-Valencia industrial axis, and in Caracas, Commander Acosta had seized control of La Carlota and arrested the head of the Venezuelan Air Force.[6] Just before 3 A.M., Chávez made telephone contact with Ortiz, who asked, *"Compadre,* what about the media?"

Chávez replied, "I'm waiting for them, too." According to Chávez, that was when "the operational plan started to unravel. Incommunicado and surrounded, the people in Miraflores didn't make it, but they achieved something I consider heroic."[7] He was referring, no doubt, to the desperate tank maneuver, carried out by two captains who would later be elected as state governors during the Chávez administration.[8] In the capital—specifically Miraflores, the power base—Operation Zamora had not turned out as planned.

By that time, the entire nation was glued to the television, witnessing a parade of overtired political leaders declare their support for the democratic regime. The coup attempt quickly made international headlines: George Bush, Sr., telephoned Pérez, and in another irony, Fidel Castro wrote a telegram filled with warmth and solidarity for his Venezuelan counterpart, claiming he was "overwhelmed with concern." Among those who lost sleep that evening was Chávez's mother, Elena, who learned of the coup from Cecilia, one of the Chávez family's neighbors.

"When that woman told me what had happened, this—" Elena Frías de Chávez said, her hands fluttering over her heart, "everything just fell apart. No, Cecilia, my son, my God!" She had last seen her son the previous Christmas. That night, her husband, Hugo de los

Reyes, was sleeping in La Chavera, the family's tiny farm outside Barinas. In a moment of desperation, Elena—who knew nothing of Hugo's insurrectionist pretensions—woke up her son Narciso, the only one at home that night, and together they called Adán. Although Adán was fully apprised of the conspiracy, he focused on trying to calm his mother down: "Hugo's not here, actually." Why hadn't he called? asked Elena. "He must be sleeping," replied her eldest son.

This distressed her even more, because they were unable to locate her daughter-in-law Nancy and her three grandchildren. So she planted herself in front of the TV set. President Pérez's face, once again, appeared on the screen. "He said that it was the battalion of the red berets. . . . That was unbearable."

By now Elena, a woman who cries easily, was beyond consolation. "It was terrible, I kept on saying to myself, 'Oh, no, will they kill him? Will they do that to me? Is my son already dead? Wounded? Oh, this is such torture!' "

At around 4 A.M., her son, while not dead, was surely feeling quite lost. The assault on Miraflores had been repelled. The tank drivers, sidestepping the wounded and the dead, were now making their way to jail. The leader of the insurrection, however, continued to remain a mystery to the Venezuelan people. At that moment, Commander Hugo Chávez felt, as he himself later declared, like "a caged tiger. I didn't know how to face it, what to do." Communications had broken down, and neither the infantry, nor the reserves, nor the artillery cannons had taken the positions they should have. A rat, Chávez claimed, must have brought down the coup. It is known that a captain[9] who was a member of the Bolivarian Revolutionary Movement had alerted his superiors of the plot, although according to military reports, nothing ever came of this tip. "The information, initially obtained at around 1 P.M. on Monday, February 3, was incomplete and vague: when army intelligence and the Directorate for Military Intelligence evaluated it, they assumed that it was limited to a series of actions that would be carried out at the International Airport at Maiquetía, to detain the president of the republic."[10]

Commander Acosta later stated that they had confirmed the participation of "around twenty-seven commanders for the operational
plan, and of that entire number, only five of us went out. The rumor
that some captain had betrayed the movement broke a lot of hearts."
The main objective of Operation Zamora, according to Chávez at
least, was to capture the president. A commando was to apprehend
him when he arrived at Maiquetía and take him directly to the
Military History Museum. If that didn't work, their backup plan was
to arrest him in one of the tunnels on the highway into Caracas. And
if that didn't work, they would make a third attempt at La Casona.

"Various attempts were made to catch him, but Pérez was slip-
pery,"[11] Chávez has said. And what was the overall objective? "That
was the idea, to create the power vacuum. We would be the ones to
fill it."[12] Ironically, the same "power vacuum" thesis would be invoked
ten years later by the men who attempted to overthrow the government of Hugo Chávez.

The failure to capture the elusive chief commander demoralized
Chávez. But that wasn't the only thing that went wrong: "The surprise didn't work, mobility was lost, the firepower fell, everything
fell."[13] It seemed to be time to surrender, but Chávez's show was still
far from over. In fact, he hadn't even gotten started.

As dawn broke on February 4, Venezuela was a country of glassy
eyes, the glassiest of which were likely those of President Pérez, who
was back in his office at Miraflores Palace preparing to issue a third
televised address assuring the country that the coup was a thing of
the past. This was not true. For starters, the La Carlota air base was
still in the hands of the insurgents, as were the garrisons in
Maracaibo, Maracay, and Valencia. At his side were Minister Avila and
General Ochoa, who already had spoken with Chávez over the phone
and tried to get him to lay down his weapons. Ochoa had also sent
Chávez a message in the early dawn with two emissaries: General
Ramón Santeliz and Fernán Altuve, a civil engineer and former
teacher at the military academy who is currently special commis-
sioner at the Defense Ministry. Ochoa was not interested in negotiat-

ing with Arias. He knew that the head of the military revolt was Commander Hugo Chávez.

Pérez had also considered bombing the museum at dawn. "I advised him against it because there were lot of people living in the area around La Planicie. And so he decided to have two F-16 planes fly overhead," says Iván Carratú, who remained at the president's side that morning.

Still indignant, the former president of Venezuela recalls how he brought in the defense minister to direct the operations from Miraflores during the coup: "And at some point, Ochoa said to me, 'Listen, it wouldn't be a bad idea to talk to Chávez, to tell him to surrender and save us more trouble.' I said to him, 'All right, but who should speak with him?' And he said, 'Right here, we've got General Santeliz, he's a friend of Chávez's. We can send him.' That was when I made the mistake of sending Santeliz out to get Chávez to surrender. Because the two of them struck a deal."

Santeliz went back to La Planicie with Altuve. They arrived at the Military History Museum shortly before 8 A.M.

"Now I really am thinking seriously about surrendering," Chávez told them. He asked them to guarantee that neither he nor his troops would be killed. Moreover, he refused to hand over his rifle because he was convinced that the men had been given orders to assassinate him. Santeliz not only agreed to his conditions but also granted an extra request during a mysterious lull in time: he promised Chávez that he and his "custodians" would leave the museum alone, in the general's car, with Altuve behind the wheel. Almost two hours went by before they reached their destination, which was no more than fifteen minutes away. What did they do during all this time? Some say they destroyed documents and compromising evidence. Despite repeated denials of Santeliz's involvement in the plot, Chávez does concede that "Santeliz and Altuve behaved very well."[14]

Neither Chávez nor Santeliz has ever offered a satisfactory explanation of this episode. A report issued some time later states that the rebel leader remained in the museum "until 7:45 A.M. of February 4, when he decided to surrender."[15] Chávez arrived at Fort Tiuna at 9:30 in the morning. According to General Iván Jiménez, at the time the head of the Joint Chiefs of Staff, the lull was even longer. In an account published four years after the coup, Jiménez reproduced a telephone conversation between himself and Chávez at 7 A.M. Jiménez had given him an ultimatum: "Either you surrender, or the museum is going to be attacked [by the air force]."

Chávez replied, "All right, General. I surrender."

"They brought me to Ochoa's office," continued Chávez, "[on the] fifth floor of the Defense Ministry, I handed over my rifle, I handed over my pistol, my hand grenades, my radio, and I sat down on a sofa and asked for some coffee." He also requested cigarettes. "And I slowly got hold of myself. Surrendering is something worse than death. When I surrendered for my men, I told them I would have rather died. I mean, I fell to pieces, and I just kept on falling."[16] That is how Chávez, some eight months before he would win the presidential elections of 1998, recalled the moment of his surrender. Vice Admiral Elias Daniels, who received the defeated military officer because Ochoa was in Miraflores, remembers him as a disciplined man who behaved in classic military fashion. "He entered the office and, in a very respectful but firm tone of voice, saluted and then said to me, in these words, more or less, 'My admiral, Commander Hugo Rafael Chávez Frías has come to lay down his weapons.' He was aware of the mess he'd gotten himself into. I asked him where he was from, I asked him about his family, and then I said, 'Would you like to speak to your mother?' And he replied, 'Yes, I would appreciate that. Mamá, it's Hugo,' he said." At the other end of the line Elena Frías de Chávez burst into sobs. Once Chávez hung up, Daniels asked him why he had done it. "And he said to me that it was because of how bad the situation was in the army, he talked about boots, military equipment, things like that . . . housing, clothes, machinery. . . . His discourse had absolutely no relation to the civilian world." Even as Chávez surrendered, his fellow insurgents held tight to their positions at the La Carlota airport, Maracaibo, Valencia, and Maracay. As time passed, the high command began to learn who they were and how many: "There are 5 lieutenant colonels who are the visible heads of this movement, followed by 14 majors, 54 captains, 67 second lieutenants, 65 noncommissioned officers, 101 troop sergeants, and 2,056 enlisted soldiers."[17] In total there were 2,367 uniformed men[18] representing ten different battalions, some 10 percent of the total number of battalions in the armed forces.

The Venezuelan people were hungry for information. Soon enough, however, they would be able to connect a face to the uprising, for history would take a surprising turn, when Hugo Chávez transformed a failed coup into the advertising campaign of the decade.

THE DEFENSE MINISTRY was in a feverish state. Top-ranking generals were stationed at Fort Tiuna, analyzing the best way to neutralize the rebel strongholds in Caracas, Maracaibo, Valencia, and Maracay. They didn't think the insurgents could cause more damage at this point, but they were afraid of more confrontations erupting. Determined to wipe out the rebellion by noon, they knew their foremost objective was to prevent "an atmosphere of ungovernability" and to keep things from "spinning out of control in public protests," as Daniels recalled. And they thought they had hit upon a solution: to put Chávez on TV, where he could exhort his fellow insurgents to surrender. The vice admiral picked up the phone to telephone Ochoa for approval.

The defense minister discussed the proposal with the president. "Pérez insisted that we tape it, but when I got back on the phone with Daniels, he framed the situation in such a way, saying that we didn't have time, that the possibility of a confrontation was very serious at that moment. So I made the decision to put Chávez on without taping him [editing him], and, without a doubt, that was a very grave mistake," Ochoa later acknowledged. The president, a precursor to Chávez in his keen awareness of the power of the media, says he warned the defense minister, " 'Right now I am telling you: Do not allow him to speak on live television. They can tape him in some room and edit a version of it.' The problem was that we wanted to resolve the problem as fast as possible, since there were a few strongholds that hadn't surrendered." According to Carratú, CAP had also ordered that they "strip him of his weapons and exhibit him handcuffed."

Daniels received the go-ahead and ordered his men to put in calls to the reporters from the TV stations, so that they could tape the message.

Chávez was very clear about the symbolism of his clothing: "I didn't have my beret or my decorations and the first thing that came into my mind was the image of General Noriega when the Americans presented him after the invasion, in his undershirt, completely defeated. And so I said to them, 'Get me my beret, I'm going to go wash my face.' 'Write what you're going to say,' Vice Admiral Daniels Hernández told me. [I replied,] 'No, no, I'm not going to write anything. I give you my word that I will tell [my men] to surrender.' "[19]

The lights went up, and the cameras were set in place. Commander Hugo Chávez appeared ramrod straight in his paratrooper's uniform and red beret, flanked by General Jiménez and Vice Admiral Daniels. Every so often, a nervous tic in one of his facial muscles would tug at his cheek, the consequence of the nasal hemorrhages he has suffered since childhood. As he stared straight ahead, he seemed confident, arrogant. He took a deep breath and exhaled a record 169 words in just over a minute:

> First of all, I want to say good morning to the people of Venezuela. This Bolivarian message is for the brave soldiers who are presently at the Paratroopers' Regiment in Aragua and the Armored Brigade in Valencia. *Compañeros:* unfortunately, *for now,* the objectives we established in the capital were not achieved. That means that we, here in Caracas, did not succeed in taking control [of the government]. You did an excellent job out there, but it is now time to avoid more bloodshed, it is now

time to reflect. New situations will present themselves. The country must find the definitive path toward a better destiny. Listen to what I say. Listen to Commander Chávez, who sends out this message so that you will please reflect and lay down your weapons, because now, truly, it is impossible for us to meet the objectives we established on a national level. *Compañeros:* listen to this message of solidarity. I thank you for your loyalty, your bravery, your generosity, and as I stand before the nation and all of you, I assume the responsibility for this Bolivarian military movement. Thank you very much.

The television crews raced off to their studios. The video was broadcast, unedited, at 10:30 that morning. The eyes of the television viewers opened wide in amazement: "Listen to Commander Chávez."

The first thing that everyone noticed was the detainee's superb communication skills. His impressive composure throughout the speech and his natural gifts as an entertainer came through loud and clear: After a sleepless night that had ended in a military defeat, after having to order his co-conspirators to lay down their arms, who else would have begun a speech with "Good morning to the people of Venezuela"? And when it was all over, two tiny phrases seemed to hang in the air: "I assume the responsibility" and "for now." The former was a rarity in a country where politicians never seemed able or willing to assume responsibility for anything. And the latter, which sounded something like a threat, was slipped in as a kind of promise, or perhaps a cliff-hanger to a cinematic thriller. It was a way of saying "To be continued." The television stations broadcast the statement over and over again, not knowing that it would become a powerful and effective promotional tool for the failed coup commander.

After speaking, says Chávez, "I was totally broken, I felt completely defeated. I mean, I felt that I had wrought the disaster of the century. I had had to surrender, our plan had failed, and on top of it I had to tell all my men to surrender, too. Santeliz sat down to my right, and gave me a slap on the back. 'Good job, damn, you really said it!' But me, all I did was look at him and say, 'What do you mean, good job? I had to tell my men to surrender!' And he said, 'For now.' I didn't even realize it. It just came out."[20] The rebellion, the attack against those in power, which he had spent fifteen years dreaming about and preparing for, had failed. But he had been its protagonist. And his fate changed drastically thanks to that chance appearance on television. That stroke of luck was what saved his coup from being a complete failure. Hugo Chávez had crossed the threshold separating anonymity and celebrity, and he would never turn back.

His parents were stunned. Elena was so distraught that she hadn't even found out what her son had said. "Like, around fifteen days later, a little piece came out in the newspaper with his little face. And so, I sit down to read, and I say to one of my sons: 'Son, when did Hugo say such pretty things?' And he said to me, 'Oh, come on, Mamá, that's what he said when he surrendered on television.' "

The other commanders were dumbfounded. And furious. What on earth had happened to Hugo? Shortly after the televised message, La Carlota finally fell, after eleven hours in the hands of the conspirators. At 12:45 P.M., Arias surrendered in Maracaibo, handing over the control that four years later he would gain through legitimate elections. The last to lay down his weapons was Jesús Urdaneta, who had been determined to fight until the bitter end. When all was said and done, Chávez's co-conspirators had fulfilled their missions superbly, successfully. The only one who had failed was Chávez himself.

By 12 P.M. on February 4, at least twenty people were dead as a result of the uprising,[21] fourteen of them military personnel, and there were scores of wounded as well. That most of the soldiers involved in the coup had been sent to fight under false pretenses remains a dark cloud over this now-historic event. In 1998, referring only to the military casualties, as if there had been no other victims that day, Chávez remarked that "On 4F [February 4] there were fourteen deaths. Fewer deaths than any weekend in Caracas, fewer deaths than [those of] the children who die of hunger every month in Venezuela. In this light I bear the burden of my violence, and the others should take responsibility for their own violence. I have never avoided this. . . . Are your hands stained with blood? Someone once asked me. Yes, my hands and everything, all of me is stained with blood, from here all the way down."[22]

AS DAY FADED INTO NIGHT, President Pérez addressed the nation once more. For the fourth time, he assured the country that everything was under control. Now he was telling the truth. More than three hundred military officers had been arrested by then, and the troops who had been used for the coup had been returned to their barracks. At Fort Tiuna, Chávez met with Ochoa for the first time that day. The defense minister invited him to dinner. Alone together, they ate their plates of fast food and talked, one on one. The minister lent Chávez his phone, and Chávez, for the first time since his surrender, spoke to Marksman. "Herma, I want you to remember to take care of yourself. I am going to answer to all this, but I don't want you to worry, because I am not in any danger anymore. And I will call you again as soon as I can." Nobody would ever learn what transpired in the Chávez-Ochoa meeting. Late at night, the commander arrived at the Directorate for Military Intelligence in the company of his friend and official escort that day, General Santeliz.

This was where he finally faced his fellow conspirators, all of them wearing the insignia that distinguished them from the rest of the world: a bracelet with a tricolor ribbon, tied to the sleeves of their uniforms. The weight of their stares bore through him.

"Many people say I was a coward. No, I am not a coward. In every military operation you have the right to fall back. . . . By the time I ended up on the news, Arias had already surrendered in Zulia,"[23] Chávez has said, contradicting every military brief and news report, to say nothing of the statements made by the other conspirators confirming that no other commander had surrendered before Chávez appeared on television.

The coup leaders spent sixteen days incommunicado, in the holding cells at the Directorate for Military Intelligence. Commander Urdaneta, the most reluctant to surrender of all the insurgents, was angry with everyone. "As they brought us out, we couldn't see one another, but as you passed by the little windows [of the individual cells], you could say a little something, very fast, to one of the other men. The first time they pulled me out, I passed by Chávez's cell and ironically said, 'Hey, man, you surrendered so fast, that was amazing!' I remember his head was a mess of curls, huge curls, and I was shocked because I had never seen him like that. He moved closer and said to me, 'Listen, *compadre,* I just felt like I was all alone.' And I said to him, 'Oh, you felt like you were all alone. Well, guess what—I was out there on my own, too. I was running out there with my battalion and my officers, I didn't have ten lieutenant colonels with me. You had your battalion and your officers with you, too. What did you want?' And he just replied, 'Well, I just felt like I was all alone.' "

He said the same to Arias. "After they put us in jail, one day Hugo and I were walking arm in arm, and I said to him, 'Shit, Hugo, what happened to you? You didn't even shoot one single cannon, how come?' And he said to me, 'Shit, I was all alone, incommunicado. . . . I really needed you.' "

The following day brought more reproaches, although of a different sort, in the provinces. In Barinas, all eyes turned to stare down José Esteban Ruiz Guevara. "His mother and father went all over Barinas telling everyone that the real guilty party was the 'guy with the beard'—me. And they said that his brilliant military career was over, all on account of me." Ruiz's ex-wife, Carmen, remembers, "After the coup, José Esteban came home and said to me, 'Do you know what Chávez's father just said to me? That I was a—' because I had turned his son into a Communist and that that was the reason they threw him in jail, that was the reason his military career was over. They cursed his name a thousand times over. Right there on the corner." Ruiz Guevara did not get too worked up over it: people had always said that his home was a "nest of conspirators." What else did people expect of a man who had spent his adolescence in the library of that man? He never visited Chávez in jail, however. He always believed that February 4 was a catastrophic mistake. That was the message he sent with one of his daughters: "I sent him a message saying that I was not going to visit him because there was no way I could forgive that kind of thing. After making it to Miraflores and having the control of the government in the palm of their hands, to let it all go to shit like that? He should have gone in even if they killed him."

The only problem with that is that a dead man can't run a country.

CHAPTER 7

A Model Officer

▬

THE ENTIRE COUNTRY HAD WATCHED THIS MILITARY OFFICER APPEAR on television and listened attentively to his message. The coup attempt now had a face. But what did anyone really know about Hugo Chávez? The first person to pipe up was General Carlos Julio Peñaloza, former head of the army. The general was quite familiar with the man who had made off with the ratings that February 4. The very evening of the coup, on a Venevisión opinion show, Peñaloza declared, "He is a man with charisma, aplomb—there is no doubt in my mind that he is a man, as we Venezuelans would say, *echao p'alante.*" That is, always moving forward, focused on the future. As the director of Venezuela's military academy during the mid-1980s, Peñaloza had, at one time, been Hugo Chávez's boss.

"When I got to the academy, I found myself surrounded by a very qualified group of officers, among them a very distinguished captain, a man with remarkable leadership qualities, and that was Captain Hugo Chávez Frías, an officer who earned the admiration of his superiors and the affection of his subordinates. A model officer."[1]

Peñaloza was not surprised to see him on television. He knew that Chávez had been plotting his coup for years and moreover that he was the leader of the movement, as Peñaloza had in fact warned the Pérez government when he handed over the leadership of the army seven months before the uprising.

The Venezuelan people, however, were wondering: What exactly were Hugo Chávez's plans once he obtained power? How would he exercise it? What measures would he take? What kind of government would he establish? What would have happened to Venezuela had the insurrection succeeded? A pamphlet circulating in the military barracks around that time, signed by the *comacates* (the commanders, majors, captains, and lieutenants), swore that the corrupt would be brought to the university stadium in Caracas and, following a brief trial, shot. Another document, attributed to the Bolivarian Revolutionary Movement, claimed that "The homeland shall be cleaned with blood." In his first interview from jail, to the newspaper *El Globo* on February 29, Hugo Chávez shed some light on the matter of his plans for Venezuela. The political objective was "in a conceptual sense, to seize power, and in the concrete sense, to capture the president of the Republic and place him on trial in front of the entire nation." And he acknowledged that the Bolivarian Revolutionary Movement was indeed the author of the document that had been circulating. "That quote is from Thomas Jefferson," he said. "It says, 'The tree of liberty must be refreshed from time to time with the blood of patriots and tyrants.' With that quote, we meant to tell ourselves as well as the rest of the world that when we decided to take this step, we knew there would be bloodshed when we emerged with thousands of armed men. It was an obligatory sacrifice, because no other revolution in the world has ever been carried out any differently."[2] This was the first time the commander had uttered, in public, the word "revolution."

Aside from revealing that they had planned to name a joint civilian-military junta and institute a series of anti-neoliberal economic measures, Chávez vowed that his movement's fight was one "against corruption and against this government" and neatly avoided specifying how he and his team intended to govern the country. In fact, it remained entirely unclear until six years later, when Kléber Ramírez revealed the essence of the new government in his book *Historia documental del 4 de febrero* (A Documentary History of February 4). First, they would have established a General Council of the Nation, made up of both military personnel and civilians, as the country's central governing body. The president would be appointed from this group and would be "exclusively subject to the decisions and mandates" of the council, remaining in the position "as long as necessary in order to guarantee the country's path . . . so that a democratic assembly might create a legal framework, via a new constitution, for a more profound democracy."[3]

The constituent act of the General Council of the Nation proposed a "national alliance to rescue the dignity of Venezuela" as a way of facing up to the crisis, and its starting point was "the exemplary punishment, as determined by ad hoc tribunals, of those people who are responsible, at all levels, for driving the country into this general morass."[4] Oddly enough, without bothering to check in with popular opinion, the second communiqué indicated that "we might announce to the nation that the new regime enjoys the wholehearted, enthusiastic support of the majority of Venezuelan citizens." The council also mapped out a dozen or so decrees. The first one declared that the legislative branch would cease to function as such, and all activities undertaken by the National Congress would be immediately halted. The following decrees offered an idea of what the new government would be like: all the regional parliaments, as well as the country's highest electoral authority, would cease to exist, as would the judicial branch, which would be entirely replaced by a group of magistrates handpicked by the council. Nothing of the previous system would remain. All democratic institutions would be completely dismantled and replaced with a sole authority that would control everything. On the economic front, the new government would freeze prices for goods and services and prohibit "the free transfer of capital, in all currencies." The privatization process would be halted as well.

"At first glance we may observe something rather surprising: the entire political system devised to govern the country after the February 4 coup was characterized by its authors as 'democratic,' "[5] states the philosopher and political analyst Alberto Arvelo Ramos. Upon reading the decrees, however, he came to the conclusion that "there are a vast number of Venezuelans who are not in agreement with the regime, who would nevertheless remain excluded if this project were to come to fruition." Among others, anyone who had been a public employee during any of the previous administrations would be excluded. But what most shocked Arvelo Ramos, who had been active with the Communists in the 1960s, was the General Council's plan to institute a Public Health Committee that was not intended, precisely, to establish Venezuelan public health policies. This seventh decree defined this committee as "the personification of the national public conscience."[6] According to Arvelo Ramos, it was created in the image and likeness of the similarly named committee that existed during the Reign of Terror following the French Revolution, and was intended to crush the opposition in the style of Lenin. The impression that emerged from all this, he says, was that the coup stagers intended to control civil society by placing military officers in jobs normally held by civilians.[7]

It was not until 1998, following the death of Kléber Ramírez at the age of sixty-one, that Hugo Chávez—a man known for moving nimbly through the terrain of ideological ambiguity—admitted to the existence of the decrees. Only then did he deem the documents fit for public perusal. He swore that "many of them would never have been enacted,"[8] though he never specified which ones. Additionally, Ramírez himself stated that he had received the order to draw up the decrees during a meeting presided over by Chávez in November 1991 and that "the final draft was sent to commanders Chávez and Arias for their respective revision and approval."[9] Francisco Arias has indicated that the decrees "served as a reference" and has also said that they would have enacted decrees to terminate all existing political parties, establish tribunals to carry out swift trials for the corrupt, withdraw "a substantial number of generals," and call for a constituent assembly to draft a new constitution when they felt that the conditions were favorable. Five civilians and four retired military officers would preside over the General Council of the Nation. The latter group, presumably, would not include any of the coup instigators. Regarding the civil candidates, Arias says that there was talk of possibly appointing the journalist and former presidential candidate

José Vicente Rangel (who was vice president until January 2007), the Christian Democrat politician Abdón Vivas Terán, the Radical Cause leader Andrés Velásquez, and others. Moreover, and perhaps to keep from violating the old Spanish maxim "There is no such thing as a coup without the Church," they discussed the possibility of having a clergyman among the group as well, specifically Monsignor Mario Moronta.

"It had been made clear that, had the movement succeeded, Hugo Chávez would be the commander of the Caracas battalion and Arias would be the head of the Casa Militar [the presidential guard]," says Pablo Medina, who agrees with Arias that the government council would have been composed of five civilians and four military retirees. It is difficult to imagine, however, that the leaders of the movement would have been willing to assume a supporting role in the new government, delegating their power after having pursued it so zealously for so many years. Arias in the presidential guard? Hugo Chávez in a second-rate job, in one of countless battalions?

Beyond the many unknowns regarding the true scope and objectives of February 4, one thing remains clear, as Arvelo Ramos points out: "the Present-day Chávez never stops identifying himself with the 1992 insurrectionist project."[10] In fact, the present head of state consistently commemorates the date of the coup, celebrating each anniversary as a triumph, the dawn of a new era. He has even officially declared it the "Day of National Dignity."

EVEN FIFTEEN YEARS LATER, certain aspects of the February 4 uprising remain shrouded in mystery. One enigma is why, at the last minute, the civilian members of the movement—who had joined the group precisely to lend some balance to the insurrection—were suddenly shut out of what was ultimately an exclusively military operation. In the city of Valencia, a small group of students sparked some disturbances that were rapidly contained by the police. But in Caracas and Maracaibo, nobody took to the streets in defense of the coup.

"I had a truck filled with rifles that were supposed to be distributed among the civilians . . . there were certain people who knew the password 'Páez-Patria' for requesting weapons, but they never materialized. It's not our fault alone, since there were people who knew and didn't show up, having been alerted in time,"[11] Hugo Chávez offered by way of explanation, years later.[12]

Some people, however, declare that the opposite was true. On the night of February 3, a group of four civilians waited in vain at a toll booth on the Maracay-Caracas highway. According to Pablo Medina, the person who didn't turn up was Hugo Chávez. "A week earlier, in Maracay, he had promised to deliver us weapons for the uprising." For no apparent reason, the commander ordered the buses to turn off the highway and onto the old road, breaking away from the convoy led by his co-conspirator Yoel Acosta, contrary to what they had planned.

Medina began to organize his troops and sent four men to the toll booth, among them Ali Rodríguez, a former guerrilla who was once foreign minister and is currently Venezuela's ambassador in Cuba. The men got tired of waiting around. "Our people make contact with his people, and they refuse to receive them. And so I said, 'This piece of shit doesn't want to make contact.' I just washed my hands of the whole thing. There was nothing I could do about it."

Chávez himself has fueled this controversy. In the first interview he granted from prison, which appeared in the newspaper El Globo three weeks after his failed coup, he pointed out that "the origins of the movement are eminently military, though the intention was to put together a civilian-military junta with the best of the nation's goodwill. During the actual military action itself . . . there was no civil participation." At the time, people wondered if this was true or if he was simply trying to protect the civilians involved in the plot. Hugo Chávez has spoken about the idea of bringing civilians into his political enterprise in the following manner:

On several occasions we carried out tests, we invited civilian sectors to stage protests in certain towns in the interior, and

then we would check their ability to summon, to mobilize people. The most strategic, essential idea was an idea I came up
with, on a trip to Panama, where I saw two Dignity Battalions
in action. . . . The idea consisted of forming battalions, or even
organizational charts for squadrons, instruction manuals for
combat battalions in certain towns. . . . We had to consider that
those small civilian groups could and should act as the driving
force behind a mass movement.[13]

Yet, at the last minute, he decided to exclude them from his attempt to gain control of the government. According to Douglas
Bravo, "The idea was that civil society should have an active role in
the revolutionary movement. That was exactly what Chávez didn't
want. Not at all, absolutely no way. Chávez had no interest in the participation of civil society, acting as a concrete force. Civil society
could applaud him but not participate—that was an entirely different
story. . . . He does not tolerate dissidence or different opinions."[14]

According to Bravo, just days before February 4, a group of ex-
guerrillas (among them Kléber Ramírez) met with Chávez and, when
they asked him about the actions they would be carrying out on
"D-Day," the commander apparently said, "After we gain control of
the government, we'll call you." These words belied an attitude that,
Bravo has said, "is not a transitory, tactical stance. It is a political con-
ception of life."[15] Herma Marksman also notes that, in reality, Hugo
Chávez "didn't trust civilians," which does seem to explain why he left
them hanging the day of the coup.

Another question that remains unclear, and that sparked perhaps
more controversy and caused greater conflict between the coup instigators, was why Hugo Chávez did not leave the Military History
Museum to aid the men fighting at Miraflores. It is a question that
Chávez has never answered very convincingly, instead suggesting that
the breakdown in radio communications thwarted his mobility. It remains a mystery. Captain Ronald Blanco, one of the men in charge of
the attack, phoned Herma Marksman from the palace at around one

in the morning on February 4 and asked her to phone his mother to tell her that he had been wounded, but not seriously.

Then he asked Herma, "What do you know about Commander Chávez? He knew he had to be here, too, and we're out here all by ourselves, falling on our faces. Antonio Rojas [the other captain in charge of the operative] is wounded, and the commander is nowhere to be found." Marksman still wonders what Hugo was doing at the museum. "I don't know, he was supposed to get to Miraflores . . . it was all part of the plan."

At least three different stories attempt to explain this sequence of events. According to one, Chávez was waiting for his men to bring President Pérez to the Military History Museum so that he could then leave for Miraflores secure in the knowledge that he had succeeded. Another theory maintains that he didn't go to Miraflores because he thought his life would be in danger if he did. According to this second version, Ronald Blanco and Antonio Rojas were going to assassinate Chávez and Arias the day of the insurrection because they believed the two commanders had struck a deal with the generals and betrayed the conspiracy. The last theory, favored by Chávez's enemies, suggests that he didn't leave the museum because he was scared. We will probably never know which of these three versions comes closest to the reality of the situation.

The role of Defense Minister General Fernando Ochoa at the time of the coup is another 4F mystery. Today, former president Carlos Andrés Pérez seems convinced that his colleague was plotting against him. After the coup, Pérez not only kept Ochoa in his cabinet but went on to appoint him foreign minister. "This is what happened: in Venezuela there was a very bad situation in the Army. There were too many generals and admirals, and there just weren't positions for all of them. This created a general state of insubordination in the armed forces. And they were very ambitious. Ochoa led one group. Every general had his group and they were all trying to figure out how to get it together to take over." As all this was happening, the military intelligence service began to keep an eye on a group of generals, among them Ochoa, that was examining corruption inside the armed forces, a task that had generated criticism among their subordinates.

Some believe that a few days before the uprising, the defense minister procured an alliance with the Bolivarian Revolutionary Movement. José Esteban Ruiz Guevara described the incident that led him to believe this. He had been driving out to Maracay with his friend Francisco Orta, another Barinas Communist like him, and Orta's son Oscar, who was behind the wheel. "At the entrance to San Joaquín, a run-down little housing complex where Hugo lived, there is a kind of alleyway, and just as we arrived at around four in the morning, a car passed in front of us and someone lit a cigarette. There was a light on inside and I managed to make out the face of Minister Ochoa Antich. And I said to Francisco, 'Look, that's the minister right there.' " When they reached Hugo's house, Hugo told them, " 'The minister just left. Now he's suggesting we stage a takeover at the palace. With him [Ochoa] as president, Hugo in Defense, and I think José Vicente Rangel . . .' 'And what did you tell him?' I asked him. 'No, man, I told him to piss off!' he said." This story was confirmed by Oscar Orta, who also claims to have seen Minister Ochoa leaving Chávez's house that night.

According to Alcides Rondón, Chávez's former classmate and current vice minister for communications, General Ochoa knew all about the preparations for the coup. Ochoa has always denied this. Rondón, who worked at the Directorate for Military Intelligence, seems certain. "The night that Ochoa Antich assumed the position of defense minister, General Carlos Julio Peñaloza grabbed me to accompany an officer who was going to inform him about all the meetings they [the coup plotters] had held and all their plans. That officer brought in the exact list of the units that were going to participate in the revolt, and he handed it over. And the meeting with Ochoa Antich was in his apartment at that housing complex in front of Tamanaco [Las Mercedes]. You can say whatever you want, but I know the truth."

Chávez has always denied that General Ochoa participated in the coup attempt. But from prison, the conspirators did have something to say to the French newspaper *Le Monde*.[16] When asked if the defense minister had known of their plans, they replied:

> Yes, he knew about it but he didn't belong to the Bolivarian Movement, he had a movement that was parallel to ours. We managed to find out about his objectives after we got our men to infiltrate his meetings. They had conceived of a "Giraffe Plan" that consisted of *allowing us to act,* and they were apprised of our movements, they had identified our leaders as well as the day and time of our operation, and they didn't do anything to stop it—on the contrary, some of our men thought that General Ochoa was the movement's leader.

Rondón, who has said he was not in favor of the coup, has his own thesis about why Pérez and his team did not snuff it out, if in fact the uprising was a foregone conclusion that had been leaked to the government. In 1992, he had been posted as an operations officer at the U.N. mission in Western Sahara. On February 3, he received a phone call from his wife, at the headquarters in El Aaiún.

"She said to me, 'I'm really worried, people from the Directorate for Intelligence called to tell me that the paratroopers are leaving for Caracas, that the coup is going ahead.' I found out in Western Sahara—there is no way to convince me that the government didn't know the coup was going to happen." The officer is convinced that President Pérez "thought it would be a minor uprising that he would be able to control, that he would come out of it looking like a hero. He never thought that the movement would have the capacity to send him running out of Miraflores. I am one of those people who believe that it was a political maneuver of Carlos Andrés Pérez."

Chávez's own girlfriend, Herma Marksman, seems convinced that the outcome of the rebellion was affected by mistrust, intrigue, and hunger for power. "Today I think that 4F was doomed to fail. It had to fail, because nobody was playing clean."

It is likely that on February 4, 1992, there were other conspiracies at work. It is not unlikely that other "model officers" were plotting to overthrow the president, and not just in response to the age-old Venezuelan tradition of the military controlling the civilian realm. The general feeling at the time was that democracy was in jeopardy. People had flatly rejected the country's political elite. Had the coup succeeded, that last point would have been critical.

"Hugo had already considered all of that. He believed that the political parties had done a lot of damage to this country and that there was a need to momentarily suspend political parties," says Marksman.

Of all this, one thing was made very clear: of the many coup plots purportedly in the works, only one was activated and made visible to the majority of the nation. Only the name of Hugo Chávez began to circulate among the populace. However, 4F would always be the project that cost him the most. In 1998, just before he crossed the threshold at Miraflores, someone asked him what he felt had been his greatest misfortune.

"Not achieving our objectives on February 4," he replied.[17]

CHAPTER 8

"Bolívar and I"

THE FIRST STOP FOR THE COUP PLOTTERS, AFTER LEAVING THE MILITARY intelligence headquarters, was the Cuartel San Carlos, a prison located in an old building almost directly opposite the National Pantheon, the eternal resting spot of Simón Bolívar. Everything was in place for Hugo Chávez to become an icon. People spontaneously turned up at the jail to meet him and waited on long lines to visit him. Overnight, he had been anointed by the angel of popularity, and according to some it would transform him entirely. At first, it seemed a novelty, a curiosity. Reporters traveled to meet the Chávez family, left cell phones in the prison to get the first few radio interviews, writing and publishing the typical articles that one might expect. But something happened: the lines of people waiting to see Chávez grew longer and longer. All kinds of people wanted to shake hands with the men behind the coup. Many impromptu visitors from the middle class wanted to meet Chávez. But he was also visited by social leaders, political figureheads, and left-wing intellectuals. Behind the prison bars, a real-life popular phenomenon was unfolding.

Herma Marksman remembers the early days of this period: "I was talking with the captains, and I was about to go over to him. When I caught sight of Hugo, he was leaning against a window, with about forty people on line, waiting, so that he would sign a little piece of paper. My daughter was with me. And I asked Francisco [Arias], 'What is this all about? Are you aware of the mess we're in? Or do you think it's a laugh to drag out a bunch of tanks, knock down the door to Miraflores Palace, and then assume that everything's fine? Instead

of getting serious, looking for some kind of solution to this problem. . . . Hugo thinks he's Rock Hudson, signing autographs!' "

Although he couldn't have possibly imagined that the phenomenon
would take on such mammoth proportions, Chávez knew something
was happening. It dawned on him when he was in his first cell, in the
bowels of the headquarters of the Directorate for Military Intelligence:
"The first human being who entered my cell was a priest, the chaplain
of the military jail. Surreptitiously, he slipped me a tiny Bible, hugged
me, and whispered something in my ear. I thought he was going to say
something to boost my morale. But instead he said, 'Get up, out on
the street you're a hero.'"[1]

The affection Chávez inspired was not just the result of his personal charisma, either. The people were fed up with the elite and
were hungry for some kind of reaction to the rampant corruption in
the government. The incident also jibed well with the traditional
Venezuelan view of the military as a bastion of order and effective-
ness not found in the civilian realm. In addition, the conditions allowed the insurgents to present themselves as victims of their own
crime, victims of history. From his very first statements, Chávez invoked the Father of the Nation to justify and legitimize his actions. In
an interview that appeared in *El Nacional* a month after the coup attempt, Chávez said that "the true creator of this liberation, the real
leader of this rebellion, was General Simón Bolívar. With his incendiary verb, he has illuminated the path for us."[2] From the very beginning, Chávez created an extremely effective symbolic relationship,
basically saying that he and Bolívar had staged the coup, that he and
Bolívar wanted the country to change.

Even after Chávez and another group of detainees were transferred to Yare, a prison two hours away from Caracas, the situation
remained the same. Without moving an inch from the prison where
he was incarcerated, Chávez was carrying out extremely important
political work. Every day he drew more and more sympathizers to his
cause. The entire country wanted to steamroll the traditional political
ivory tower. All the parties had dismal reputations. Though isolated in

jail, Chávez was becoming more of a public figure with each passing day. In the middle of his mushrooming popularity, his girlfriend began to wonder: "I said to him, 'Hugo, this is transitory, ephemeral. And it would be terrible for you to believe all this, because look at how those famous artists all end up when their popularity dies down.' And he said to me, 'I'm clear about that. That's not going to happen to me.' " But it did, according to Marksman. She feels that this process transformed him, that a messianic fire had begun to burn inside him.

According to Chávez, his relationship with Simón Bolívar began in childhood. "Instead of Superman, my hero was Bolívar," he has said, recalling that "in my village, my grandfather would say to me: look, there's Bolívar's mountain. And I would imagine Bolívar crossing the Andes. Ever since I was a child, I was always shocked at the way they betrayed him, how he died alone and betrayed."[3] Ever since becoming president, Chávez has developed a penchant for novelizing his life. But there is also something of a national culture of identification with the founding father. Bolívar is the glorious father of the nation, but he is also the glorious son the Venezuelan people abandoned, allowing him to die alone in a foreign land, Colombia. Bolívar is always a superlative, an everything: military leader, thinker, strategist, writer, *caudillo*, genius, lover, model, guide, God. . . . The relationship with him is part of an absolutely religious culture that the historian Luis Castro Leiva termed "Bolivarian theology."[4] In 1970, Germán Carrera Damas published *El culto a Bolívar* (The Cult of Bolívar), a seminal text about the mythification of the national hero and how it has evolved over time: "Its initial manifestation as the *cult of a nation*, a direct form of admiration and love, has evolved toward the formulation of a *cult for a nation*, with a liturgy dedicated to caring for this worshipped object and promoting its development."[5]

From his first days in jail, Chávez presented himself as the high priest of this faith, insinuating that he had rescued a hero whom all Venezuelans, with their corrupt governments, had betrayed. Chávez revived and empowered the myth, revitalizing the symbol's function as judge and censor, commandeering its ability to inspire hope and some kind of emancipation. He brought back the idea of a paradise on the horizon. The historian Elías Pino Iturrieta maintains that by creating a new Constitution "based on Bolívar's doctrine" and adding the word "Bolivarian" to the country's official name, Chávez has carried out a baptism of sorts, closing a circle that began two centuries ago: "Through a new civic sacrament, a single historical actor has come to embody the destiny of Venezuela, within an incontestably legal framework. The manual of nationality has bestowed a holiness upon the great man's thoughts. The Liberator, then, has reached the apex of secular liturgy. But he does this much like those lucky souls who approach the altar and pass through the filter of the Vatican and receive the blessing of the Popes: with no doubts and for all eternity."[6]

This is the faith, the belief system that suggests that Bolívar is eternal and present, a light that dispels shadows, a path toward salvation. But this phenomenon is also an exercise in fidelity, in the act of believing that Bolívar is the origin, the true repository of Venezuelan identity.

"What we propose," said Chávez to the Argentinian newspaper *La Nación,* "is the idea of reclaiming this primordial notion, beneath the aegis of which our Republic was born. Simón Bolívar's idea. We don't need to go around copying models from other latitudes. . . . Bolívar had a pluripolar vision of the world." During their years in jail, the insurgents produced a document they entitled "How to abandon the labyrinth." The title was inspired by *The General in His Labyrinth,* the Gabriel García Márquez novel based on Simón Bolívar that is said to be Chávez's favorite book. By that point it was clear that the coup masterminds had earned themselves a symbolic victory by appropriating the figure of the liberator and monopolizing it for their own purposes.

From the jail, however, a popular uprising seemed like a rather remote illusion. On November 27 of that same year another attempt was made to overthrow the government. Clearly, there was a connection between the new military insurgents and the ones behind bars.

The group on the outside had been in constant contact with those in prison, and they all remained determined to take control of the country by force; the possibility of assassination was even included in their plans. They were still obsessed with removing Carlos Andrés Pérez from Venezuelan politics and history, no matter what. Everything suggests that Chávez kept himself apprised of the other group's actions until the end—according to intelligence reports, Chávez used his brother Argenis to send messages to the conspirators from inside the jail.[7] A wiretapped phone call intercepted a week before November 27 substantiates those claims.

That day at 4:30 in the morning, as the rest of Caracas was sleeping, the insurgents activated their plan to occupy Miraflores, the presidential residence of La Casona, the La Carlota air base, and other key points on the map. Led by two air force admirals and a general,[8] they commandeered the antenna that controlled the signal of three commercial television stations and then launched a violent assault on the state-run television station, murdering anyone who resisted. After successfully executing these maneuvers, they broadcast a video of Hugo Chávez expressing his support for the uprising and exhorting the people of Venezuela to join in. By sunrise, fights had broken out at the gates to Yare, as some thirty soldiers and a smattering of civilians boarded a tractor and attempted to gain entrance to the section of military detainees, in an effort to rescue Chávez. In a few hours' time, things were not looking good.

The insurrectionists were unable to control the commercial TV station Televén, channel 10. And in an almost exact replica of the entanglements of 4F, President Carlos Andrés Pérez appeared on TV to let the country know that he was safe and sound and that this second coup attempt had failed just as the first one had. For several hours, however, the conspirators managed to create a situation that was deeply frightening to the nation. On the state-run television channel, armed civilians and soldiers speaking in primitive, violent Spanish spouted off lengthy tirades, exhorting the audience to unearth whatever sticks, bottles, and homemade weapons they could find to overthrow the government for once and for all. In some neighborhoods at the western end of the capital, pockets of riots broke out, and the city was paralyzed by the thunderous boom of the four airplanes that attempted to bomb La Carlota and Miraflores. Most of the armed forces, however, supported the government and resisted the attack. By noon, the coup leaders stated that they were ready to surrender, which they did at around four in the afternoon. By then it was clear that no popular revolt was going to rise up and unseat the government in power. In contrast to February 4, few Venezuelans supported these insurgents, viewing them instead with fear and trepidation in light of their violent statements and bloody actions. The government had also learned its lesson and did not offer microphones to any of the coup leaders as they laid down their weapons. Seventeen planes were damaged, and four were taken down. A group of 93 conspirators fled the country by plane and sought asylum in Perú. According to official reports, the casualties amounted to 171 dead (142 civilian and 29 military), 95 wounded, and 1,340 people arrested in connection with the attack—500 officers, noncommissioned and otherwise, 800 enlisted soldiers, and 40 civilians.

No matter how much the men behind the events of February 4 tried to distance themselves from the second coup, it was impossible not to connect the two actions. This new frustration demoralized Chávez. Despite his popularity, the situation in prison with some of his fellow conspirators had changed considerably: "During those months, December 1992 and January 1993, I was quite a loner, in the same jail, and there, for the first time in my life, I felt the bile of bitterness for having been singled out by my friends as the one responsible for the failure."[9]

None of this stopped him in his tracks, however. If he had ever envisioned his personal destiny as inextricably linked to that of his country, his experience in jail would serve as part of that romantic, woe-filled episode that heroes always endure before attaining victory. It was a test, the purpose of which was to purify his vocation for power. William Izarra has stated that Chávez "was convinced he had an earthly mission to fulfill, guided by a force superior to that of human beings."[10] This jibes with the heroic nature of Bolivarianism. The Great Father, Simón Bolívar, however, was not the lone historical figure being resurrected here. Inside this new altar were two other warrior icons: Ezequiel Zamora and Pedro Pérez Delgado, better known as Maisanta.

Ezequiel Zamora (1817–60) was a small-town merchant who got involved in politics under the flag of the Liberal Party, spearheaded a peasant revolt in 1846, and became the icon of the Federal Revolution under the slogan "Free land and free men." The romantic left tends to exalt this bit of history, overlooking the fact that during the administrations of José Tadeo Monagas (1847–51 and 1855–58), Ezequiel Zamora held government posts and even married a wealthy widow, which left him a very prosperous landowner. In 1858, when Monagas was overthrown, Zamora was exiled, but he later returned as the military leader of the Federal War and went on to found the state of Barinas, where, one hundred years later, Hugo Chávez was born. The leader of a popular army and a renowned military strategist, Ezequiel Zamora died on January 10, 1860. During a military operation aimed at occupying the city of San Carlos, he was shot in the head, though, according to legend, the bullet came not from the enemy but from his own comrades in arms.

Nedo Paniz, in whose home Chávez lived for a time after his release from prison, recalls, "Once we were walking along, and he said to me, 'You know something? I haven't told this to too many people. I think I am the reincarnation of Ezequiel Zamora.' After that I began to see that he had a strong tendency to that sort of thing."

Jesús Urdaneta, Chávez's friend and companion from his days at the military academy, heard the same confession. "Once he said to me, 'I'm going to tell you something I have never told anyone before, but I know it's true. I am the reincarnation of Ezequiel Zamora.'" Urdaneta described another anecdote from their years in prison:

"When we were prisoners—he was in Yare and I was in San Carlos—we kept our cell phones hidden so that we could call each other. One day he called me up and told me that they wanted to kill him. And then he said, 'Remember about Zamora, they killed him from behind his back.' And I said to him, 'Stop thinking about that kind of nonsense. Don't talk to me about that. Who's going to try and kill you, come on?' But he's always got that idea floating around his head, especially around the anniversary of Zamora's death. That frightens him. He's terrified that someone is going to kill him the way they killed him [Zamora]."

Chávez rescued Ezequiel Zamora in the theoretical sense as well, by turning him into the pillar of his political enterprise. Along with Simón Bolívar and Simón Rodríguez, Bolívar's teacher and mentor, the federalist hero completes the tripartite theory that Chávez is fond of calling the "tree with three roots," the ideological source of his revolution, borrowed from the ideas of Douglas Bravo and his Party for the Venezuelan Revolution. With this proposal, Chávez claims that "we have boldly tried to search for an original, indigenous reference point, of an ideological model that might fit around the premise of Bolívar, Zamora, and Rodríguez. . . . We are a revolutionary movement, a popular movement working on behalf of the subjugated of this country and this planet, on behalf of justice, revolution."[11]

Before the failed coup of February 4, Chávez wrote a book entitled *El libro azul: el árbol de tres raíces* (The Blue Book: The Tree with Three Roots), which attempted to articulate the theoretical foundations of his Bolivarian Revolutionary Movement. He presented "an autochthonous ideological model rooted at the very deepest level of our origins and in the subconscious of the national self," which he identified as "the EBR system," the tree with three roots of which "E" stands for Ezequiel Zamora, "B" for Bolívar, and "R" for Simón Rodríguez. E, B, and R also happen to be the initials of the Ejército Bolivariano Revolucionario, the Bolivarian Revolutionary Army. Chávez underscores Zamora's role as the leader of a peasant rebellion against the "conservative oligarchy" with his mottos "Free land and free men," "popular election," and "horror in the face of the oligarchy."[12]

Néstor Francia, an author and intellectual connected to the Chávez government, defines the significance of each character in the following way: "Bolívar is the Liberator and the principal historic reference of *chavismo,* and he is also Venezuela's great foundational myth. Rodríguez is the teacher and wise man, the innovator, the great figure of all that is universal within the national consciousness. Zamora is the fire of the land, the great champion of social causes, of justice."[13] The historian Elías Pino Iturrieta sees things differently, pointing out that the "tree with three roots" is "a military composition," with deep-seated roots in a very specific vision of Venezuelan identity.

"Chávez," says Pino, "believes that politics is the work of men of action and confuses men of action with men of weapons, but this perception is not exclusive to Chávez. In the nineteenth century, Venezuelans always confused the man of action with the man of weapons and always tried to place power in the hands of men with weapons. Life has revolved a great deal around men of weapons—they are part of a very necessary mythology in Venezuelan society. The last representation of that myth is Chávez and the helmets and military boots that surround him."

Another book by Hugo Chávez, *Un brazalete tricolor* (A Tricolor Armband),[14] is a collection of six texts written between 1974 and 1989. An apologia for the army and the military life in general, the book includes a prologue by the author that borders on patriotic kitsch, with phrases like "the armband fluttered over El Avila against a sky of midnight blue." In his analysis of *Un brazalete tricolor,* Pino Iturrieta points out that "for Chávez, the laws of Venezuelan history have led to a never-ending war that will only reach its conclusion through the one transcendent entity that allows this history to exist, an entity which is to be wholly trusted because it pertains entirely to the tradition of liberty: the army that springs back into action to scrub clean the honor of 'the humiliated mother.' "

PEDRO PÉREZ DELGADO is perhaps a minor saint, especially when compared with figures like Simón Bolívar and Ezequiel Zamora. But in the personal devotional scheme of Hugo Chávez, his role is primordial because he and Maisanta are united by bonds of blood. Chávez is Pérez Delgado's great-grandson. One of his most vivid and oft-recalled childhood memories acknowledges the importance of that connection: "When I was a boy, they told me I was the descendant of a murderer. . . . When I was a teenager, I tried to analyze the situation a little, because I was really very confused, it was all so vague: a great-grandfather who was a guerrilla or an assassin? I wasn't sure of anything."[15] As far as anyone knows, Pérez Delgado was a guerrilla who, at the beginning of the twentieth century, stood up to the dictator Juan Vicente Gómez. Historians have argued about him: some believe he was much closer to a common criminal than a revolutionary hero, but his war cry did go down in history, giving him the nickname by which he would always be remembered. Whenever he headed out to war, he would yell out, "Mai Santa!" which was his way of saying "Madre Santa!" or Holy Mother. It has also been said that this might be a reference to the Virgen del Socorro, the Virgin of Succor, of Valencia, whom he worshipped.

As the family story goes, Maisanta had fathered two sons in the village of Barinas, Pedro and Rafael Infante, without the benefit of marriage. The latter of the two was Chávez's mother's father, although Elena Frías de Chávez admits that she does not remember Maisanta and in fact never even laid eyes on him.

In 1974, the Venezuelan doctor and writer José León Tapia wrote the book *Maisanta, el último hombre a caballo* (Maisanta, the Last Man on Horseback). "Maisanta," he writes, "was something like one of the last popular *caudillos* who galvanized multitudes for a revolution, the purpose of which even he was unable to describe with any clarity. . . .

He had the very bad luck of living at a time in which revolutions with no real content had slowly begun to disappear, giving way to revolutions of the purely ideological kind, about which he only had the very foggiest ideas, which were only occasionally reflected by his actions."[16] Perhaps, in the same way, Tapia was attempting to explain Pérez Delgado's rather ambiguous fame, the two sides of his legend. In 2004, when Tapia won the National Literary Award, sponsored by the government, he declined the honor, stating that he did not want his book used for political ends.[17]

Chávez, however, saw the book as a revelation. After reading it he felt himself rediscovering the heroic strain of his origins. Tapia himself recalls this: "When the book came out, I received a letter from a man I didn't know at all, and to my surprise it was an army lieutenant who was terribly moved because his great-grandfather had been a military officer of the same rank, and his image of this man was that he had been a bandit. He went on to say that the book had opened his eyes to the person his great-grandfather had been, and I got the feeling that this young man had been very affected by that fact."[18]

Chávez was so affected that he began to research and revisit the life of his great-grandfather, rescuing it and incorporating it into his own existence. While doing this, he learned of a filial relationship that made him even nobler and greater than he had presumed: he discovered that Maisanta's father had been a colonel in Ezequiel Zamora's army. This historical detail may well have reinforced Chávez's conviction that there was a larger story, that he was part of a family saga, bound by blood, that directly linked him to the revolutionary struggle. These were the seeds of his fervor, his need to impose this new idol on those around him. His childhood friend Rafael Simón Jiménez recalls that in 1985, when the army sent Chávez to the plains town of Elorza, "At headquarters, next to the portrait of Bolívar, he had someone hang a portrait of Pedro Pérez Delgado, Maisanta. . . . In the afternoon he would order his soldiers to pay tribute to the Liberator and Maisanta."

In 1989, Chávez met Ana Domínguez de Lombano, Maisanta's

daughter, who was seventy-five at the time. Chávez would visit her from time to time, and she remembers how he would always offer a military salute to the portrait of Pedro Pérez Delgado that hung in her home whenever he came over: "And when he brought soldiers around, he would have them stop right here, in front of the photo, so that they could pay him tribute. Once he took the photo so that he could make a copy of it; he has it in his house. Hugo would pray to Maisanta for everything he did."[19] Just after Chávez was sent to jail at the Cuartel San Carlos, she sent Chávez a gift: Maisanta's scapular, an amulet he had always carried with him, just as a Catholic would a crucifix. In a way, there was something sacramental about this act, and it was duly noted by the press. The news reports describe how Ana's son brought Chávez the scapular in "a kind of ceremony that unified everyone there." " 'My cousin,' said the man, visibly moved, 'I impose this scapular upon you so that you, too, may call out the war cry just as Maisanta did. He has now been reincarnated through you."[20]

Francisco Arias recalls how, one night in prison, he went over to Chávez's cell. "Hugo was wearing a pair of shorts, holding Maisanta's scapular and a huge cigar. Some people had brought us some soft drink bottles filled with rum, kahlua, whisky. . . . And there he was, with one of those bottles of rum and with that tobacco and the smoke pouring out. 'We are summoning the spirits,' he said to me. I walked in, bit my lip, and lay down in his bed. Suddenly, something came over him and he began to tremble and speak like an old man, 'How are you, boys?' he said. One of the kids who was sitting next to me immediately jumped to attention and said, "General Bolívar!" Chávez answered, 'No, I'm not General Bolívar. Don't flatter me.' Then Ronald Blanco jumped up: 'General Maisanta!' 'That's right, my son, here I am,' Chávez said."

Had Chávez not rescued him from the forgotten annals of history, Pedro Pérez Delgado would probably be just one more Los Llanos legend, a shadowy figure whom historians would never know quite how to label—as a political activist or an outlaw. José Esteban Ruiz Guevara has his own view of the man: "It is very hard to write anything about Maisanta because there are no sources—all we have are oral sources, and some of them are not particularly reliable."

Ruiz Guevara also states that the blood relationship between Hugo Chávez and Pedro Pérez Delgado may in fact be "questionable." In any event, it is impossible to prove. There are no legal records, no papers. It is the stuff of legend—not the legend of Maisanta but of Hugo Chávez.

As for Bolívar, at one point a rumor began to circulate that Hugo Chávez's devotion to Simón Bolívar bordered on delirium. People often told of how at meetings Chávez would ask to leave a chair empty, promising attendees that the spirit of the Liberator would descend and sit in the chair, to enlighten them as they talked. Nedo Paniz, a close collaborator who gave Chávez a home to live in after his release from jail, confirms the anecdote about the chair. In his office, which Chávez used for a while, Paniz points to the chair in question and says, "That was the Liberator's chair!"

The historian Elías Pino Iturrieta consulted with at least six people who attended those debate sessions. "As they discussed things, drafted work plans, and organized projects for more immediate activities, the solitude of that chair would attest to the presence of the hero. Occasionally the commander's eyes would gaze at that space, occupied by no one, because in reality it was just a lone chair, an empty hole."[21]

This type of legend fuels the perspective of those who see Chávez as someone imbued with a special historical mission. These people speculate that even before his spell in prison, Chávez already felt marked by destiny, though perhaps to a slightly lesser degree.

Other testimonies, however, from those close to him, suggest something else. Yoel Acosta, another of the leaders of the 1992 uprising, says that the process began when Chávez's popularity began to swell during the furor that followed the coup attempt. After February 4, the men behind the uprising were kept in basement cells at the Directorate for Military Intelligence, where they remained for days, incommunicado, their movements recorded by video cameras, with the light shining twenty-four hours a day. They had absolutely no contact with the outside world. "When we left the Directorate for Military Intelligence," says Acosta, "and headed to the jail at the Cuartel San Carlos, that was when we realized that we had really made an impact, that we had shaken the foundations of the system, and that there was a mob of people out on the streets, anxious to see who Chávez was. . . . Exactly two weeks after the coup attempt, as we were riding in a caravan, we saw all those people in the street. . . . Wow, we said, we're like stars, so it wasn't such a failure after all."

While Chávez was in jail, his movement grew stronger and his star rose. Without a doubt, he enjoyed the acclaim. In a 2002 interview, though, he depicted himself as a victim of history: "They lit candles for me, next to Bolívar. The people actually invented a prayer: 'Our Chávez, who art in jail, hallowed be thy name.' How was I supposed to fight something like that?"[22]

It was also during this time that Chávez's marriage came to an end, as did his nine-year relationship with Herma Marksman. Chávez had become a sex symbol, and the gossip about his presumed love affairs, even while in jail, spread like wildfire. His relationship with Marksman soon imploded because of his fame.

"He would receive these letters," says Herma, "from all over Venezuela: from children, from entire families, and from women saying the most unbelievable things. . . . He told my daughter that it may be my love just wasn't strong enough to be able to endure all that without getting hurt." From one day to the next, Hugo Chávez became a heartthrob. Although Marksman does not deny that the gossip took its toll on the relationship, she also insists that the popularity phenomenon affected Hugo Chávez himself, transforming him into another person.

"I said to Francisco Arias, 'Listen, Francisco, I think this has to be stopped, because Hugo is becoming a messianic figure.' And he said, 'Oh, it doesn't matter, right now that's what we need. Because, aside from the fact that it keeps the attention focused on the jail, it may help get us out of here sooner.' " That was, in fact, exactly what happened. They got out of jail much earlier than anyone expected. But as far as Marksman was concerned, Hugo had died. "Yes, I feel a lot like a widow." The metamorphosis that occurred as a result of his dizzying popularity was so profound that she says she no longer sees even the slightest trace of the man she loved and conspired with for so many years. The Hugo Chávez who walked out of the San Carlos jail was another man, someone she did not know. "I'd sure like to meet him," she says dryly.

CHAPTER 9

The Skinny Guy in the *Liqui-Liqui*

"Before this century is over, without a doubt, we will be the government." This is how Hugo Chávez expressed his desires, as a kind of premonition. At the time, though, most journalists noted this comment with boredom and disdain. By late 1996, the former conspirator barely managed to capture 7 percent at the polls.[1] One of the main contenders for the votes at stake back then was a former beauty queen, Irene Sáez. Also an outsider, she was nonetheless the antithesis of Hugo Chávez and had recently enjoyed a successful stint as mayor of a Caracas municipality. With two years to go before the 1998 presidential elections, the only person in Venezuela who would have bet everything on a Chávez candidacy was Chávez himself.

At that time, the ex-conspirator, in the cynical slang of Venezuelan journalism, was hastily deemed a *galápago*, a *caliche*: a man who was not newsworthy but who did everything he could to get his face in the news. With neither fanfare nor entourage, Hugo Chávez would visit the newsrooms of the country's major dailies. He was discreet, friendly, self-confident, and without a trace of arrogance. And he always wore the favored outfit of the Venezuelan plainsman: a *liqui-liqui*, preferably in olive green.[2] This suit, similar to the one worn by Gabriel García Márquez the day he received the Nobel Prize in Literature in 1982, highlighted his nationalist sentiment, and in it he felt elegant, at ease. In Caracas, people said he wore it on the recommendation of the comedian Julián Pacheco, but Chávez has always denied this: "I decided to use it after I got out of jail."[3]

Once he made it to Miraflores, he never again donned the suit, with its straight pants and Mao collar that made him look so slender. But during those early days many people looked at Chávez as part of the past: just a skinny former insurgent wearing a *liqui-liqui*.

Though his army training developed his chest and back, Chávez is naturally thin, in part because food has never mattered much to him. During this period in his life, he would eat poorly and at odd hours. For months he lived like a gypsy, traveling in his van to the remotest corners of the country in his endless quest to promote himself by shaking people's hands and showing his face in person. Without a job, without a political party, and at the nadir of his popularity ratings, he had run out of possibilities. Apart from a few breaks here and there, this was what he did for the two years following his release from prison on March 26, 1994.

"Nobody thought that Mr. Chávez had even the remotest chance of becoming president of the republic," sighs ex-president Rafael Caldera, with the gloom of someone reflecting upon the inexorable. To this day, there are still those who will never forgive Caldera for letting Chávez out of jail, though it was certainly something of a fait accompli: during the 1993 presidential campaigns all the candidates promised to free him. The political temperature at that time was highly unstable and the institutions exceedingly fragile. February 4 had shaken the armed forces to their core, and another wave of tremors shook the country when Carlos Andrés Pérez was removed from office[4] after being found guilty of misappropriating public funds. At the time, it was believed that the mastermind behind February 4 was more dangerous inside the prison, where he had become a constant source of conflict, than outside. The consensus was that once Chávez was out on the street, his myth would deflate.

"He had to be sentenced, and after the sentencing, he could have been pardoned, but that would have left him inoperative politically. [Instead,] Caldera dismissed the case, got him out, and handed him the opportunity to be president," recalls Carlos Andrés Pérez. "Caldera dismissed the case, in effect telling Chávez, 'You have not committed any crime.'"

There had been, in fact, two possibilities for Chávez's release: on one hand, he might have been brought to trial and then pardoned. Today, many people reproach Caldera, a renowned constitutional lawyer, for having taken the shortcut of possibility number two, that of discontinuing the proceedings. Some even claim he took this route as a way of thanking Chávez because the February 4 coup allowed him to give a much-vaunted speech, broadcast on live television direct from Congress, that paved the way for his own political resurrection.[5]

"I have to say that on February 4, I was quite positively impressed by Chávez, as was everyone. Those few moments Chávez spent on television presented him as a sensible, well-balanced man. He said what he had to say quite well, and he came off as a real television artist, without a doubt," remarks Caldera, who denies any previous contact with Chávez, despite the coup leader's best efforts to connect with him. While in Yare, Chávez "called my house, and María, the woman who works for us, answered the phone. And so we made jokes with her, saying 'Oh sure, you're one of Chávez's friends, aren't you?' because she had had the chance to speak to him when she picked up. But after that I don't remember if we ever exchanged a single word. And if we did, it was very brief, because I was very careful . . . there were no conversations, nor any kind of negotiations."

In his faint voice, Caldera defended his decision to free him: "Dismissal does not imply a value judgment. When you dismiss a legal proceeding, you are not saying that the proceeding is relevant or irrelevant, nor are you pardoning anyone. You simply put an end to the case for reasons of acute national interest. In that sense it was much easier to make the decision to dismiss the case." The veteran Christian Democrat leader invoked this logic as a way of thwarting any attempt to blame him for the ex-insurgent's political victory and the country's situation, present and future. Those who made Chávez president, he says, are the ones who voted for him.

While they tended to present themselves to the press as something of a fraternity, there was actually a great deal of friction among the officers behind the February 4 coup. The sixty insurgents who had not been returned to their barracks were split up among four prisons: San Carlos, Yare, Lino de Clemente (inside Fort Tiuna), and the eighth floor of the military hospital. The men at Yare were widely considered the most volatile, recalls Raúl Salazar, a commander of the Third Army Division, who was in close contact with the prisoners known as the "Gallows 13": "There was a severe lack of discipline in there. They were rebellious, didn't listen to anyone. There were problems among them, as well. After a while it calmed down." According to Salazar, who later became Chávez's minister of defense before distancing himself from the movement in 2002, the great majority of the detainees were "dreamers conquered by historical theory, who believed that they could change the course of Venezuela without any political knowledge."

A few days before his release from prison, Hugo Chávez and his close friend Jesús Urdaneta spoke about their imminent liberation. Of the entire group of insurgents, they were the only two still behind bars. They were likely stunned by their good luck, for they had spent only two years in jail, at a time when the crime of military insurgence was punishable by a thirty-year prison sentence. The only consequence was that they would have to hang up their military uniforms forever. As they prepared to go, Chávez turned to his friend and said, "You go first. I'll go out after." Then he added, "Caldera wants to talk to us, do you want to talk to him?"

Urdaneta replied, "Yes, I think we ought to thank him for being willing to resolve the issue of the officers in jail."

According to Urdaneta, Chávez bristled at that, and said, "No, *compadre*. I'm not doing that! That old slob, I'm not talking to him. He only did it because the whole country pressured him into doing it."

Urdaneta then said, "Well, you have your reasons, then, and I have mine. I am going to talk with him because anyone else could have kept us in jail for as long as he pleased." That, says Urdaneta, "caused some unpleasantness between the two of us."

One month after their release, Caldera phoned Urdaneta, who went to see him with his family. "I told him how grateful I was that he had allowed the officers involved in the uprising to reintegrate back into society . . . my military career was over. He told me that he wanted me to start my life over and offered me a job in the foreign service." Shortly afterward, the former insurgent Jesús Urdaneta moved to Spain as head of the Venezuelan Consulate in Vigo, where he remained for five years. Arias had also accepted an olive branch extended by the Caldera government, when he agreed to head the Food Program for Mothers and Infants, which served as a launching pad that helped him secure the governor's seat of the oil-rich state of Zulia one year later. Yoel Acosta was offered a job at the communications ministry. Hugo Chávez, however, held his ground, refusing to budge. Or offer his thanks.

"The word 'gratitude' doesn't really exist in Mr. Chávez's vocabulary," Caldera observes.

Pushing forty, with a pension of some $170 a month, Hugo Chávez started a new life. For the first time ever, he dedicated himself freely and openly to politics.

ON THE SATURDAY, before Holy Week, there was a festive atmosphere in the neighborhood around the military hospital, where Chávez was on the eighth floor. He had been transferred there "because of the internal problems at Yare. They were arguing too much, so we separated them. Chávez took advantage of the transfer to have his knee operated on," said Salazar, who says he had "the pleasure of picking him up so that he might leave [the prison]." Rather anxiously the coup commander removed his military uniform, the same one he had used during his twenty-six months of incarceration, and donned civilian clothes. Anyone else would have raced home instantly. Not him. A man of rituals, he asked to be taken to the military academy. When he arrived, the place was shrouded in silence, emptied of students and teachers, all of whom had left for vacation. Standing in the courtyard, he stopped in front of what was presumably the great-grandson of the mythical Samán de Güere, the spot where he had sworn the initiation oath of the Bolivarian Revolutionary Army in 1983. He stood there talking by himself, uttering words that Salazar was unable to hear. After that he walked out, a free man.

Among the many people waiting to carry him off on their shoulders was the architect Nedo Paniz. A tall man with bushy hair, familiar with the military world thanks to his affinity for parachuting, Paniz had supported the February 4 uprising and helped, as did other civilians, plan the coup of November 1992. Toward the end of that year Paniz met Chávez for the first time, appearing at the prison even though the authorities were under orders to capture him. Using false identification, he entered the prison and came face to face with the conspirator for the first time.

"He was really something of a snake charmer: very interesting, captivating. That is definitely the word: captivating. I was one of those people captivated by him. When he was freed, the relationship grew closer. I traveled to the interior of the Republic with him, and I supported him, giving him a place to live and an office, helping him with logistics."

The former insurgent had no intention to return to his modest home in Maracay. Caracas was the power base. And new women began to parade through his life, though only one would intrigue him enough to make him suffer. In reality, he had little desire to settle down with any of them. Nedo Paniz offered him a space in his home, a small guest cabin in the well-to-do Caracas neighborhood of La Floresta. Chávez moved in with what few possessions he had.

"In those days, he was very detached, very different from the way he is now. He had two pairs of pants, a few shirts, and three *liqui-liquis:* one green, one blue, and one beige. Material things meant very little to him—he didn't even have a passport or a car. All he had was a house in Maracay that he had given his wife. He had nowhere to go."

Chávez did not allow himself a moment's rest. Despite the failed coup and the time in jail, his goal remained intact though distant: Miraflores. He spent many long nights receiving people in the little guest cabin. Food was irrelevant: occasionally he would order fried chicken, fast food. Every so often, he would accept an invitation to dine with the Paniz family.

"He was always pretty reluctant, though, and tended to isolate himself with the little group of lieutenants and second lieutenants who were around a lot." This "little group" included three disciples who would pick him up and drop him off regularly, taking him wherever he needed to go. They were the former military officers Juan Carlos Castillo, José Calatayud, and fellow Barinas native Pedro Carreño, who had become Chávez's disciple after taking his military history class at the academy.

"He was a very demanding person who liked to give long, stirring speeches, intended to inspire people," recalls Carreño, who worked directly with Chávez as his personal assistant in 1987.

As expected, the Chávez myth deflated a bit once he was outside prison walls. Shortly after his release, the media lost track of—and interest in—Chávez, and his name stopped appearing in the headlines. The former conspirator began traveling like mad from one end of Venezuela to the other in *la burra,* as he and his collaborators baptized the Toyota Samurai that Paniz bought for him. Together he and his three inseparable companions traveled around, taking turns sleeping and driving. After some time, Luis Alfonso Dávila, another former military officer Chávez met through Paniz and who would later become his first foreign minister, came up with the idea of fixing up a van so that Chávez might do some preaching in more remote towns and villages.

"The agenda would begin very early in the day, and Chávez would do his number even if there were only five or six people. He would get out of the pickup truck, climb up onto the truck bed, and fire off a speech as if he were standing before the kind of throngs that nowadays pack the Avenida Bolívar whenever he comes out to speak. He was inexperienced politically, hasty," Carreño notes. Hugo would often end up hoarse from speaking so much and eat ginger to get his voice back. Sometimes he would get depressed, but he never lost his spirit, because he was guided by a blind faith in himself.

During those "endless hours," Chávez would read and revise documents in silence. Sometimes he would tell jokes and sing to entertain his companions, or they would listen to music or regale one another with stories of Barinas and life in the military academy. They were free men, and nobody could stop them.

"In the middle of all the bad things, we were lucky in that we were all divorced. . . . In those days we were convinced that you had to abandon your family." Hugo's relationship with his children was checkered, subject to the ups and downs of military life, the conspiracy, his time in jail, and, after that, his political adventures. He would have liked to spend more time with his children, but there was a goal that stood between them: power. He missed his children and on occasion would carve out the time to see them. He often spoke with Nancy, whom he had divorced on good terms, to see how they were. During the period when he lived at La Floresta, he had them stay with him for a little while.

"Without a doubt, it was a very fractured family nucleus. During a few of our tours, we brought the girls along with us, Rosa Virginia and María Gabriela, or Huguito," Paniz remembers.

Nobody—not even those who eventually became his archenemies—has ever questioned Hugo Chávez's devotion to his children. He loves them deeply and has always been an expressive, affectionate father. In the middle of those interminable road trips he would telephone them. At the other end of the line there were never reproaches. They knew their father.

"Yes, he loved them very much. But I don't think it went deep enough. He had a lot of other things to do, more important things. I don't think that affectionate words and comments over the telephone are substantive enough for a father-child relationship," says Paniz. In any event, the Chávez children indeed celebrated their father's then-limited fame and when possible would join him—especially the girls—at some of his events, and they generally seemed happy and content to be at their father's side.

Nedo Paniz had given Chávez an office in the exclusive commercial and business district of Las Mercedes and, later on, on the first floor of a house in Chuao, a neighborhood in east Caracas. In La Floresta, things had gotten a bit difficult. The inhabitant of the small guest cabin was no ordinary man. He was someone who spent twenty-four hours a day focused exclusively on his political future. The breaking point finally came when the lady of the house, sick to death of having a minigarrison in her backyard, with people coming and going at all hours of the day and night, asked her husband to figure out some kind of solution. "Tell him to have people come to the office and use the guest house to rest," she told him.

As Paniz recalls, "Even though I said this to him with all the humility in the world, he told me that this was his way of operating." This was the first confrontation between benefactor and benefactee. "After a while he left, leaving his clothes and things behind. But he stayed on in my office."

A multitude of anonymous people who would later become government ministers, ambassadors, congressmen, and government employees passed through the doors of that office, including one curious man who looked something like an anorexic Santa Claus. Every day he would arrive first thing in the morning, sharpen about twenty pencils, climb the stairs, and disappear into Chávez's lair on the first floor, eating little and working for hours on end. This mystery man was Jorge Giordani, a professor at the Center for Development Studies at the Central University of Venezuela. Eventually, he would become the mastermind and head guru of Chávez's economic policy. The other regulars at the office, as one might expect, included scores of men who marched through the place like warriors. Most were former conspirators, and all of them were no doubt drawn by the tenacity and daring of the *comandante*.

After his release from prison, Hugo Chávez began a crusade to get people to abstain from voting, arguing that the system was "fraudulent, illegal, and illegitimate." His period of wearing the *liqui-liqui* suits marked a phase of political radicalism that was not necessarily opposed to violence.

"During those first years, 1994 and 1995, we had not yet ruled out the possibility of another armed struggle, but when we went out to evaluate our situation, our actual power, our real power, we came to the conclusion that we just didn't have it."[6] When he finally left Paniz's guesthouse in 1995, Chávez moved to a new home very close by in the Universe building in Altamira, which was located on the plaza that, years later, would become a stronghold of the most radical anti-Chávez activists. In that building, he was offered shelter by yet another of those people who had been waiting outside the military hospital the day he was freed: Luis Miquilena. An old ex-Communist, Miquilena became his new mentor, giving him the political polish he lacked, showing him how to fight with the big boys, introducing him to certain members of the economic elite. In time, Miquilena would become the single most influential figure in the first years of the Chávez administration.

BY THE TIME HE crossed paths with Hugo Chávez, Luis Miquilena was so far removed from the Venezuelan political scene that he was a virtual unknown to anyone born after 1960. The leader of a bus drivers' union, he had broken away from the Venezuelan Communist Party to form his own radical organization, the Proletarian Revolutionary Party, which opposed the brief presidential term of the writer Rómulo Gallegos, from February to November 1948. The members of Miquilena's party were known as "black Communists" and *"machamiquis."* Chávez's new host spent the Pérez Jiménez dictatorship in prison, and in the mid-1960s, after an extremely active period of participation in his country's political life, he distanced himself from the public sphere. In his mid-eighties, Luis Miquilena is as vigorous as ever, smoking a cigar as he recalls meeting Hugo Chávez: "A friend of mine told me he needed a cell phone, so I sent him mine. And a few days after he got it, at around ten in the evening he called me up—using the cell phone—to say hello and thank you. Then he invited me over to see him."

After meeting Chávez, the veteran became convinced that the former coup leader "was absolutely committed to the idea of a project to change things, a project that would serve that immense territory of silent souls, people without voices, without resources, the poor people of this country." This was how their relationship began, an "almost fraternal" relationship that grew closer when they lived under the same roof. The apartment they shared was tiny, some two hundred square feet at the most. Miquilena slept in one room with his wife, and Hugo Chávez had the other room. They were so close that they could practically hear each other breathing.

During this period with Miquilena, Hugo Chávez was sure that he would never be able to obtain power through democratic means. He had never considered becoming a councilman, a congressman, or a governor. It was a path that didn't interest him. He clung to that old teenage fantasy of being a celebrity, of playing in the big leagues. And he continued thinking about an assault on Miraflores. How could he land himself in Miraflores without having to go through all that business of small-time political leadership? In December 1995, as all the politicians in the country set their eyes on the gubernatorial elections, Chávez devoted himself to creating an "abstentionist caravan," which had little or no impact. He still hadn't realized that the moment would soon be ripe for the outsiders. He wasn't the only one: the traditional political parties were also unable to see their own agony. The two-party system was foundering, as demonstrated by the victory of political veteran Rafael Caldera, who sensed the crisis early in 1993 and had had the nerve to break away from COPEI, the party he himself had founded, and present his candidacy through a party of his own creation, Convergencia.

Luis Miquilena, almost twice as old as Hugo Chávez, opened the *comandante*'s eyes. "He was very taken with the idea of armed conflict, the idea that armed conflict was the only path. In that, we had many differences, and I was not in agreement with him on that. From his first meeting with a group of followers, we began to discuss the different paths to be considered, and I told him that here, armed conflict was not a possibility, that he needed to understand that there were many possibilities; that a project like his, the kind of project he was putting together, along with me, was viable within a democratic regime." By January 1996, two thirds of the population had lost faith in the existing political parties, and the main concerns of the Venezuelan populace were inflation, insecurity, unemployment, and the poor quality of public services.[7]

Around that time, Hugo Chávez appeared at a protest in front of the congressional building. Wearing a red beret to draw attention to himself, he climbed onto the hood of a car and fired off a heated speech in support of the protesters, calling for President Caldera to resign from his position immediately and allow a transitional government to come in "before this explodes." At that moment in the center of Caracas, in one of the wings of the legislative palace, a U.S. flag was being burned in opposition to "the imperialism of the *yanqui* aggressor." A small article in the newspaper *El Nacional* termed it "an extemporaneous, folkloric protest." Still two years away from the elections, Miquilena and a number of civilians began to persuade Chávez to disengage himself from the violent path. "Finally, it was life itself, which is very determined and speaks louder than words, that made him realize the virtue of the other path, the peaceful one, because every time we would bring our proposals to the popular sectors and the economic sectors, he would start to see that the plan we were offering, a plan to effect change, was perfectly viable and accepted [*sic*], that is, if it had a solid enough social base to win electorally," said Miquilena.

Chávez later recalled, "We focused on finding out what people thought . . . we realized that a considerable portion of our nation was not interested in violent movements but was in fact expecting us to organize a structured political movement so that we might be able to take a peaceful path. From that point on, we decided to take the electoral path."[8] Still Chávez hesitated. When he finally took the leap, he did so in an ambiguous, provocative manner, so as not to disappoint his most hard-line supporters. And he made sure not to alter the combative tone of his discourse: it was with the old military-barracks language that Chávez began to effect the change, in February 1996.

"We are advancing toward the exercise of power through the peaceful path,"[9] he said, but a bit later on, close to the two-year anniversary of his release from prison, he noted that "if forced, we are willing to achieve it through force."[10]

For some time, Chávez had been trying to attract William Izarra to the movement, and in the middle of 1996, Izarra finally joined the group. From his perspective, what prevailed in the Chávez realm of those days

> was a tendency toward a revolutionary vision, and its ideological core was the Marxist interpretation of attaining power . . . the tendencies ranged from hard-line militarism to the most radical revolutionary positions. We also had individuals who came from right-wing political activism, who did not agree with the military sector, but who were seeking a change for the country. . . . There were also fanatical followers of the Chávez myth. . . . Generally, because of their excessive zeal, the militants did not allow the incorporation of people who came from the parties that represented the status quo or individuals who wanted nonviolent change.[11]

"I remember how, when we decided to go with the electoral route, we always talked about the 'tactical window,' "[12] Chávez has said. And the person to open that little window was Miquilena, of whom the *comandante* once said, "If I had had to pick my father, it would have been him."

According to Izarra, Chávez's lack of "ideological substance" was what allowed him to "change concepts" with "relative ease." For Izarra, Chávez was

> very wise and with a great deal of political intuition, which allowed him to decide, quite categorically, who was useful to

him and who was not. . . . Who could influence him and make him change his initial positions, and whom he could ignore. . . . A swift learner with a prodigious memory, he assimilated the theoretical elements that he needed to understand in order to take political action in a given situation. . . . He always held fast to the position that he would not be beholden to anyone. Anyone who joined him did so to achieve an end, in which he was the leader and the objective was to get him to Miraflores.[13]

WITH THIS IN MIND, the extraordinary assembly of the Bolivarian Revolutionary Movement unanimously decided, in April 1997, to go to the polls. Hugo Chávez, former coup leader, was now a presidential candidate who intended to achieve his goal "with the conviction of transforming the status quo." His first slogans were "For the Constituent Assembly, against corruption, In Defense of Social Services, For higher salaries and wages across the board, Bolivarian Government Now." He looked healthier. He also changed his uniform. Out went the *liqui-liqui,* and in came an entirely new look: a casual shirt and sweater for the campaign and suits made by the renowned Portuguese-Venezuelan tailor Clement for more elegant occasions. No longer did he look like an old-fashioned insurgent. On the eve of a trip to London, he admitted, "We have been making an effort, a logical one, out of necessity, to change clothes and get some more or less typical Western-style suits. . . . There is no such transmutation from the *liqui-liqui* to Clement. I have my combat uniform with me. And if a riot were to break out, I would get out my combat uniform to fight. It is a question of a man and his circumstances."[14]

It is the man and his quest for power.

PART TWO

CHAPTER 10

State of Grace

THEIR PERSONAL HISTORIES, WHICH IN MANY WAYS REPRESENT THE
history of modern Venezuela, had crisscrossed circumstantially for
years. But for the first time, the three men found themselves together,
under the same roof at the same hour. Hugo Chávez, Rafael Caldera,
and Carlos Andrés Pérez. The first man was an enigma; the other two
were symbols of a time, a system, and a particular way of practicing
politics. The date was February 2, 1999. In the modest chamber of the
Venezuelan National Congress, the former military officer who had
led an armed rebellion seven years earlier was poised to receive the
tricolor taffeta sash, to be placed on his person by the outgoing president. Outside, a throng of supporters in red berets were yelling themselves hoarse shouting *"Viva!"* over and over again in celebration of
their leader, an outsider whose antipolitical discourse had transformed the apathy of his countrymen into hope and enthusiasm.

"When God created the world," Chávez had said a month earlier
on a visit to Paris, "He gave Venezuela aluminum, oil, natural gas,
gold, minerals, fertile land—everything. But He realized that this was
a lot. 'I am not going to make everything so easy for the Venezuelan
people,' said God, and so He sent us politicians!" Now, however,
within this very special vision of things, it seemed that God had taken
pity on the country and sent them Chávez, who would never call or
consider himself a politician. Though he has refused to budge on this
point, the facts have proven him a very political animal indeed:
blessed with a great deal of intuition, astute and perceptive when it
comes to the exercise of politics, beyond his hegemonic inclinations.

Inside the congressional building, elation and chagrin were the two sentiments visible on the faces in the crowd, which included congressmen, a dozen or so foreign presidents (including Fidel Castro), and the members of Venezuela's diplomatic corps. It would not be a typical inauguration ceremony in any sense. A tight, bitter grimace stretched across the features of President Caldera as he walked onto the dais to surrender the presidency to the ex-commander whose liberation he himself had ordered. This was not an easy task for him, though in the symbolic and technical senses he did not fulfill it. Contrary to tradition, Caldera did not swear in the new president. In his place, another former military officer who was now the president of the Congress, Luis Alfonso Dávila, did the honors.

"Without a doubt, I had no desire to confer that sash on Chávez, because I could already sense all the negative aspects of his presidency," recalls the former Christian Democrat president.

There was, in fact, some precedent for Caldera's gesture. The first time he had assumed the presidency back in 1969, his Social Democrat predecessor, Raúl Leoni, had "refused to confer on me the sash. He gave it to the president of the Congress, José Antonio Pérez Díaz, who then gave it to me. So it wasn't anything shocking." Caldera notes that even back then he could see "that what predominated in Chávez was his ambition, his desire for power. An ambition not simply to be president for a period of time, but to take over all public authority, and all aspects of the [nation's] administrative life." It may also have been a way of making Chávez pay for having tried to hustle himself into Miraflores. Publicly and privately, "through emissaries," Chávez had asked Caldera to step down from the presidency the day after the elections.

"I made a categorical statement that I would hand over [the presidency] on the day stipulated by the Constitution," said Caldera. In other words: two months after the election results were in.

But nothing and nobody could spoil Hugo Chávez's joy that day. He, too, had several surprises up his sleeve that would make the moment even more bitter than his predecessors might have imagined.

His first surprise, a remarkably irreverent comment, made it clear where he was coming from. Standing straight as a rod, he raised his hand in front of the president of Congress and in a thick voice solemnly thundered, "I swear before God, I swear before the Nation, I swear before my people that upon this moribund Constitution I will drive forth the necessary democratic transformations so that the new Republic will have a Magna Carta befitting these new times. I do so solemnly swear." The impact of this death knell was not minor. And the new commander in chief was aware of the weight of his words. Not only was he inviting the Venezuelan people to the funeral of the country's most foundational laws, established in 1961, but he was also inscribing the gravestone of the two-party system that had ruled the nation for four decades.

Following this was an acceptance speech that was more like a two-hour tongue lashing, which began—of course—with a quote by Bolívar. The youngest-ever president of the country, born four years before the start of the democratic era, offered an evaluation of the crisis, stating that "Venezuela has received a blow to the heart, we are teetering on the edge of our tomb." Then he rattled off a statistic that news agencies, foreign correspondents, and even local journalists would repeat over and over again without bothering to confirm it first: that 80 percent of the Venezuelan people were living in poverty. At that moment, the real poverty statistics were grim enough; they needed little embellishment. In 1999, more than half the population of Venezuela—specifically 57.2 percent, more than 13 million people—did not have what they needed to subsist.[1] This, however, in no way minimizes the overwhelming predicament Chávez inherited, which he defined as "a time bomb" ready to explode. He announced his intention to deactivate that time bomb and exhorted his countrymen to join him in revolution to bring about a new political system. The audience was probably reminded of his past right then, and so was he—in fact, he took a moment to reflect upon it, saying that "the Venezuelan military uprising of 1992 was as inevitable as the eruption of a volcano." He followed this by expressing his hope that the future would not hold any military insurrections like the one he had staged. During this speech, which lasted an hour and forty-five minutes, Chávez was interrupted by no fewer than thirty spontaneous bursts of applause.

Hugo Chávez is not just a man of words. He is also a man of action, and showed it that day. During this address he enacted his first measure, a decree calling for a referendum to push forward his idea of creating a Constituent Assembly to bury the Constitution for once and for all. A new Constitution would not only give his country a new law, either.

"At that time, it was urgently necessary to transform the political map in order to continue pushing forward the revolutionary project," Chávez later remarked. "We had only three governors connected to the process . . . and the National Congress was in their hands: we were the minority."[2] In reality, Chávez's Patriotic Pole had come out with eight of the twenty-three governorships in dispute during those elections. But for the new commander in chief, this was not enough. In Congress, his party, the Fifth Republic Movement, was in the minority with less than 20 percent, and though the presidential party might have been able to boost its numbers by forging alliances with smaller parties, Chávez would never have been able to come close to a simple majority. The regional and legislative elections held in November 1998, a month before the presidential elections, had left him with an opposition-controlled congress.

When the new head of state stepped down from the dais, that new Congress's days were numbered. At that moment, Chávez allowed himself one more marvelous, magnanimous gesture, a final surprise for the audience, the press, the whole country, and, most especially, for one man in particular. The *comandante* turned on his heel and began to walk toward the first row of seats, where the country's senators were sitting.

"I walked away from the front row so that I wouldn't have to say hello to him, but he came right over to where I was and extended his hand, without saying a single word," recalls ex-president Carlos

Andrés Pérez, one of the people most despised and most severely damaged by Chávez. And then, when it was all over, as if to prolong the glory of his rise to power, the former insurgent walked the few blocks to Miraflores as his followers cheered him on. The presidential guard was unable to contain them, and the throngs entered the palace with their new president. His first official act as president was an improvised ceremony "in memory of those fallen during the events of February 4." An old woman, who had somehow managed to outsmart the wall of bodyguards surrounding him, hugged him tightly during the moment of silence.

THE WILL OF THE new president would be done, and fast. The opposition was demoralized, not only by Chávez's landslide and his enviable talent for reading the pulse of his people but also by their own lackluster performance in the elections. The echo of this punishment vote was felt on every street corner and especially at the doors to the congressional building, where the congressmen who were now among the opposition were heckled by Chávez's most radical supporters: "Corrupt thieves, go look for a job!" Chávez quickly baptized the previous forty years of Venezuelan politics a "corruptocracy," a newfangled expression that quickly found its place in the popular lexicon. But it wasn't all a bed of roses.

"In the beginning, the president did not know how to run a cabinet, despite being versed in the ways of the General Staff, because in fact a cabinet was more or less like a General Staff," remarks his first defense minister, General Raúl Salazar, the man who had accompanied Chávez on his walk to freedom when he was released from prison in 1994.

His first team, made up of fourteen ministers, included few people with experience in public administration. Two well-known journalists, Alfredo Peña, minister of the secretary of the presidency, and José Vicente Rangel, foreign minister, had spent most of their energies railing against the public administration, but always from afar.

Power had a magnetic attraction for both men, but neither had ever exercised it from inside the government. And Chávez's party was not rife with leaders experienced in the ways of officialdom, whether on the municipal, regional, or legislative level. According to Salazar, "They were ignorant in terms of managing the public sector."

Chávez, however, proved himself an able politician when it came to dodging obstacles. In an unexpected but well-received maneuver, Chávez confirmed Maritza Izaguirre as treasury minister, keeping her in the post she had held under Caldera. The state of the country's budget was delicate. According to Salazar, "The [1999] budget was calculated at $13 per barrel of oil, and it went down to $7.20. He had to formulate a new international policy, to make not just Venezuela but OPEC competitive, so that the price would go up by July. There wasn't enough money in the Treasury to pay salaries. . . . There were 76 billion bolívars in the National Treasury [approximately $130 million], and 540 billion were needed for the first trimester, and there was no more income. The president learned along the way, but he has a serious problem: he always acts as though he were still campaigning."

As he faced the task of leading his government, Hugo Chávez chose to rely mainly on Luis Miquilena, his interior minister, who soon became his right-hand man. According to General Salazar, during the first two months, the new commander in chief accepted suggestions and criticisms with goodwill, but after that point, "it seemed that his circle had deified him and acted as if they knew everything." During those early days, those not in his camp gave him the benefit of the doubt, at least for the time being, and hoped that he would fulfill his promises to combat corruption and reduce the level of poverty. At that moment, it seemed unpatriotic to hedge bets on his failure.

"As soon as Chávez won, I spoke with Miquilena and José Vicente Rangel, saying, 'All right, now that we've got this man on our hands—who is going to be a dictator, I don't doubt that one bit—at the very least we have to make sure that he remains on the path of democracy,' " said Pérez when he was still a senator for life, though this status would be revoked some months later. "On Chávez's first trip to Colombia, I called President [Andrés] Pastrana to make sure he would be well received, and I also called the Brazilian [president] Fernando Henrique Cardoso, because that was my idea: now that this man had gotten himself in there, let's see if we can get him on the democratic path."

After hearing Chávez's speech in the congressional building, those who had hoped he might change his tone after settling into the presidency were disappointed. The *comandante* abandoned neither his campaign rhetoric nor his antiestablishment discourse. From his position as the most powerful man in the land, he continued to invoke the defense of the have-nots against Venezuela's powerful, a concept that swiftly took hold among the populace. "Hurricane Chávez," as some called him, did not let up. And in just a few months' time he did away with entire generations of politicians that had taken decades to evolve and devolve. His first confrontations were with the opposition Congress and the Supreme Court of Justice, an institution he had inherited from previous governments and that questioned his authority to call for a referendum by decree. Resistance was useless. His campaign to impose a Constituent Assembly was simply an extension of his successful presidential campaign. And he was bound to win: the Venezuelan people were hungry for change, and the polls gave him an 80 percent approval rating.

His newfound authority gave him the tools he needed to consolidate his leadership and confirmed the fact that he was indeed a tenacious man. Maripili Hernández saw this up close as his campaign adviser and, later on, as president of the state-run TV channel Venezolana de Televisión. (She was also vice foreign minister for North American Affairs between 2005 and 2006.)

"Chávez is a visionary," Hernández says. "He starts talking about things that one doesn't understand until a year later. One clear example of this is the Constituent [Assembly]. I remember how, the first time we heard him talk about the Constituent [Assembly], we all said, 'What is that about? What does that have to do with anything?'

Moreover, communicationswise it was a problem for us because Chávez constantly insisted that we include the topic in every speech he gave, and we just didn't think it was promotable. But he kept insisting that it was. And so we put all our energy into making the Constituent [Assembly] an electoral offer that people would buy. And he did it, with his insistence. One or two years later we began to understand how important the Constituent [Assembly] was for the country, and if you think about it, it really was a revolution."

Less than three months after assuming the presidency, Chávez would savor one of his great moments: on April 25, the people of Venezuela voted, via referendum[3] (albeit with a 62.5% abstention rate), to convene a National Constituent Assembly. In May 1999, as head of state, Hugo Chávez became the president of his party, the Fifth Republic Movement. It is a tradition in Venezuela that presidents formally disassociate themselves from partisan activities. Chávez ignored this tradition.

"What interests us is that Chávez is the principal militant of this political project that we call 'revolution.' The other thing is a problem of formal character. It would be hypocritical to claim that the president is not also the president of a party. As it stands, things are genuine and transparent. Don't tell me that when CAP was running the country he wasn't an AD militant." This is how Maripili Hernández sees things. As such, the president himself devised a campaign for the election of the Assembly members. Three months later, the Venezuelan opposition endured one of its blackest days ever. On July 25, more than one thousand candidates vied for the 128 seats at stake,[4] and the result was a thunderous upset, as the Venezuelan people summarily expelled the traditional political parties from their positions. The progovernment party, the Patriotic Pole, having presented just over a hundred candidacies, won 95 percent of the seats in dispute. Only six spots went to the opposition.[5]

As the day came to an end, the man from Barinas stepped onto the "people's balcony" at Miraflores to revel in the radiant night, a "home run with the bases loaded," as he called it. He was as ebullient in victory as his opposition was silent and crushed in defeat. In an unusual gesture, he placed a very public kiss on the lips of his also-triumphant first lady, Marisabel, whose name had quickly been placed on the list of candidates, thanks to a rather idiosyncratic mechanism known as the "Chávez lottery." Marisabel, it turned out, received the second highest number of votes of all the candidates for the Constituent Assembly. Among the new delegates were Chávez's closest collaborators: nineteen military officers, three former presidential candidates, well-known journalists and personalities like the historian José León Tapia, the psychiatrist Edmundo Chirinos, and even a singer of *llanera* music.

Three days later, his forty-fifth birthday, his first as president, was celebrated with a party complete with giant cake, fireworks, and mariachi band that sang *mañanitas* in Plaza Caracas in the city center.

"I feel as if I'm twenty, as if I were just starting out," he said as the crowd of ten thousand roared its approval. Could that young boy in Sabaneta, the one who envisioned standing ovations during his childhood daydreams about becoming a great baseball player, have possibly imagined this? Chávez's passion for baseball would never wane, and later on in his presidency he took special delight in inviting Sammy Sosa to Caracas, where the big-league baseball star pitched to him in the university stadium. Back then, every time Chávez or any member of his family entered a stadium, the crowd would break out in booming applause. He was the man of the hour and he enjoyed it, though he never lost sight of his real goal: power and everything that went with it.

Chávez is known for speaking his mind. "He is totally transparent," Maripili Hernández swears. But at other times, he seems the opposite. It is never easy to read him. Following his party's victory in the Constituent Assembly, resulting in a governmental hegemony, he had this to say: "We will not see a concentration of power in the Assembly." That, however, was precisely what people saw when the presidency of the Assembly went to his right-hand man, Luis Miquilena.

"These are just a few ideas for discussion," Chávez said, handing over a ninety-page volume of proposals for the new Constitution. "I stayed up late writing them all down." Nobody would doubt that: Hugo Chávez is a man of little sleep.

"Caffeine is his great drug," says his friend and onetime psychiatrist Edmundo Chirinos. "He drinks twenty-six to thirty cups of black coffee a day." A hyperactive insomniac, he has been known to sleep three or four hours a night and wake up in mint condition. Energetic. Ready for battle.

"He is a tireless worker. At the pace he goes, nobody can keep up with him. He works twenty-five hours a day," says Hernández.

With few exceptions, everything the president proposed was included in the new Constitution. The progovernment constituents worked for four months straight, like industrious tailors determined to design and execute the most perfectly appointed custom-made suit for their president. Among the many points they wove in: reelection; the extension of the presidential term from five to six years, which would give Chávez the opportunity to remain in power for twelve years uninterrupted; the creation of a Moral Power, based on an idea of Simón Bolívar; suffrage for military personnel; and even a new name for the country: what was once the Republic of Venezuela was now the Bolivarian Republic of Venezuela. Another novel and rather risky proposal was slipped in as well: the possibility of revoking the jobs of public employees, including the head of state himself. At least two of Chávez's initial proposals either were not granted by the team drafting the new constitution or were withdrawn by the president himself: the provision for runoffs in the presidential elections, and the creation of various vice presidencies that would answer to a first vice presidency. In the end, the Constitution was approved via popular referendum, although there would not be any fireworks this time around.

"The hour of our nation has arrived. Of turning, once again, to a national referendum, the second in our entire history as a republic . . . it will be another magnificent day for history,"[6] announced Chávez, battling the flu as he issued a brief address to the nation the day before the vote. Unable to resist temptation, he then offered his countrymen a dramatic quote by Bolívar, to convince them to get out and vote despite the dismal weather: "If nature opposes us, we will fight against her and force her to obey us." The Liberator had uttered these very same words after the Catholic Church had suggested that the 1812 earthquake that leveled Caracas had been God's way of punishing them for the independence movement. And just as if Chávez had cast a spell on Mother Nature, a thunderstorm of biblical proportions crashed down on Wednesday, December 15. More than half of the voting public stayed home, resulting in a 55 percent abstention rate.

The birth of the Bolivarian Constitution was a difficult one, and though it was approved with 71 percent of the votes of 45 percent of the electorate, it was not a night for celebration. In fact, few Venezuelans were particularly concerned about the Constitution at that moment. They were far more focused on what was going on half an hour outside of Caracas, where one side of the graceful mountain that separates the city from the sea crumbled away. The avalanche occurred on the side that faces the water, home to the people of the state of Vargas.

The early dawn hours of the following day were spent counting victims rather than votes. The death toll reached the thousands. The coastal city of La Guaira, the capital of Vargas state, was virtually buried beneath the mud, which broke free and slid down the slopes of Mount Avila, dragging massive boulders along with it. The country's main port was leveled entirely. The main airport had to be shut down. It was the most devastating natural tragedy ever to hit the country, and on that day Venezuelans forgot about the differences that separated them, about whether they were pro-Chávez or anti-Chávez. Everyone waited for the president to declare a state of emergency, and the sleepless populace asked themselves the same question over and over again: Where was Chávez? Hypotheses abounded: some said he was on La Orchila, the island where Venezuelan presidents vacation, and couldn't get into town because of the bad weather. Nobody knew. The following day, the newspapers did not help to clear up the mystery.

On Thursday, around noon, a stunned Chávez finally turned up on television in a military uniform after flying over what was now an unrecognizable coastline. With a religious timbre to his voice, Chávez said that twenty-five thousand victims were being transferred to parks and gymnasiums and that it was still not possible to calculate the number of dead and missing. He explained that he had ordered the Directorate for Intelligence and Prevention Services and the Metropolitan Police to stop any and all looting attempts in the area. He expressed his pain, and was then speechless.

It was the saddest December in Venezuelan memory, and the country's citizens canceled their end-of-millennium parties and donated all they could. The casualty estimates were in the range of 15,000 dead, more than 90,000 displaced, and some 400,000 people in need of medical attention. During those nights, Hugo Chávez found neither solace nor advice in his bedside book, *El oráculo del guerrero* (The Oracle of the Warrior). For a few weeks, he would sheathe his sword, as he liked to say, but it wouldn't be long before he would brandish it again, for the benefit of the gringos, the communications media, the Church, and anyone else who crossed him—or whom he suspected of doing so.

THE TRAGEDY KICKED UP a lot of mud, far beyond Vargas state. Thirty-six hours after the catastrophe, Washington sent four Chinook helicopters, eight Black Hawks, two Galaxies, and 146 soldiers to join the aerial aid shuttle.

"The U.S. got here in a day and a half," recalls General Raúl Salazar, who was defense minister at the time. Salazar had solicited the aid of Bill Clinton's government, after receiving authorization from Chávez. "The head of the Southern Command, Charles Wilhelm, came to visit the area on December 23. We began to discuss the idea, which I communicated to the president, of taking a look at the future of La Guaira, because it would take ten years and ten billion dollars to recover." The U.S. engineers, who would take care of building the paths and the reservoirs for a considerable stretch of this area, would arrive by boat. "It was all going very well until January 2, when I received a call from the president at four in the morning, ordering me to stop the entire thing. That has to weigh on Chávez's conscience. Whom did he talk to on the night of the second? I think it was someone in the Caribbean," says Salazar, in a clear allusion to Fidel Castro. The boat, however, had already set sail from the United States and was heading for Venezuela. "Twelve helicopters and 150 gringos were already here. That aid should never have been rejected." Days later, Salazar argued with Chávez about the incident. "I told him, 'You are wrong.' But he said it was intervention, he said some things about sovereignty, and that they could spy. . . . I think he got confused and was very poorly advised."

Chávez's bitter falling-out with his old friend Jesús Urdaneta, after twenty years of friendship, is another incident that reveals just what kind of power battles were raging inside the government. It was also Chávez's first stumble in the world of corruption, a word that until then had not been part of the vocabulary of his administration. Urdaneta, who was the first government employee designated by the new head of state (as well as Chávez's one-time roommate), was one of the first to abandon the government, after thirteen months on the job. "All throughout that period I had many differences with Chávez and his circle, because of things I learned and later reported."

In one year, Urdaneta tracked at least forty cases of corruption inside the new administration. By mid-1999, he says, he was considering resigning from his position. "At one lunch in particular I was very hard on him. I said, 'Listen, Hugo Chávez, I fought against a crooked, corrupt government, and your government is the same! I have given you the details of Luis Miquilena's shady deals, of the entire infrastructure of power and corruption that he has built, plus what José Vicente Rangel has done, and you do not seem at all disposed to do anything about it. On the contrary—you have obstructed and hampered my efforts. I don't want to keep on playing the useful idiot. I don't want to stand by your side in this administration for one second more.' I threw so many things in his face that day. . . . I do remember, though, that he exhibited a patience and a humility that were unsettling. He said to me, 'The problem is that you, *compañero,* want to achieve change overnight.' " The head of state placed the situation in metaphorical terms, telling him that they were "in the middle of the Guaire River [a sewage stream that crosses Caracas], and the important thing is to get to the other side, not to end up getting carried off by the river."

Urdaneta says he replied, " 'The river's going to carry you away, because it just isn't possible to try to cross it with guys like them, Miquilena and José Vicente.' And so he said to me, 'Don't worry, *compañero,* just be a little patient, because when I have my new tools in place, the National Constitution, I'll get rid of them. Those two are the kind of old political operators I need right now, because none of us [military officers] has what they have. I can't force a friend to stay with me. Of course I need you there." Urdaneta decided to wait. But he eventually realized that his condemnations had rendered him an inconvenient government employee. By year's end, the Vargas landslide gave Chávez a reason to relieve him of his duties. According to Urdaneta, the government linked the Directorate for Intelligence and Prevention Services, which he supervised, to a series of supposed executions in La Guaira during the efforts to control looting.

Urdaneta tendered his resignation in protest against what he considered unwarranted interference by Foreign Minister Rangel, who criticized the Directorate for Intelligence and Prevention Services for calling in a journalist to testify about the crimes his employees had been accused of committing. Urdaneta was also bothered that Chávez did not authorize him to speak to the press to clear up any doubts regarding the Intelligence Services' actions in Vargas.

"He said to me, 'You're not giving that press conference.' 'Why not?' I asked him. 'Because I'm going to look really bad.' I told him that I didn't understand, because the one who was going to end up looking bad was me. 'It's an order from me, and I am the president of the Republic,' he said. That was the definitive break."

Urdaneta was later accused of building a house that he could never have paid for, given his salary, though he said that "it was a lie and they never proved anything." After resigning, he says that Chávez offered him the Spanish ambassadorship.

"I told him I was outraged that he thought he could buy my conscience. He insisted, though, and asked me why didn't I re-enter the armed forces so that he could promote me to general. I told him that I couldn't believe what I was hearing. 'I will not accept anything you offer me.' And so he asked me, 'What are you going to do? Raise pigs?' That made me even angrier, and I said to him, 'If I can do it honestly and decently, yes.'" Though he hadn't suspected it at the time, Urdaneta is now convinced that Chávez and Rangel engineered a "setup" to neutralize his negative claims. He says he discovered this when Chávez called the head of investigations at the Directorate for Intelligence and Prevention Services, ex-commander Luis Pineda Castellanos, and asked him to hand over "the files on all the corruption cases I had been handling." The president apparently said to Pineda, "Jesús is very uncomfortable for me. I need you to go to Vargas and submit a report that implicates him in human rights violations." This was confirmed by Pineda, who now opposes the Chávez government. Urdaneta was the first important resignation from Chávez's government. Before long, all the other men behind the February 4 rebellion would tender their resignations as well.

Around this time, the bestselling book among the roving street vendors in the center of Caracas was *El oráculo del guerrero* (The Oracle of the Warrior), by the Argentinian Lucas Estrella. It was the latest literary fetish of the Venezuelan president, who had begun to cite it frequently in his speeches. The author, a biologist and martial arts practitioner, came to Caracas and stated that the message of his book was that "the ego must occupy the place of least importance, and service to others, the most."

When asked what it was about the book that fascinated Hugo

Chávez, Estrella replied, "I suppose he feels that the only way he will be able to carry out the massive undertaking that lies before him is by following the principles of the warrior." One of these principles, for example, says, "Warrior, when you win a battle, don't lose time sheathing your sword, because tomorrow will only bring more battles." The head of state waxed on and on about the Oracle until someone came up with the idea that the book had been written in a code of sorts and intended for a gay audience.

"All summer long I have talked on and on about how, compared to Chávez's favorite book, my novel is downright heterosexual," joked the ingenious Boris Izaguirre, Venezuela's most illustrious gay celebrity, while promoting his latest book in Spain. Apparently, this revelation was more than enough for Hugo Chávez to throw Estrella's book straight into the garbage.

As his first year in office came to a close, the Venezuelan president decided to offer the world an assessment of sorts of "a process of profound change, carried out peacefully, without the rivers of blood that other nations have waded through and continue to wade through as they try to change a political regime."[7] His cornerstone program was the Plan Bolívar 2000, a $113 million social welfare project administered by high-ranking military officers employed by the administration. Soldiers would participate in the construction of state-subsidized residential buildings, and they would also work selling at the stands in the new local markets, an idea that dovetailed with Chávez's plan to create a stronger bond between the armed forces and the populace. The state bureaucracy was now a sea of epaulets, as Chávez entrusted this aid work to his former *compañeros* in the barracks. Not long after the program was launched, some of the uniformed men close to Chávez became linked to a few very public corruption scandals. Overpricing, nonexistent or fraudulent bills and invoices, ghost employees, and a host of other irregularities that were long-standing traditions in Venezuela began to drag Plan Bolívar 2000 through the mud.

The president continued to use the vocabulary of war in public, but he may well have thought back to Lucas Estrella's aphorisms as he faced his next battle, one that would affect him deeply. On February 4, 2000, the eighth anniversary of the 1992 uprising, his collaborators in that daring endeavor, close friends with whom he had spent long nights hatching plots, accused him of betraying the revolutionary objectives for which they had staged their rebellion. Jesús Urdaneta, Francisco Arias, and Yoel Acosta (Jesús M. Ortiz, the fifth ringleader, had died in a car accident in Paris) surprised him one day with a press conference.

"Revolutions happen with revolutionaries, not with the same people that were part of the destiny that we, the Venezuelan people, do not deserve," the former insurgents declared. Analysts interpreted this split as evidence of the power struggles that had erupted within the government. The leaders of 4F had turned against the more seasoned politicians, whom they accused of being part of the "old guard." The former conspirators had already tried to express their concerns to Chávez in private, but, as they claim, he had been shunted away from them by then, isolated behind the wall that tends to encircle and protect the powerful.

Miquilena, considered the number two man in the administration, accused the former insurgents of lacking "the courage necessary to confront Chávez themselves and directly express their dissatisfaction with the political line he is pursuing; they are using us as a pretext to attack him." Chávez, probably very hurt, left it at this, at least in public: "True brothers work as an eternal team, beyond the difficulties, beyond interests, beyond individual sentiment."

Chávez's opposition was delighted by this first conflict within the government, never imagining that two years later Miquilena and Arcaya would also abandon Chávez. At the time, however, the opposition was still against the ropes. The antipolitical stance favored by the president was not going out of style. Any Venezuelan who had spent a few years out of the country would have had a difficult time identifying the government officials who now appeared on the TV news. With few exceptions, the usual suspects had all but disappeared. And on the horizon was the campaign for the popular election that would be the last step toward ratifying the powers granted by the Constituent Assembly. The swell of popular support behind Chávez in 1998 had not died down, and the anemic opposition desperately searched for a candidate who could challenge Hugo Chávez. Ironically, they turned to a man with credentials similar to those of the man they wished to defeat. A onetime coup stager, though considerably more moderate than the *comandante* from Barinas, the man chosen for this task was none other than Chávez's old ex-comrade Francisco Arias. A real face-off.

Though by now the president had stopped quoting *El oráculo del guerrero,* he continued to act like a warrior when running the country, for he has always thrived on confrontation. With no effort at all he would find people who would take his bait and get caught in conflict with him: the communications media, the Church, trade unions, the United States. Making enemies has always come easily to Hugo Chávez. Puffed up by his tremendous popularity, he has always reveled in provoking his adversaries with irreverent, over-the-top remarks. "Christ is with the revolution!" he would cry, and the Church would lunge at him.

For Chávez, the 2000 campaign was a racecourse with one minor obstacle: just two days before the May election, technical difficulties forced the government to postpone the "megaelections," so nicknamed because for the first time in Venezuelan history, president, governors, national and regional congressmen, mayors, and councilmen would be voted in on the same day. Election day was rescheduled from May 28 to July 30. On that day, more than 36,000 candidates would be vying for 6,241 elected positions. Along the way Chávez lost a great deal of support in terms of public opinion.

"In fifteen months as president, he has, with his intolerance and his language, clashed unnecessarily with a great deal of people. He has alienated the support of sectors that previously endorsed him. He has alienated the middle class, the Catholic Church—which supported him quite strongly—and the organized sectors of the working class," said Teodoro Petkoff, critic, editor, and historical leader of the Venezuelan left, in May 2000.

The face-off with his rival, his former "soul brother," was tough. In his campaign advertisements, Arias satirized Chávez with a picture of a hen, in an allusion to Chávez's performance—or rather, lack thereof—on February 4, though later he would regret this. Hugo Chávez, confident of his popularity, used the same formula that had worked for him in 1998. On the day of the election, the president emerged looking relaxed. After casting his vote in the morning, he played baseball with the members of his honor guard. The majority of the Venezuelan voters that day once again placed their bets on the charismatic man with the incendiary discourse, the man who continued to blame the "corruptocracy" for all the evils that plagued Venezuela and fashioned himself as an avenger out for justice. The election results, of course, were yet another blow to his desperately weakened opposition: the head of state had not lost one bit of his hold on his nation's people. On the contrary: his voting index rose more than three percentage points. While 3,673,000 people (56.2%) had voted for Chávez back in 1998, that number went up to 3,757,000 (59%) in 2000.[8]

The Chávez style, so deeply reviled by a certain sector of the middle class who consider him vulgar and common, continued to incite the fervor of Venezuela's more impoverished citizens, who gave him carte blanche to do what he wanted. Some three fifths of the unicameral National Assembly fell into the hands of the progovernment party (99 seats out of a total of 165), allowing him to legislate as he so desired and nominate key government officials. The head of state was clear about this: "In my first campaign speech I said that I would exchange all the governorships and mayoralties for the National Assembly" he declared, aware that "that majority would determine the composition of all the other instruments of power: the Public Prosecutor's Office, the Supreme Court of Justice, the Electoral Power, the Attorney General's Office, the Comptroller General, and the Public Defender's office."[9] But that wasn't all. His popularity had

had an exponential effect, catapulting unknown candidates into no fewer than fourteen governorships. In addition, their allies in the Movement Toward Socialism party gained control of two more governorships. Previously with sixteen governorships under its aegis, the pro-Chávez platform now controlled a total of twenty-three, in what the president himself called a "spectacular knockout." The most widely remarked example of what the local press termed as Chávez's "aircraft carrier effect" was the case of Hugo de los Reyes Chávez, Chávez's father, who was voted in as governor of the state of Barinas. It was the dream of absolute power come true. The road was wide open for Chávez, far wider than it had ever been for any Venezuelan president before him.

Supporters banged at the doors to Miraflores as the opposition leaders glumly conceded their defeat. Before eleven that night, the heavy gates of Miraflores Palace opened, as hundreds of admirers poured in, gathering beneath the balcony that Chávez had baptized "the people's balcony." As the president emerged with his wife, Marisabel, the crowd roared their approval, sounding like an audience at a rock concert welcoming their idol onstage. These were the *comandante*'s most fervent devotees, the ones who sang, "Hungry and jobless, I'm sticking with Chávez." They then spontaneously broke into a rendition of "Happy Birthday," just two days late. And as all this was happening before him, Chávez overcame the knot in his throat enough to call out, "Thank you for your love . . . and as José Martí, the Cuban apostle, once said, 'Love is repaid with love, and I have no choice but to love you.' " That night he made them his and transferred his importance to them: "All of you are sublime, for you have defeated all the campaigns that have come out against us." As always, he improvised his speech, recalling the days when he had only just emerged from anonymity: "This path comes from the glorious and epic 4F." Once again, the failed coup was invoked as a symbol and a starting point for the new Venezuela. And just as in 1998, he made a call for unity, "to push the nation forward, so that we can push the ship out to a good sea and into a safe port." With companies going out of business left and right and foreign capital fleeing the country, the economic situation was depressed, but Chávez promised to launch a new model. When it was all over, at around twelve-thirty at night, he bid the crowd good night in classic *llanero* style, singing a *copla* for his audience. Up on stage, the president would never disappoint his followers: a night with Chávez was and always is quite a spectacle.

THE HEAD OF STATE continued to stun his adversaries at every turn. His appetite was insatiable. Even now, with a majority in the parliament, he wanted more authority, and to this end he behaved like a real *caudillo*, a real Latin American strongman. Now he wanted to legislate directly from Miraflores, and he solicited extraordinary powers from the National Assembly—which was controlled by docile supporters—to put together a reform package. In the long run, however, the reforms served only to infuriate half the country and inspire his most reactionary enemies to stage a coup of their own. For almost two years Hugo Chávez had been operating in a state of grace. With one triumph after another, he was acclaimed by the masses, but as 2001 approached his fortunes turned. The first people to seriously express their disapproval of the *comandante* were middle-class teachers and housewives, who felt that their children's education was being threatened. For the first time in history, the well-to-do ladies of Caracas marched into the city center toting megaphones and signs and yelling out, "Don't mess with my children!" Two issues were responsible for igniting their ire: the decision to make premilitary instruction a mandatory course in secondary schools, and the approval of Resolution 259, which allowed the Education Ministry to rewrite history textbooks. Disgruntlement in the education community only grew as word spread about the revised contents of the textbooks, which included, among other things, a damning recap of the previous forty years of democratic government in Venezuela and praise-filled descriptions of the 1992 coup and the Bolivarian Revolution.

But it was the announcement of the new National Education

Project designed by the Marxist professor Carlos Lanz, a radical who denounced McDonald's hamburgers for their transculturizing effects, that put Hugo Chávez's government to the test. Private schools suddenly became hotbeds of assemblies and meetings among parents and teachers who meticulously pored over the project, analyzing it from every angle. Out of this controversy emerged the first NGO specifically dedicated to combating Chávez policies: the Civil Association Education Assembly. As terms like "ideologized supervisors," "indoctrination," and "Cubanization" were heatedly bandied about at these meetings, the middle class began having nightmares about *pioneritos,* pint-sized Communists, and these nightmares were only exacerbated by the announcement of a new prize to be awarded by the Education Ministry: the Ernesto Che Guevara Prize. On January 20, 2001, parents and teachers took to the streets in the very first anti-Chávez protests, a phenomenon that only grew as time went by. In response to the crisis, Education Minister Héctor Navarro was forced to clarify that the government was attempting not "to Cubanize education but to create a pedagogical model tailored to our culture."

Chávez was not about to cave in to a group of parents he called "selfish and individualistic," who had begun to ruin his honeymoon. In an unprecedented move, he placed himself at the head of a rally in support of Decree 1.011, employing a discourse filled with clichés that his opponents termed as entirely divisive: "They live quite well, quite comfortably, tremendous house, tremendous apartment, they have no problems, their children attend good schools and travel out of the country. Nobody criticizes them, but some of them don't realize that a December 6, 1998, took place here. . . . The thoughts they express when they say, 'Don't mess with my children' are contrary to the social life of a democracy. That indeed is fundamentalism, contrary to the mandate of God. . . . They look down their noses at everyone else, as if the rest of us were insignificant rabble. Yes, we are the same rabble that followed Bolívar. . . . The decree will be enforced, and I will be supervisor number one."[10]

The head of state responded to the protests with provocations, exhibiting the qualities that most irritated his adversaries: "Come out to the street and look at me! The more dirt you throw at me, the more I'll throw at you. That is who I am!" He ended his harangue, as he often liked to do, with a song: *"No soy monedita de oro pa' caerle bien a todos"*[11] (I am not a gold coin to be tossed around to make everyone happy). In the end, this controversy marked not only Chávez's first experience with resistance but his first concession, as well. The government finally backed down on Resolution 259 and abandoned Decree 1.011 in favor of a consensus-based educational program.

Beyond its successful results at the polls, the Fifth Republic Movement, as a political party, did not come together as Chávez had hoped it would. For this reason, the president organized units from the popular sectors to revive the Bolivarian Revolutionary Movement. He announced this in mid-2001[12] on his television show, *Aló, Presidente*, urging his supporters to register with the Bolivarian Circles so as to create "a great human network" to defend the revolution.

"They will be made up of honest Bolivarian journalists, cameramen, *conuqueros* [farmers who own small plots of land], fishermen, true leaders who will come together to work; they may be created at universities, hospitals, Bolivarian schools, at businesses . . . they will need organization. We can't wander around adrift. This project will need true leaders in every unit, on every street corner." To organize the Bolivarian Circles, the president would avail himself of public funds. And he would not hide this. "The command post is where it needs to be. Where? At Miraflores. That is the home of the Political Headquarters of the Revolution." There, he said, "the direct link will be created and the lists compiled." The person assigned to head up this little operation was the former military officer and coup stager Diosdado Cabello, then the minister of the secretary of the presidency.

Although their inspiration likely came from the Panamanian Dignity Battalions, the Bolivarian Circles were inevitably compared to Cuba's Committees for the Defense of the Revolution. Equally inevitable, of course, was the anxiety that broke out among the media, the business community, and the middle class. One week later, Chávez endured an avalanche of criticism and was threatened with charges of embezzlement for having used public funds to attract and organize political supporters while president.[13] He responded to these accusations with outrage: "Put me on trial, then! Put me on trial. For organizing the people? For fulfilling my obligation? This is ridiculous . . . they say that I am violating the Constitution, well, they must have another Constitution. . . . They can do what they want, because the Bolivarian Circles are mechanisms of direct participation." The objective, he said, was to attract one million volunteers and swear them in by December.

Nobody would ever know if he managed to get those million volunteers. By December 2001, the Circles were pushed into the background. The country was up in arms over the ratification of a package of laws drawn up at Miraflores, thanks to the extraordinary powers the parliament had granted the president. The laws in question were in fact forty-nine law decrees, practically one for every week of the year. The Venezuelan business community and the media sharply denounced the hermetic manner in which the law decrees had been conceived, without consulting the specific sectors that would be affected by them. Of all the legislation, the piece that caused the greatest consternation was the Law of Land and Agrarian Development, which Chávez himself acknowledged as very controversial, adding, "I worked on it personally and directly."[14] As far as the commander in chief was concerned, it was "a truly revolutionary, modern law that does not trample upon anyone, it is just fulfilling the constitutional mandate to put an end to the *latifundio;* to establish a tax; to regulate the possession of land; to subordinate the possession of land to productivity and national interest with the goal of achieving high levels of agroalimentary self-sufficiency."[15] The main objection to this measure was that agricultural and livestock activities would be subject to the dictates of the government, since the government would have the power to make decisions regarding private farms. If the government determined that a particular property needed to cultivate sorghum, it would have to cultivate sorghum even if it was a cattle farm.[16] Contrary to what many people outside Venezuela would believe, the new laws did not effect much change with respect to the *latifundio,* the large, privately owned ranches. In fact, the *latifundio* would continue to be defined as "all tracts of idle land" covering more than 5,000 hectares. According to the Institute of Superior Studies of Administration, at the time there were "900 *latifundistas* in existence in a universe of, depending on the sources, somewhere between 350,000 and 500,000 units of production."

Fetishistic about historic dates, the president decided that the controversial law would be enacted on December 10, the anniversary of the 1859 battle in which his federalist idol Ezequiel Zamora defeated the forces of the landowning oligarchy. He decided to celebrate the event in Santa Inés, in Barinas state, at the very spot where Zamora's battle took place. Picking up on this war-oriented motif, the opposition got out its artillery that very same day and responded with a general strike, the first ever to be staged in protest of the government, and the first strike ever to be jointly organized by the country's largest trade union, the Venezuelan Confederation of Workers, and the national chamber of commerce, Fedecámaras. Their leaders, Carlos Ortega and Pedro Carmona, respectively, soon became the spokespeople of the opposition. Ortega, an oil industry union leader with ties to Democratic Action (the Social Democratic party), gave the Chávez government its first electoral defeat in the union elections on November 2, which the government called fraudulent. Chávez went on to claim that "the business leadership of Fedecámaras has turned into a political party. It has become the binding factor of the opposition, because there are no opposition parties. Where are the opposition parties? Where is the opposition leader who could bring these groups together? They simply do not exist, and so they are taking on this role."[17]

The strike proved that, though fragmented, the opposition was no longer as "anemic" or "scrawny" as Chávez scornfully termed it. Soon the affected parties initiated a series of legal actions and, amid the ensuing unrest, the parliament agreed to debate observations regarding twenty-four of the new laws. The president, however, stood his ground. There is a postcard snapshot of Chávez at a Caribbean summit on Margarita Island, in a field uniform, flanked by Fidel Castro, brandishing a pair of pliers given to him as a gift by someone who attended the enactment of the Fishing Law. "You have to turn the screws in favor of those who are the weakest, the poorest," he said on that occasion. And there, with a crystalline bay as his backdrop, he announced that his renewed hard-line stance was a response to the fact that "we have discovered a conspiracy against the government, an attempt to destabilize the country . . . we cannot allow people to confuse democracy with self-indulgence so that they can do whatever they please."

By that time, Hugo Chávez had already earned his place in history as the president most loved and most despised by the Venezuelan people, the president who inspired the greatest zeal and the deepest revulsion at the very same time. His "chains," continuous and prolonged television broadcasts with which he would interrupt commercial TV programming at whatever hour and for whatever reason—to talk about some recently granted microcredits, a military decoration ceremony, a desertification conference—generated a great deal of irritation and frustration. Didn't he realize he was going too far? Was it provocation or simple egomania?

"I think there's a lot of those two adjectives. There is egomania, there is narcissism, and to a certain degree he is unaware that he is not charming. He needs to be admired, that is the narcissistic part," states his friend and onetime psychiatric adviser Edmundo Chirinos.

In addition to the natural and typical fluctuations of any president's popularity ratings, Chávez's image eroded further because of his adversarial style and overexposure in the media. After almost three years in office, he was still extremely difficult to pin down. His opponents on the right called him a Communist and an autocrat, while the anti-Chávez left said he was a neoliberal. Despite his invective against savage capitalism and globalization, Chávez opened the telecommunications, gas, and utilities sectors to foreign investors and continued to follow the guidelines recommended by the International Monetary Fund. He paid Venezuela's debt punctually and was not allergic to taxes. According to the pro-Chávez congressman Tarek Saab, "his idea is to use protectionist capitalism to generate social balance." Hugo Chávez began 2002 with a certain level of popularity, but he could no longer boast of an 80 percent approval rate. And he knew this. It had been a long time since he had dared set foot in a stadium to watch his favorite team play ball. When the well-known baseball player Endy Chávez would come out onto the field, the crowd would roar, *"Endy sí, Chávez no!"* People had started banging on their *cacerolas*, their kitchen pots. And nothing irritated Chávez more than the sound of people banging away on those kitchen pots. Whenever he heard that noise, his proverbial good humor would instantly evaporate. On his Sunday television show *Aló, Presidente,* he would ask his followers to respond to the *cacerolas* with firecrackers, even though fireworks are theoretically illegal. For every kitchen pot banged on, he said, "we will hear the sound of five hundred firecrackers, from the great majority that supports the revolution."

The year 2002 would be one of thunder, full of surprises. The first was a loss that would leave him feeling a bit like an orphan. The man he long considered his political father and his right hand decided to resign from the government: Luis Miquilena quit the Ministry of Justice and the Interior. As he did this, Miquilena swore that "this is not a good-bye but a 'see you later' . . . my commitment to and my belief in the project of change will not abate, not for one second."[18] But it was a good-bye. He stayed on temporarily as the chairman of Chávez's political party, but a couple of months later he cut his ties with the president altogether. By that point, he says, he had seen too much of his pupil's disturbing metamorphosis. Chávez's radical rhetoric was bothering him more and more. "That fake revolutionary language . . . I would say to him, 'But you haven't touched a single hair on the ass of anyone in the economic sector! You have created the most neoliberal economy Venezuela has ever known. And yet you go on deceiving the people by saying that you are starting the bla, bla,

bla revolution. Which means you deceive the crazy revolutionaries we have here, plus you scare the people, the businessmen who could help you build the country.' "

Miquilena also questioned Chávez's tendency to attack people who disagreed with him. He criticized Chávez, for example, for publicly denigrating a renowned caricaturist—saying that he was an illustrator for hire—"simply because the man drew a caricature that he didn't like." Chávez promised to tone it down, but he would inevitably go back and do the same things all over again. The straw that broke the camel's back was the package of laws drafted and enacted from Miraflores.

"The day I resigned, he came here at three in the morning and asked me to accept the vice presidency but I refused. Then he offered me the U.S. embassy. 'Are you crazy? I don't even speak English!' I said to him. 'And the last thing I'm good for is as an ambassador. No, kid, you know that I can't stand by you anymore because I just don't agree with you," recalls Miquilena. In his view, Chávez was a humble man who got carried away "by the temptations of power, for they are too seductive to resist for anyone who isn't sufficiently prepared. Very shortly after he took over the country, Hugo was another man."

CHAPTER 11

Around the World in an Airbus

"HE ASKED, HE ASKED, AND HE ASKED. HE ASKED FOR LA VIÑETA SO that he could settle in there, airplanes for flights, travel expenses. I don't know how much, but without a doubt Chávez's inauguration was the most expensive Venezuela has ever seen. And in the middle of all that, he was making noise about having to cut costs, having to sell planes . . . all the while spending more and more, astronomical amounts, on the inauguration, all of which reveals his inconsistency."

Former president Rafael Caldera does not exactly recall Hugo Chávez for his austerity. Unlike all his predecessors, who continued to live in their own homes during the lull between electoral victory and inauguration, the former conspirator abandoned the borrowed apartment he had been occupying in Alto Prado the morning after his triumph in the 1998 elections.

He had gotten his bags ready and demanded to move into La Viñeta, a residence for state visitors within the Fort Tiuna complex. There "he would have lunch with a hundred people and would organize dinners for two hundred," recalls José Guillermo Andueza, who served as interior minister under Caldera. "All of that was fun and games for him and his friends. The situation got so out of hand that they decided to send the chef from Miraflores over to La Viñeta, because it was cheaper that way. With Chávez, everything went off the charts. We would have to write up two expense reports just to cover his costs." Caldera recalls seeing Chávez for the first time when the *comandante* turned up one day at Miraflores following his election.

"Once we were alone, he leaned over and made some excuses for the way he had behaved during the campaign. I don't remember being impressed in any sense. I got the feeling that he was an astute politician, that he had managed well with the media, and that he projected a likable quality, because that's what he was always after in his relationships with people."

Soon after being elected president, Chávez said he would sell everything that he deemed to be excessive: "I have already signed a decree . . . to auction off the big lot of airplanes. There is no justification for so many. My God, 128 airplanes!" In no time, the fleet of the mammoth state-run oil company, Petróleos de Venezuela, was reduced from fourteen to six. Chávez ordered a portion of the proceeds from the sale to go to the Centralized Social Fund for the construction of schools, health clinics, and housing units. He also promised to trim a thousand soldiers from the Honor Guard regiment, leaving him with just four hundred men.

Chávez had always been known for being frugal and detached from material possessions, the kind of person who cared little for things like cars or saving money to acquire the kinds of things that most people dream of: a house, creature comforts, a certain level of well-being. Jesús Urdaneta recalls, "Chávez was a man who never, not in his entire life, worried about buying himself an apartment, not at all. He would take his salary and spend it all, when the rest of us, from a very young age, were always paying off [loans]. When we were lieutenant colonels, Chávez had the worst car, a Fairmont that was all but useless. He really seemed like someone totally detached, without any sense of belonging. I remember saying to him, 'You're going to do what all of us have to do [the insurrection], and you haven't even thought about leaving your family with a roof over their head?' He would be in my room when we took the General Staff course, and I would say to him, 'Come on, be responsible.' And then he bought a little house somewhere in Mariara, which he left to his wife, Nancy."

Urdaneta also recalls how Chávez reproached people who demon-strated an interest in material things. "When I bought a bigger, more comfortable apartment in Maracay that was 120 square meters, he came over and said, 'Boy, is this apartment luxurious.' I told him that I didn't know what luxurious meant for him, but that as far as I was concerned it was no sin to live comfortably if the money was earned honestly. I said to him, 'I don't know, maybe for you, being a good Venezuelan means living under a bridge,' and he said don't be like that, that he knew I had worked like hell. Chávez is a man who never made sacrifices, he was lucky—when we ended up in jail, his house had just been paid off by people who identified with him, sympathiz-ers. He always managed to get people to help him. In a speech he gave just after we made it to the government, he said, 'Anyone who has two apartments has to give up one,' and I said to him, 'Oh, sure, isn't that fine and good—and completely irresponsible of you to say things like that! If I have two apartments, it's because I worked to pay for them, why should I have to give up anything? It's easy for you to say—you've never had to pay for anything yourself.' He finally came around, but he wasn't very happy about it."

By the time his presidential campaign was under way, Chávez was comfortably ensconced in an apartment financed by his supporters in a middle-class neighborhood in southeast Caracas, but he did not know true abundance until he reached the presidency. From the very start, Chávez has spared no expense when it comes to promoting himself, using government funds to show the world that he is neither a military "gorilla" nor a recalcitrant Communist and most especially to destigmatize his "revolution," which he knows is viewed with trep-idation by many. His efforts to this end are tireless. Paradoxically, his rhetoric has always earned him a reputation as a radical, which he has then had to refute, especially outside Venezuela.

As president-elect, he broke travel records, making it to twelve countries in the space of six weeks. In the Americas, he traveled to Brazil, Argentina, Colombia, Mexico, the Dominican Republic, Canada, and Cuba. In Europe, he visited Spain, France, Germany, and Italy. In Paris, at a forum of French businessmen, he said, "My tour of Europe is an effort to show that I am not the Devil, or that combination of Mussolini and Hitler so many people have talked about. And I am not a tyrant." He saved the United States for last and visited with Bill Clinton for fifteen minutes, just enough time to give him a little gift, a book entitled *Bolívar Forever*. This was his first visit to Washington. He also met with U.S. Energy Secretary Bill Richardson, and with Michel Camdessus, then the president of the International Monetary Fund, which Chávez would later call a "revolting instrument of exploitation at the service of the world's powerful."[1] In all the capitals he visited, presidents and prime ministers received him with a degree of curiosity. During all of these encounters, he made a point of appearing a modern, moderate politician.

"We are facing a new century, and I am its legitimate representative," he immodestly declared in Washington. In what remained of 1999 he visited twenty-three more countries, outdoing even Carlos Andrés Pérez, who had previously been known for being Venezuela's most globetrotting president.

At the close of 1999, his debut year as president of Venezuela, Chávez had logged fifty-two days out of the country, traveling in an old Boeing 737 that had been in service for twenty-four years. It was hardly the most appropriate plane for transatlantic voyages: a single trip to Europe required four stopovers, a logistical nightmare that took some eighteen hours. The aircraft, moreover, was occasionally refused by certain airports because of the loud noise it made upon landing. The head of state prohibited the consumption of alcohol on the presidential plane, a rule that was not well received by some of his ministers. He did not like unusual food, either, and when he traveled he would bring his own cook along, as well as his doctor, Luis Chang Cheng, an internist of Asian descent who watchdogged his cholesterol. On occasion he would be joined by his daughters from his first marriage. The first lady, who had a fear of flying, traveled little with the president, joining him only when she managed to overcome her nerves or when her jealousy reached the breaking point. When she did make it onto the plane, it was always with a rosary in her hands. Hyperkinetic and sleeping little, Chávez would pass the time reviewing papers and meeting with his ministers, turning the presidential plane into his personal airborne office.

The former military officer from Barinas was literally charmed by the world that opened up before him. In some ways, he was like a VIP tourist, and he left behind the antineoliberal sermons to smile and pose for photos when he rang the bell at the New York Stock Exchange and tossed out the first pitch at a baseball game in Shea Stadium. At a businessmen's breakfast in Houston, he crossed paths with former president George Bush and his son, then governor of Texas. Both of them, of course, were unaware that in a few years' time, once George W. Bush was president of the United States, Chávez would call him enemy number one and claim that the American chief executive was attempting to destabilize and even overthrow his government. From then on, Chávez would refer to George W. Bush as "the man who owns the Venezuelan opposition."

Three months later, the Venezuelan president returned to New York to speak for the first time at the U.N. General Assembly. At the U.S. mission to the U.N., he had his second meeting with President Bill Clinton, this time for an hour. He also had the opportunity to shake hands with former secretary of state Henry Kissinger, who tried stroking Chávez's ego by praising his "energy and dedication." One wonders if the figure of Salvador Allende flashed through the mind of the anti-Pinochet ex-*comandante* right then. In Washington, he couldn't resist the temptation of playing baseball again, this time with the officers from the Inter-American Defense College. Then, in a move that would leave more than one of his left-wing comrades flabbergasted, Chávez declared that as a member of the armed forces, he had once dreamed of attending this U.S. military institution.

At the Vatican, he fell to his knees when he laid eyes on Pope John Paul II, placing his hands in front of his face, as if deep in prayer. Exuding serenity, he spoke quietly and gesticulated tactfully, exhibiting a discretion that was quite out of character. Away from his home turf, Chávez's actions began to reveal a particularly intriguing quality, one that had only just begun to emerge during his campaign. Like the protagonist of the eponymous Woody Allen film, Chávez was a kind of Zelig, or at least a tropical version of him—a mastermind of mimesis, adept at blending in with his environment and his interlocutors. He was spontaneous and irreverent at times, unyielding only when it came to military rituals. He would subvert civil protocol every chance he could, but he would always take care to toe the line to some degree.

At the end of 1999, he embarked on an extensive tour through ten countries in Asia, Europe, and the Middle East, traveling with a team of close to a hundred people. Around this time he began to be perceived as something of a ham, a folksy character. In China, he was received by Jiang Zemin in Tiananmen Square. When taken to see the legendary Great Wall, he broke into a run, leaving his ministers and the rest of his companions dumbfounded. "It reminded me of Rocky, the only thing missing was the music; he communicates that same vitality," said the famous Venezuelan chef Helena Ibarra, who had been hired to supervise the cocktails for the Chávez delegation during the trip.

His spontaneity and sense of humor—at times ill advised and unsophisticated, at times downright vulgar—have a way of wounding people's sensibilities and making them uncomfortable. On his first visit to Moscow in May 2001, he tried out a little joke with Vladimir Putin before the two men had formally met. As the Russian premier walked toward him, Chávez jumped into a karate pose before shaking his hand. For a few long moments Putin seemed stunned, until it finally dawned on him that Chávez was making a joke, at which point he smiled courteously. Chávez then changed positions, assuming the stance of a baseball player stepping up to bat, and said with a broad smile, "I've heard that you're a black belt in karate. I'm a baseball man myself." On another occasion, just after meeting Rosario Green, the former foreign secretary of Mexico, Chávez suddenly began crooning the Venezuelan song "Rosario," leaving Green bewildered. Some time later, at a Caribbean summit, Green was sitting with a group of colleagues when Chávez suddenly walked up behind her and placed his hands around her eyes as if to say, "Guess who?" His efforts to be likable often have the opposite effect: Green probably interpreted his actions as macho and presumptuous.

Chávez often seems uncomfortable with formalities and protocol, as if he wants to dispose of them as quickly as possible. What he wants is to be loved, says Chirinos, his one-time psychiatrist. "[He is] a man for whom all protocol is simply anathema. To a large degree, [this is] because he was raised and educated in the countryside, humble, simple, where there is no protocol. In a town like Sabaneta, I don't know if people respect the priest or the civil authority, but in general it is a '*tú a tú*' with everyone," says Chirinos, referring to Chávez's affinity for speaking with people in the familiar. This is a curious characteristic given that he spent more than twenty years, from 1971 to 1992, in an institution as formal, hierarchical, and strict as the army.

In Japan, the Venezuelan president shocked the guards of the Imperial Palace when he broke protocol by giving Emperor Akihito a tight good-bye hug before leaving. It must have amused the emperor, however, judging by the smile that came over his face. Chávez then bid farewell to the guards by thanking them and shaking their hands one by one, a gesture he frequently repeats wherever he goes.

"He plays that affection game to disarm people. Whether or not it works, it's definitely not the kind of thing you forget. It's a side of him that is disrespectful but naïve. He plays with that, and I think he does it on purpose. It's a ploy for seducing people. And it delivers results," Ibarra notes. In Tokyo, Chávez was yet again unable to resist the temptation to test his pitching arm at Meiji Jingu Stadium. In between sessions of back-to-back meetings, as a kind of parenthesis, he would order his aides to put together moments of diversion. There, he revealed himself to be a man with an astonishing attention to detail, noticing everything that went on around him. One day he surprised Helena Ibarra in the lobby of the luxurious hotel where the delegation was staying. Standing around with a lost look in her eyes as a group of Venezuelan musicians (also part of the delegation) played a tune, she suddenly felt a hand come to rest on her shoulder and a thick voice whisper in her ear, " 'What's the matter? Why are you so down?' Evidently, I was thinking about things," Ibarra recalls. "That's the way he is with people, and that's what gets them hooked, he grabs them in the emotional sense. On the airplane he would stop at every aisle, remembering each and every person's name, telling them anecdotes. That was what it was like the entire trip."

Once, she recalls, the president's bodyguards spent all night asking her to bring some *hallacas,* a kind of tamale that Venezuelans typically eat at Christmastime, up to the president's suite. By the time Chávez's meetings ended at around three in the morning, he wanted to eat some of Helena's *hallacas,* but there were none left; his guards had wolfed them all down. In response, the president gave them a military-style punishment, making them do leapfrogs on command.

Though she was not in charge of preparing the commander in chief's food, Ibarra quickly sniffed out the presidential culinary genome. "He just can't get enough of things that connect him to his culture, his customs, his history. For him the *hallaca* and the *chigüire* are the absolute best. There are certainly people with bolder culinary tastes, people who like to discover new flavors. Not him, he's very stuck on the things he has always liked. In that sense he's pretty square." According to Ibarra, Chávez "seems to eat a lot out of anxiety," which is easy to see—that is, if the change in his body and all his excess weight are any indication. While in office, he has gained no less than thirty pounds, a far cry from the reedy Tribilín of his childhood.

AFTER A NUMBER OF MISHAPS with the old Boeing 737, the president decided it was necessary to purchase a new aircraft. As the air force began to weigh the options, Chávez placed only one condition on the purchase of the new plane when he discussed it with the experts advising him in the matter: it must not come from the United States. With this in mind, they recommended an aircraft manufactured in France, with VIP furniture and fittings, including an executive office, bedroom suite, and a luxury bathroom. When it came to light that the president with the Robin Hood airs had finally settled on this plane, an Airbus 319 that would cost a total of $65 million, the public went ballistic, for it was quite a contrast to his constant wheedling about the need for austerity. The transaction was protracted, but this did not slow Chávez down in the least. During his first three years as head of state, Chávez spent 170 days outside the country—in other words, more than five months. Visiting seventy-one countries on four continents, he circumnavigated the earth.

Finally, when the new plane arrived in Venezuela in March 2002, the Airbus spent an entire week in the hangar because it was deemed unwise to exhibit it in a country where antigovernment protests had reached a boiling point. On April 6, when the gleaming new aircraft, named FAV 0001, performed a test run at La Carlota air base, a massive human chain—complete with *cacerolas*—surrounded the airport to protest what they felt was extravagance that was inconsistent with the president's preaching. A week later, a fleeting coup attempt against President Chávez threatened his chances of ever sitting down in seat number 1, behind which hung a painting that he had personally ordered, of his hero Ezequiel Zamora. As fate would have it, he would make it back to Miraflores and debut his new plane. Months later, a video of its luxurious interior (which also boasted portraits of Bolívar and Simón Rodríguez) were broadcast on television. It was an extraordinary sight to behold, with beige leather seats and gold fixtures. According to an air force pilot familiar with the matter, the new plane had in fact been necessary, and he even added that of all the Airbus models in existence, Chávez had selected the smallest one, with forty-two seats. This, however, did not stop the newspaper *El Universal* from baptizing it *el chupadólares*, "the dollar drain."

The old aircraft, Chávez decided, "is going to become the first plane to be used in a new tourism program for the masses, so that the poor may see Canaima [national park] and visit the islands of the Caribbean." Until the middle of 2004,[2] this was not the case. The next time anyone heard anything about the old Boeing 737, it was during the protests that erupted when people learned that it had been used to take Chávez's ex-wife, Marisabel, and her two children to Disney World. Later on, the former presidential pilot Juan Díaz Castillo caused a scandal when he resigned from his position and stated that the presidential plane was being used to give members of the pro-Chávez Bolivarian Circles a lift here and there on occasion. It is worth noting that during his first days as president, Chávez questioned whether the planes belonging to the national oil company, Petróleos de Venezuela, were being used to take certain government employees on little excursions. Díaz also stated that security regulations had been violated because people with firearms had been allowed to travel on the plane, and he also added that a colleague of his had once been assigned the "mission" of delivering, via Cougar helicopter, a box containing cereal and milk to the first lady, who was at the beach.

The new head of state had started his term by reducing the number of government ministries from seventeen to fourteen, but by 2004 that number had risen to twenty-three. He also cut back on the security detail for former government officials and changed the names of autonomous institutions and organizations to distinguish his administration from previous ones. And he vowed to save money. The word "poverty" clung to his lips. Upon his arrival at the presidential residence, a colonial mansion tucked away in a leafy Caracas neighborhood, he expressed outrage at the luxurious accommodations. "I declare myself a socially anguished man, and that anguish only grows when I arrive at La Casona, when I contemplate that luxury and those gigantic salons and those gardens. When I am there I cannot sleep thinking of all the children who don't have enough to eat," he announced shortly after moving in.[3] La Casona, an old coffee hacienda built in the eighteenth century, boasts four square miles

of constructed space and twenty square miles of gardens. Bought in
1964 as the presidential residence, it has thirteen rooms for the family's living quarters, two guest rooms, ten for the service and guard
staff, plus ten sitting rooms, two dining rooms, seven interior patios,
a pool, a gymnasium, a bowling alley, and an open-air movie theater.

"I don't need such a big house. I could live in an apartment with
my wife and children, and I would only need one bodyguard just in
case someone decided to throw a rock at me,"[4] he said during one of
his first press conferences as president, but he didn't move out.

"I don't want to live like a king as long as there are children who
clothe themselves with newspapers. I don't want imperial parapherna-
lia,"[5] Chávez said, and although he questioned the fact that the mansion had a swimming pool and "even a movie theater!" he would
nonetheless give the okay four years later to a remodeling job so that
his family could enjoy the pool. Chávez would put up with the luxuries of La Casona for his first three years in office. Later on, the ghost
of assassinations and conspiracies, to say nothing of his neighbors
banging away on their kitchen pots, would send him running to safety
at the Fort Tiuna military base, where he decided that the house normally occupied by the defense minister needed refurbishing.

Thanks to all of Chávez's revolutionary-minded preaching, presidential travel and expenses have become the subject of unprecedented scrutiny. The opposition congressman Carlos Berrizbeitia,
vice president of the parliamentary Commission of Administration
and Services, keeps a detailed account of the president's every trip. By
mid-2004, the Venezuelan chief executive had taken 98 trips, visiting
135 countries—not counting lightning trips of less than three days,
which do not require approval from the legislature—and had been
out of the country for a total of 248 days. It was quite a record: eight
months and three days. The countries he visited the most were Brazil,
Colombia, and Cuba. Ever since controls were placed on the foreign
exchange rate in early 2003, the Foreign Currency Administration
Commission, which had overseen the restriction, approved $7,499,800

in presidential travel expenses for 2004. This was not the only item on the presidential balance sheet that shot up drastically.

Hugo Chávez, who has always ascribed a symbolic value to clothing, abandoned his *liqui-liqui* as soon as he crossed the threshold of Miraflores. And soon thereafter he would abandon the suits fitted for him by Clement, turning instead to Giovanni Scutaro, the Italian tailor preferred by the very wealthiest men of Caracas. The military uniform, however, would always be his preferred outfit—in fact, he liked it so much that he began to use it for official events, despite being retired from the military and despite his advisers' admonishments to put it away. Within the armed forces, people took umbrage whenever he donned the full dress uniform of the army general, since he had never actually graduated to that rank. Technically speaking, the failed coup of 1992 had put an end to his military career. Nevertheless, one day, he came up with the idea of restaging a scene that brought Venezuelans of a certain age back to the days of the Pérez Jiménez dictatorship of the 1950s. Chávez arrived at a military parade on Caracas's Paseo de Los Próceres riding in a convertible and wearing the dress uniform of a general, with a tricolor sash across his chest, and a jacket heaving with military decorations. The first lady was at his side, dressed in pink and wearing a hat that recalled the confections favored by the former dictator's wife. The mise-en-scène provoked resentment among many in the barracks and outrage among Chávez's adversaries. Months later, during the act of contrition he performed at his first public appearance following the failed coup against him in April 2002, his first promise was to hang up his uniform for good.

During his early days in Miraflores, Chávez demonstrated a predilection for shirts with wide stripes and white collars and cuffs. For more informal occasions, he favored a safari-style hybrid shirt-jacket with shoulder pads, which made him look even more corpulent than he was. Local gossipmongers swore that the outfits were gifts from Fidel and made of bulletproof material.

Chávez has often remarked that his favorite color is blue, but during this period he was most frequently seen in green, and for proselytizing purposes, he began to favor red, for its associations with both his party and his Bolivarian Revolution. On one occasion, he spoke of the distress he had felt one day upon opening his closet to find more than one hundred suits. Someone had bought them, he said, without his knowledge. "Someone, I don't know when, gives me these suits, and I don't have any other choice but to put them on."[6]

His time spent in the corridors of power has only refined his tastes. In mid-1998, as he pounded the campaign trail in plaid long-sleeved shirts and heavy sweaters, the cream of Caracas's designers agreed that he was the worst-dressed candidate, but today he is possibly the best-dressed president in the history of Venezuela. And perhaps all of Latin America. Nowadays Chávez wears only the finest suits, according to the society columnist and local fashion arbiter Roland Carreño: "Brioni, the Italian house, sends President Chávez his suits directly from New York." In mid-2004, the ex-*comandante* appeared on TV looking sharper than ever in an impeccable dark suit as he announced the campaign to defend his presidency in anticipation of the recall referendum slated for August 15, 2004. The suit, by Lanvin, had cost somewhere in the vicinity of $3,000, according to Carreño, who says that "President Chávez possesses one of the most magnificent wardrobes on the continent," with ties by Hermès and Pancaldi. He has also developed a penchant for watches by Cartier, Boucheron, and Rolex. In 2003, the attorney general's office, headed by Chávez's former vice president Isaías Rodríguez, who is a member of Chávez's party, received a formal complaint regarding the presidential expenses, which had ballooned by 1,000 percent. Predictably, the investigation went nowhere.

Berrizbeitia, who was a member of the Venezuelan Congress from 2000 to 2005, began to keep track of Chávez's expenses in early 2002, when he heard the president, in a televised address, ask the people of Venezuela to make sacrifices for the revolution even if they were "naked and hungry." According to the information he has gathered, based on the official budget report, Chávez as president has cost the nation between $6,000 and $7,000 a day. By 2004, the presidential expenses had increased by 54.3 percent over the previous year, placing the Miraflores budget at $60,894,764.[7] According to his old mentor Luis Miquilena, "there is an abyss between the humble gentleman Chávez once was, the man who wanted to sell La Casona when he arrived because it was just too much for him, who wanted to do away with Miraflores Palace and establish a university in its place, and the dandy who dresses up in Gucci and wears Cartier watches. The Chávez of today is a Chávez completely beholden to the concupiscent pleasure of power."

SOME BELIEVE, THOUGH without much evidence to support their claims, that Chávez's newfound taste for luxury is the result of the relationships he has cultivated with the sumptuous world of the Arab elite. Ever since taking office, Chávez has led the crusade to defend the price of Venezuelan oil, which in 1998 closed on a downward spiral at $10.80 per barrel.

"Look at the inheritance you have left me: oil is at less than $10 a barrel," he complained when he became president. He became fixated on the idea of orchestrating a meeting of OPEC member states in Venezuela, undaunted by the fact that ever since the establishment of the cartel in 1960, the member countries had convened only once before, in Algeria in 1975. The second OPEC summit was held in Caracas in September 2000, thanks to the initiative of the Venezuelan president, who traveled to the Middle East to extend his personal invitation to the kings, emirs, and heads of state in question. Chávez and Libyan leader Muammar Gaddafi took an instant liking to each other: Chávez had long admired him and was extremely familiar with Gaddafi's *Green Book,* from his days plotting the 1992 coup. And defying the U.S.-imposed isolation of Iraq, he was the only head of state to visit Baghdad after the Persian Gulf War. When a U.S. government official asked him to cancel the trip he responded with outrage: "Can you imagine that? How unbelievably disrespectful! . . . I'll go to hell if I feel like it," he said. A photograph of Saddam Hussein driving a Mercedes-Benz with Hugo Chávez in the passenger seat traveled the globe shortly thereafter.

In the space of two years, the Venezuelan president got what he wanted, and by late September 2000, Caracas was another city altogether. The government made a Herculean effort to fill potholes, collect garbage, repair tunnels, and hide the hundreds of roving merchants who normally battle it out on the streets of the city center, in a massive effort to show his guests a clean, tidy Caracas that the city's residents had surely never seen before. At the closing ceremonies of the summit, attended by eleven foreign dignitaries and delegates,[8] the Venezuelan president reiterated that with the Caracas Declaration "we have relaunched a united OPEC!" It wasn't just rhetoric, either: from that point on, the cartel would act as a bloc, respecting fixed export quotas, making reductions, and encouraging the price of oil to rise. Hugo Chávez was so jubilant that at the end of the event, held in the Ríos Reyna Auditorium in the Teresa Carreño Cultural Center, he burst into song, crooning the tune "Venezuela." Since then, the price of Venezuelan crude oil has more than doubled: by September 2006 the price was over $50 a barrel.

Later on, the oil issue landed Chávez in his diciest predicament since the attempted coup of April 2002, though the outcome allowed him to stop feeling miserable, as he acknowledged. In December 2002, Chávez's opposition organized a national strike, accompanied by protest marches that paralyzed the oil industry, which represents approximately 80 percent of Venezuela's export business.[9] As a result, the country was without oil for several days. According to political insiders, the strike was to last for only a few days, but a sector of the opposition, independent of party affiliation, imposed an agenda it had been hatching for a long time: an indefinite strike that would paint the government into a corner and force Chávez either to resign or to agree to a referendum that would decide his fate as president. The country's economy fell to pieces, but Chávez refused to be bullied. After swiftly militarizing the oil facilities, he turned to his Middle Eastern allies for help in meeting his export obligations, hired retired oil industry employees and foreign technicians and engineers, and headed off his dwindling supply problem by importing food and fuel, principally from Brazil.

The strike, which left the country paralyzed for sixty-three days and which the government called "sabotage," ended on February 2, 2003, the fourth anniversary of Chávez's rise to power. The strike cost the country 10 percent of its gross national product, approximately $9 billion, and crippled the industry for months. By the end, the strikers were exhausted and the populace was fed up. The Venezuelan president emerged triumphant and ordered the dismissal of some 19,500 oil workers, about half of the country's oil industry workforce.[10]

The following year, in his annual address to the nation on January 15, 2004, President Chávez stated, in front of the National Assembly, that "2003 brought with it the task of reclaiming Petróleos de Venezuela and its operations, and the management of its finances. And as I stand here today I can tell you that yes, I am able to take charge of PDVSA [Petróleos de Venezuela], whereas before I was not. And do you know how I felt? Like a miserable wretch. Bolivarian that I am, I cannot help but recall Bolívar's words: 'To call yourself a leader and not act like one is the height of wretchedness,' the very height of wretchedness. That company now belongs to the Venezuelan people, and it always will." Then he offered the following revelation: "Often, crises are necessary. Sometimes, they even have to be generated— within reason, of course. The PDVSA crisis was necessary even when we, well—it's not that we didn't generate it, we did generate it, but when I blew the whistle on *Aló, Presidente* that day [on April 7, 2002] and started to fire people, I was provoking the crisis; when I named Gastón Parra Luzardo and that new board of directors, well, yes, we were provoking the crisis. They [the oil workers] responded, and the conflict came about."

Chávez admitted that the problems within the oil industry had started months before, in April 2002, when the workers went on strike to protest the changes at Petróleos de Venezuela. That conflict, sparked by the president's words, exploded just a few days before a coup d'etat removed him from power.

CHAPTER 12

Entangled April

H UGO CHÁVEZ THOUGHT ABOUT IT FOR A MOMENT. PERHAPS HE FELT that everything had just happened too fast in the past few hours. Perhaps he couldn't quite figure out how that thing people call "reality" could just come to a halt, right there in the barrel of a gun. Was that the solution? What is the defining moment that leads a person to decide that the only way out is by firing a bullet? Seated next to him was his vice president, José Vicente Rangel, who urged him to fight, to resist, whatever the consequences. Suddenly someone informed them that there was a call for the president. It was Fidel Castro. The president picked up the receiver, said a few words, and listened. It was midnight. Fidel said, "Save your people and save yourself, do what you have to do, negotiate with dignity, but don't go and sacrifice yourself, Chávez, because this isn't going to end, do not go and sacrifice yourself."[1] Chávez hung up and asked to be left alone. He sat down, and he thought hard about things. And then, for the second time in his life, he decided to surrender.

There were many April elevenths in Venezuela, for there are many, many different stories about what happened on this fateful day. Unfortunately for Venezuela, it was a day that left many dead and wounded. Between the eleventh and fourteenth of April 2000, in less than forty-eight hours, Hugo Chávez was expelled from and then returned to the presidency; an authoritarian project materialized and then evaporated; a coup d'état met with failure; and the armed forces impeached and reinstated a president. In less than forty-eight hours, 20 people died and more than 110 were wounded. After all the investigations, all the books, all the movies, there are still many unresolved mysteries from that day, murky areas in which the explanations for what happened were no match for the onslaught of accusations that the government and the opposition hurled at each other. To this day, it is a story filled with shadows and dense, bitter silence.

Chávez believes three main factors triggered the events of April 11. The first dates back to September 11, 2001. "That brought about a new attitude on the part of the U.S. government, which started to encourage the Venezuelan opposition."[2] The Venezuelan president maintains that the U.S. Embassy facilitated meetings between opposition leaders and groups. The government obtained this information through "a Venezuelan they mistakenly invited [to one of the meetings], because they sometimes make mistakes, too, and this Venezuelan—who is not a *chavista*—left very alarmed and told a mutual friend what he had heard the people in the opposition say back there, that Chávez had to be either overthrown or killed. And they said these things while talking to Pentagon officials."[3]

The second factor, says Chávez, also dates to 2001 and the approval of a package of law decrees in November. According to the president, these forty-nine laws complied with the constitutional project and set guidelines for certain aspects of the country's infrastructure including taxes, land, hydrocarbons, finances, but they were also perceived as an attack against some powerful elements of Venezuelan society.

The third detonating factor, a consequence of the first two, came into play when a group of military officers within the national armed forces banded together and allied themselves with certain sectors of the opposition, with the intention (according to Chávez) of staging a violent overthrow of the Bolivarian government.

The official analysis, however, neglected to mention additional factors that the opposition identified, such as the overwhelming social tension in Venezuela at the time and the increasingly heated and volatile relations among the country's politicians. After the oil-industry strike, for example, Chávez publicly fired seven top executives of the state oil company, PDVSA, because of the controversy they generated over the government's decision to appoint a new corporate board—a move that had been intended to provoke a crisis that would give the executive branch more control over PDVSA, as Chávez himself admitted two years later.

At the same time, the government was waging another battle with the radio stations whose programming Chávez had recently been interrupting with his long "chains." Eventually they reached a breaking point with the president and his communications policies. In the end, a constellation of elements came together that day in a highly charged atmosphere, and many Venezuelans did little to hide their disgruntlement. Without a doubt, there had been a massive amount of social mobilization, but there are many indications suggesting that a conspiracy was also at play.

General Raúl Baduel, commander of the Fourth Paratroopers' Brigade at the time, acknowledges that he was not exactly shocked by all that came to pass. "It wasn't a complete surprise, because a number of incidents had already served as indications of what was to come: the whole national strike situation, the protests both here at the level of the capital, as well as in other regions. . . . And I have a calendar where I made a note on April 5, right there I wrote, 'The coup is imminent.' I marked it and I tried to talk to the president, but I couldn't."[4]

It is slightly surprising that Chávez and his closest aides underestimated the internal crisis in the armed forces. There is a good deal of evidence to suggest that, for a long time, some sectors of society had been determined to force Chávez out of office. Those intentions were never a secret, not even in the middle of the crisis. On the night of April 11, when the president's fate was still a mystery, Colonel Julio Rodríguez Salas, the spokesman for the insurgent military officers, made the following announcement on TV: "Nine months ago, a solid, serious movement began to come together, a movement that fortunately has materialized on this day."[5] There is also evidence suggesting that the coup was far from an isolated plot hatched by a coterie of military officers, and that members of the business community, the

HUGO CHÁVEZ FRÍAS AS A CHILD, IN BARINAS.

Courtesy Herma Marksman

CHÁVEZ'S GREAT-GRANDFATHER MAISANTA (RIGHT).

Courtesy Herma Marksman

AS A TWENTY-YEAR-OLD CADET IN
LIMA, TOASTING WITH HIS FELLOW
CADETS FROM COLOMBIA, ECUADOR,
BOLIVIA, AND PERÚ. CHÁVEZ IS
SEATED THIRD FROM THE RIGHT.

Courtesy Herma Marksman

HUGO CHÁVEZ, SHORTLY
AFTER ENTERING THE
MILITARY ACADEMY.

Courtesy *El Nacional* archives

AS EMCEE OF A
BEAUTY PAGEANT
AT THE MILITARY
ACADEMY, 1975.

Courtesy Herma
Marksman

Alférez Hugo Rafael Chávez Frías

El día 28 de julio de 1954 vino al mundo este dinámico muchacho en la muy noble y leal ciudad de Barinas.

A nuestros tímpanos suenan todavía las pintorescas, ilustrativas y no menos jocosas letras de sus joropos, corridos y pasajes, con los que se empeñó en dar a sentir y conocer lo que es su terruño llanero, cosa que lograba

a toda costa. Su número favorito y que en todo momento llevara en sus labios era aquel que empezaba: "Furia se llamó el caballo..."; llegando a identificarse tanto con su melodía que nosotros decidimos llamarle "Furia".

El ejemplo fue la base de toda su actuación y exigencias.

Por baluarte siempre tuvo la camaradería, que impartió entre todos nosotros.

Aplicado estudiante de Ciencias, donde se mantenía en duro combate contra Morfeo.

Dentro del base-ball fue de los mejores, el zurdo "Furia" llegó a ser el mejor pitcher del equipo y excelente primera base. Dentro de su afición deportiva también cabe mencionar sus grandes dotes de submarinista y buceador del fondo de las piscinas, deporte que practicaba durante la Semana Santa en el Instituto bajo el fulgurante sol.

Pertenece al servicio de Transmisiones.

THE PAGE
DEDICATED TO HUGO
CHÁVEZ, JUST SHY
OF HIS TWENTY-FIRST
BIRTHDAY, IN THE
SIMÓN BOLÍVAR
YEARBOOK, 1975.

CHÁVEZ (CENTER) CARRIES THE FLAG DURING AN EVENT IN BARINAS IN 1976.

Courtesy Herma Marksman

CHÁVEZ IN MILITARY FATIGUES, 1982. Courtesy Henry Delgado

DURING A MILITARY DRILL
IN 1983.

Courtesy Herma Marksman

CHÁVEZ AND HIS LOVER
HERMA MARKSMAN (LEFT)
IN THE LATE 1980S, WITH
HERMA'S DAUGHTER MERCEDES
(BOTTOM) AND SISTER
CRISTINA (MIDDLE).

Courtesy Herma Marksman

CHÁVEZ'S
MOTHER, ELENA
FRÍAS DE CHÁVEZ,
IN 1992.

Courtesy La Prensa,
Barinas

CHÁVEZ URGES HIS FELLOW CONSPIRATORS TO SURRENDER ON
FEBRUARY 4, 1992. THIS WAS CHÁVEZ'S FIRST TELEVISION APPEARANCE.

Courtesy Jesús Castillo

CHÁVEZ'S FIRST WIFE, NANCY COLMENARES, AND THEIR THREE CHILDREN,
NEAR THE PRISON, FOLLOWING THE FEBRUARY 4 COUP.

Courtesy Jesús Castillo

DURING THE FIRST
INTERVIEW
CHÁVEZ GRANTED
WHILE IN PRISON.

Courtesy Laura Sánchez

CHÁVEZ IN HIS CELL AT
YARE PRISON FOLLOWING
THE COUP ATTEMPT.

Courtesy Herma Marksman

HUGO CHÁVEZ
SHORTLY AFTER HIS
RELEASE FROM
PRISON, WEARING
A *LIQUI-LIQUI,*
A TRADITIONAL SUIT
WORN BY MEN IN
THE REGION OF
LOS LLANOS.

Courtesy Jesús Castillo

ON A VISIT TO
COLOMBIA IN 1994,
WITH HIS FRIEND
JESÚS URDANETA
(MIDDLE) AND HIS
BENEFACTOR NEDO
PANIZ (RIGHT).

Courtesy Herma Marksman

CHÁVEZ ON THE CAMPAIGN TRAIL DURING HIS 1998 BID FOR THE PRESIDENCY.

Courtesy Alex Delgado

TAKING THE OATH OF OFFICE ON FEBRUARY 2, 1999, IN THE PRESENCE OF THE PRESIDENT OF THE CONGRESS, LUIS ALFONZO DÁVILA, WHO SWEARS HIM IN, AND OUTGOING PRESIDENT RAFAEL CALDERA (MIDDLE). Courtesy Ernesto Morgado

CHÁVEZ IN 2000, HOSTING ONE OF HIS FIRST RADIO SHOWS.

Courtesy Alex Delgado

WITH HIS SECOND WIFE, MARISABEL RODRÍGUEZ, DURING AN OFFICIAL PARADE, 2001.

Courtesy Manuel Sardá

WITH MARISABEL AND
THEIR DAUGHTER ROSINÉS.

Courtesy Henry Delgado

CHÁVEZ'S ELDEST
BROTHER, ADÁN.

Courtesy William Zurek

CHÁVEZ'S YOUNGEST
BROTHER, ADELIS.

Courtesy *El Nacional* archives

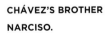

CHÁVEZ'S BROTHER
NARCISO.

Courtesy *El Nacional* archives

**CHÁVEZ'S BROTHER
ARGENIS.**

Courtesy *El Nacional* archives

**CHÁVEZ'S BROTHER
ANÍBAL.**

Courtesy *El Nacional* archives

HUGO DE LOS REYES
CHÁVEZ AND ELENA
FRÍAS DE CHÁVEZ.

Courtesy Iván Aponte

A RECENT PHOTO OF
ELENA FRÍAS IN
BARINAS, WITH HER
PUPPY COQUI.

Courtesy *La Prensa*, Barinas

CHÁVEZ IN FULL-DRESS UNIFORM FOR THE MILITARY
PARADE ON PASEO LOS PRÓCERES, JULY 5, 2000.

Courtesy Jesús Castillo

HUGO CHÁVEZ FRÍAS, PRESIDENT OF THE
BOLIVARIAN REPUBLIC OF VENEZUELA,
IN HIS MILITARY UNIFORM, 2000.

Courtesy Jesús Castillo

media, and certain political parties were also involved. According to this version of the story, the real political operator who served as the nexus among the different groups, was the cardinal of Caracas, Monsignor Ignacio Velasco.

A few weeks before the coup, certain representatives of the political and business elite of Caracas met in that city. After offering a blessing to all those present, Monsignor Velasco spoke about the very urgent need to remove the president from office and said he was sorry that the "greens" had not made it to the gathering. This was the prelude to another meeting, held on April 9 at a home in a luxurious neighborhood in southeast Caracas. Apparently, representatives from the military and civilian sectors worked on their conspiracy plan that day. Monsignor Velasco, yet again, served as the link between the civilians and the military personnel and asked them for a vote of confidence that would empower him to designate the person to lead a possible transition government, if it became necessary. It seems probable that, beyond the social predicament and the general friction in Venezuela at the time, a group of opponents of the Chávez government was indeed plotting a coup.

Teodoro Petkoff suggests the following hypothesis: "Both initiatives moved forward in a kind of parallel, and at a certain point, the conspirators galloped over the popular movement. I don't believe that the popular mobilizations of the previous months were a response to the conspirators' strategies, but the conspirators—in the last few weeks—most definitely took advantage of them."[6]

ON APRIL 11, 2002, a massive protest was staged by the opposition leaders in Caracas. While the most ambitious estimates claim that one million people participated in the march, even the less enthusiastic assessments said there had been at least 500,000 attendees. Whatever the real number, in the middle of the fervor generated by the crowds of people, their temperatures rising as they demanded the resignation of the president, some of the organizers of the protest relented and decided to let the march continue beyond its original desti-nation and on toward Miraflores Palace, despite the fact that they had not been authorized to do so. The protesters needed little encourage-ment. The collective mood only grew more heated and the crowds were all too anxious to get to the palace and clamor for Chávez's res-ignation. At the same time, the pro-Chávez mayor Freddy Bernal summoned the president's sympathizers to the palace to defend the government. It was just barely noon.

As for the president, he was inside his office at Miraflores, analyz-ing the situation, receiving information, making decisions. At around one in the afternoon, things began to happen, and fast. National Guard officers blocked the arrival of the protesters outside the gates to Miraflores, and the situation rapidly degenerated into chaos. Bullets seemed to fly in every direction, without warning, without any particular target—just the nearest body. And as blood began to spill onto the multitudes, all of a sudden anything seemed possible.

One hour later, Lucas Rincón Romero, inspector general of the armed forces, accompanied by a group of officers from the High Military Command, appeared on the state-run television station to deny rumors that they had resigned and that the president had been arrested. Rincón Romero explained that there were a few pockets of unrest in the center of Caracas but that Chávez was in his office work-ing. "The situation in the country is one of normality," he stated.

The situation around Miraflores, however, was anything but nor-mal. To date, it has been impossible to come up with a credible recon-struction of the events of those few hours. The opposition accused the government of unleashing its armed troops, officers, and subordi-nates on the protesters. The government, on the other hand, accused the opposition of hatching a cynical plot with mercenaries and mem-bers of the Metropolitan Police (which reported to the anti-Chávez mayor Alfredo Peña) to open fire on the protesters and foment mas-sive chaos, in order to spark an institutional crisis and pave the way for a coup d'état. Photographs from that day support both theses, and in-vestigations and testimonies have allowed both sides to defend the argument they find most convenient. There have even been documentary films promoting respective versions of the events of April 11. Sadly, there were also many dead and wounded on both sides of the story, people who are no longer pro- or anti-Chávez.

At 3:45 P.M., Chávez decided to "chain" all the television stations in the country to deliver a message to the Venezuelan people. For the first time, he actually seemed nervous, uncomfortable, and tense, and his usual aplomb had all but vanished. He repudiated the intentions of the protest march and, paradoxically, also claimed that the country was doing fine, that everything was normal. It was then that the privately owned television stations decided to take a stand against the official story by dividing their screens in two, placing the president on one side and the painful, bloody images of the confrontations in the city center on the other. This was a very overt challenge to the president's authority, and in response the government cut the private stations' signals while the chief executive said his piece. After Chávez delivered his message, the signals went back up and they continued broadcasting images of downtown Caracas. The city was in complete upheaval choked by the acrid smell of tear gas.

After that point, little is known about what was happening with Chávez, who did not reappear on television until early dawn the following day. At approximately 5:30 P.M., he activated Plan Ávila, a highly repressive security operation carried out by military personnel. A few months earlier it would have been all but impossible to imagine Chávez resorting to a measure like this, given his oft-repeated refusal to use the army as an instrument of civil repression. In addition, within the armed forces a complex crisis had suddenly come to a head. The book El acertijo de abril (The April Puzzle), which offers a meticulous analysis of what happened in the armed forces between the eleventh and fourteenth of April, describes one detail that seems to be a telling sign of the nature of things that day: when the president finished his television message, he went back to his office and "changed his clothes. He put on a field uniform."[7] This one image speaks volumes about the direction in which things were headed and reveals that the country's problems could be resolved only by calling in the military.

Starting in the early afternoon of April 11, certain high military officers began to carry out acts of insurgency. As the night wore on, more and more people made statements against the president declaring he no longer had authority as president. This is the point at which discrepancies begin to appear regarding the day's events. Some people maintain that it was an orchestrated, highly organized plan to overthrow the government. Some of the generals implicated, however, claim that they had simply been reacting against the order to execute Plan Avila when they refused to lead their soldiers onto the streets to control the disturbances. Chávez, meanwhile, remained inside the palace trying to assess the situation and figure out which forces were on his side. A number of his closest aides were with him by this time. The president had announced his plan to hold a meeting after his television broadcast with the governors loyal to his cause, but the meeting never happened. His mother and his father, the governor of Barinas, were with him in the palace that afternoon. Elena recalls, "It was worse, worse than the fourth [the coup attempt of February 4, 1992]. I was sobbing, begging God to just give me a heart attack."

The entire country seemed on the verge of a heart attack. Army commander Efraín Vásquez publicly declared that "Until today, I was loyal to you, President." After that, a considerable number of generals and other high-ranking officials stated that they held Chávez responsible for the violence that had erupted. The first lady and her children were taken to the city of Barquisimeto, in central Venezuela. The signal from the state-run television station was suddenly cut off, and the government's screen went blank. Luis Miquilena sharply criticized the day's events, marking his definitive split from what he called a "bloodstained" government. Everything, right then, seemed fraught with tension, uncertainty, and tightly controlled fear. Venezuela was a flurry of whispers, speculation, muffled negotiations. The entire country remained glued to the television and the radio, waiting for something, anything. Maripili Hernández, one of Chávez's close aides, confirms that by this time "a ton of people were saying that the only answer was to fight to the end and defend Miraflores Palace. Chávez said no. He was going to surrender, he said."

At around three in the morning, Elena spoke to her son. "He said to me, 'It looks like we're leaving, Mamá.' And I said, 'All right, we're leaving, my darling. But don't you worry because your house is waiting for you. The little house in Barinas, we'll live there. And if all we find is a banana or some noodles, then that's what we'll eat, but we will always be the same family.' And my son hugged me and then said to me after a moment, 'Oh, Mamá, I really have made you suffer.' Without shedding a tear, I said to him, 'Don't you say that. The suffering is nothing compared to the great pride I feel as your mother.' After that I blessed him, kissed him, turned around, and left." It wasn't the last time she would see her son that early dawn. A bit later on, outside on the palace grounds, she watched as her son left for Fort Tiuna with a group of military officers.

"Well, I went running [after him], but he was already inside the car. I clung to the car door and wouldn't let them close it. The kid that was riding in there with him said, 'Ma'am, we're leaving now.' And I said, 'No, I have to go with him,' but the man said to me, 'No, no. You can't go.' Then my son Adán, who was somewhere around there, heard from someone that I was holding on to the car, that I wouldn't let go. . . . Hugo didn't say anything. He didn't speak to me. And I just stayed where I was, hanging on to that door, with that man trying to shut it, and me trying to open it to get inside. That was when Adán arrived and grabbed me and said, 'Come on, Mamá.' I felt as though they had ripped my heart and soul out of me."

AT AROUND 3:25 A.M., General Lucas Rincón suddenly appeared on television screens all across the country, to say, "The high military command condemns the appalling incidents that occurred yesterday in the nation's capital. In light of these facts, the president of the republic has been asked to resign, and he has agreed to do so." With this brief statement, Lucas Rincón would go down in Venezuelan history for prompting an extensive catalog of confusion regarding Chávez's absence from the government. That moment was what gave rise to the theory of the "power vacuum," which challenged the government's theory of a conspiracy and a coup. A mysterious military negotiation, followed by an evasive resignation, was the crux of the mystery that unfolded during those few hours. The president acknowledged that he was prepared to fight but then, after evaluating the situation, desisted. At that point, a providential telephone call came in from Fidel Castro. Chávez confessed to him that he was facing "a major dilemma. It isn't easy for someone, for the president of the republic, with a rifle at his side, a soldier, to hand over his weapon and agree to become a prisoner, because I agreed to become a prisoner. . . . I could have gone to another city, or at least I could have tried to with an armed column, or I could have gone to some other part of Caracas, armed, with some three hundred, five hundred men, [I could have] summoned the people, but that might have been the first step toward a civil war."[8]

Once the decision was made, the head of state and the military officers who had orchestrated the coup began negotiating. In all likelihood nobody was clear as to what was going on inside the military high command. Not even Chávez. And while an organized group had executed a plan to seize power, there was another group of military officers who never quite defined their position as the events unfolded. The best evidence of this tense ambiguity, and of the general befuddlement that followed, is the fact that General Lucas Rincón, the man who had refused to set Plan Avila into motion and publicly declared that Chávez had resigned, later reemerged as a faithful supporter of the president, who would go on to honor Avila with military decorations and appoint him minister of justice and the interior.

ANOTHER SOURCE OF CONFUSION is the question of Chávez's resignation. In retrospect, it almost seems like a word game. Monsignor Baltasar Porras, president of the Venezuelan Episcopal Conference, received a telephone call from the president at midnight the evening of the eleventh. The idea was that Porras might act as a kind of guarantor in the negotiation.

"There is a huge debate regarding whether he resigned or not," Porras explains. "He did not use the word 'resign' with me. He said, 'After three hours and a lot of consultation, I have decided to relinquish my power, and I am willing to sign if you can guarantee that they will let me out of the country.' " Out of the country, in this case, meant Cuba. In a taped conversation from the period when he was in custody, Chávez told a colonel who was standing guard over him, "It's time now, I need you to tell me where I am going. If not, I'm not leaving here."

The officer replied, "The plan is to take you to La Orchila [a militarized island in the Caribbean, some 80 miles from Caracas], because it is possible that you will then be transferred out of the country."

The president stated, "Well, if I go to Cuba, or wherever I decide to go, it cannot be something forced on me. Cuba is one of the possibilities I have been evaluating."[9] In fact, by early dawn of April 12, the Cuban government had contacted twenty-one different embassies to have Chávez transferred to the island.

The issue of Chávez's resignation was key because it would determine the legitimacy (or lack thereof) of the steps taken by the military and the provisional government that existed for a few short hours that day. The resignation, unsigned yet publicly announced, suddenly became a critical factor in the case. Thanks to this nuance, the Supreme Court of Justice ruled in favor of the "power vacuum" theory, and the military and civil conspirators involved in this case were absolved of all criminal responsibility.

Chávez himself has used different versions of his own story. On several occasions, he has maintained that he surrendered to avoid a bloodbath. When interviewed by the journalist Miguel Bonasso of the Argentinian newspaper *Página 12,* however, he said that his decision to surrender to the insurgent military leaders was a strategic maneuver, because he wanted to shift the situation to his natural environment, among the military officers at Fort Tiuna. He then claimed that when he was face-to-face with the conspirators in the dawn hours of April 12, he categorically refused to surrender and in fact berated them, saying, "I am not going to sign that paper, it seems that you men don't know who I am. I am not going to sign that. . . . You don't seem to know what you're doing; when the sun comes up in a little while, you are going to have to tell the country what it is that you are doing."[10] During this episode, one witness remembers the adversarial attitude of General Néstor González, who forced the head of state to remove his military uniform. This is yet another symbolic detail underscoring the military's predominant role throughout this entire incident. Chávez, reduced to civilian garb, was stripped of the one kind of authority that could keep him in the presidency.

In another bit of testimony, the president recognized that his decision to go to Fort Tiuna was almost inevitable, the logical conclusion of a man who had finally realized that he had lost almost all his military support. He gathered the aides who had stood by him and told them, " 'I am capable of resigning, but only if four conditions are met.' The first was that everyone's physical security had to be respected . . . the second was that the Constitution had to be respected—that is, if I were to resign it had to be before the National Assembly. The vice president would then assume the presidency of the republic until new elections were called. The third condition was that I had to be allowed to address the country in person. And the fourth: my staff had to be allowed to join me."[11]

Monsignor Porras says that Chávez refused to accept the first resignation speech that was handed to him for his signature: "He rejected it simply because it announced his resignation, and then he told them, so as to move things along, to put in [a passage stating] the dismissal of his cabinet ministers and of Diosdado Cabello as vice president, 'because he isn't good for that kind of thing.' And so after that, the new version had to be written up.

Chávez's initial willingness to resign turned sour when he was not granted his demand to leave the country. He felt betrayed and feared for his life, as he no longer knew whom he could trust within the military circle. By the time the conspirators finally agreed to grant his request, a day and a half later, it was too late; the scales had already tipped back in favor of the president's return to Miraflores.

No letter bearing the resignation of Hugo Chávez Frías was ever signed by the president. There were many drafts, but the signing kept getting postponed for various reasons: at first because some of the conspiring military officers did not want to let Chávez out of the country and insisted he stand trial in Venezuela; then because the two sides were unable to reach a definitive agreement over the resigning president's demands; then again when Chávez rejected one of the draft proposals; and yet again when he vowed that he would sign the document only when he was climbing onto the plane that would take him out of the country. After it was all over, in the kind of narrative that is typical of the victorious, Chávez himself would tell yet another version of the story that did little to shed more light on the situation: "I never had any intention of resigning from my position because I was being pressured to do so. The only thing I considered was abandoning my position [of my own volition]."[12] In any event, all the delays allowed Chávez to follow the very wise advice dispensed by José Vicente Rangel, the most skillful, shrewd political operator: "Hugo, don't sign; then it will become a coup d'état."

Hugo Chávez had still not signed anything when, just before the sun rose on April 12, Pedro Carmona, president of the Venezuelan business association Fedecámaras, announced that he would be assuming the presidency of Venezuela, as the head of a transitional civilian-military government.

Carmona's news and the announcement of a new administration elicited mixed reactions from the populace. Some people celebrated it, some bemoaned it, and still others were too perplexed to know what to think. Some radical opponents of the Chávez government gathered together in front of the Cuban Embassy and staged acts of violence. Those sympathetic to Chávez also tried to mobilize and plan their reaction to this new circumstance.

Carmona put his lawyers to work preparing his decree of self-proclamation and began to negotiate with various different sectors to put together a new governmental team. Using a cell phone lent to him by one of the soldiers guarding him, Chávez made several attempts to communicate with one of his daughters: "Listen, María, listen to me, call someone, call Fidel if you can. . . . Tell him I haven't resigned, that I'm in custody and that they're going to kill me but that I haven't resigned."[13]

Monsignor Porras recalls Chávez during those hours as "a man who was without a doubt battered, reflexive . . . the only thing he did was recall a series of events from his childhood, of his life as a military officer at the various posts he had been assigned to . . . at times it seemed that he wanted to cry, and he would put his hands here [between his eyebrows] as if to keep the tears at bay, and then he would continue talking."

As all this was happening, the internal crisis in the armed forces was escalating quietly. General Baduel later admitted that nobody in the High Military Command seemed prepared to jump in and defend Chávez; little by little, however, as the conspirators' project began to reveal its arbitrary and totalitarian side, some military forces began to reevaluate the situation.

As all this was occurring, an administration that wasn't yet an administration had begun to confront its first crises in Caracas. The military sector underwent an internal reshuffling, and General Efraín Vásquez, the army commander at the time, was a key figure in this process. Despite the fact that he had publicly disobeyed the president and refused to execute Plan Avila, it was Vásquez who called his generals and mid-level officers into a meeting, where they decided not to recognize the legitimacy of Carmona's transition unless important changes were made to the Act of Constitution of the new administration. In the meantime, María Gabriela Chávez had done her duty, announcing to the world that her father was in custody but had not resigned.

That same afternoon, Isaías Rodríguez, attorney general of the Republic, informed the media that a coup d'état had indeed taken place and that the Carmona government was unconstitutional. More and more people began pouring into the streets, calling for Chávez. At five-thirty in the afternoon, Pedro Carmona, completely blind to the reality of what had begun to happen, declared himself president of the Republic and read a series of decrees dissolving all the existing public authorities and removing the word "Bolivarian" from the name of the country.

"The objective was very clear: to begin a very brief de facto period, respectful of citizens' rights, so that we could call a first parliamentary election in ninety days—that is, in July 2002—and then, six months later, a presidential election, so as to hand over the presidency in January 2003,"[14] assures Carmona, who neglected to make such relevant clarifications on the day of the coup. His book Mi testimonio ante la historia (My Testimony Before History) devotes many pages to justifying the legitimacy of his decrees, but most Venezuelans, even a significant number of Chávez's opponents, felt it was an untenable political enterprise.

Teodoro Petkoff feels that "the decree was absolutely fundamental in terms of effecting a change in the power dynamic within the armed forces; it was what caused the abrupt shift that reinstated Chávez in the government. And the attitude of the armed forces reveals very clearly that the [country's] forty years of democratic life were not in vain: when it found itself in the throes of a coup d'état, [the military] perceived that the country was isolated internationally and that you couldn't break out of a government that had been accused of all sorts of antidemocratic perversions with a dictatorial regime. The same people who accepted Chávez's departure as a solution to the political crisis said, 'Go get him.' That decree was the inflection point. That was what broke the coup."[15]

ON APRIL 13 THE country awoke with an oddly fragile sensation. A strange premonition had permeated the collective consciousness of the nation. Support for the interim government began to dwindle. A few minor manifestations of support for the detained president were silenced. People began saying that a witch hunt had taken place, and in fact, a progovernment minister and congressman had been arrested and jailed in a maneuver that denied them due process and violated their human rights. The previous night, a flurry of meetings had taken place. Those loyal to the government finally managed to organize a popular reaction in defense of Chávez. Within the military a project had already begun to take shape, led by General Baduel and supported by Generals Jorge García Carneiro, commander of the Third Division, and Luis García Montoya, secretary of the National Defense Council. A Plan for the Restitution of the National Dignity was quickly drafted. Even left-wing leaders, political analysts, and intellectuals unsympathetic to Chávez made a point of distancing themselves from the political scheme that Carmona and his team had hatched. On that day, from an undisclosed location, Chávez's wife, Marisabel Rodríguez, and Diosdado Cabello told CNN that the president had in fact not resigned. The delicate, uncertain circumstances became clearer and clearer to Pedro Carmona, who, by the end of that April 13, would go down in Venezuelan history as "Pedro the Brief."

In the early afternoon hours of that same day, General Efraín Vásquez went public with his decision not to support the Carmona government, and Carlos Alfonso Martínez, inspector general of the National Guard, endorsed him. Both generals felt that the new government had, very simply, broken the constitutional thread.

At almost the same time, Chávez was shuttled to another military garrison in Turiamo Bay, off the coast of Aragua state, close to Caracas. The deposed president says he began to sense that his death might be imminent.

"I said to myself: My moment has come, and I began to pray, reciting the Our Father with my crucifix," he later confessed.[16] He also stated that "Carmona gave orders to some admirals and generals that I was to be dead by morning but that they were to apply the fleeing fugitives' law, so that it would look like an accident."[17] The source of this information, according to Chávez, was a waiter at Miraflores Palace who said he heard the order while serving coffee to the new employees of the recently established government. Pedro Carmona has categorically denied this, saying,

> Chávez has very irresponsibly begun to claim that on the twelfth, people were planning to assassinate him and moreover that Carmona had issued the order to kill him. This statement is untrue and paranoid, not only because that order never came from my mouth, nor would I have ever endorsed it, being a man of principle, but because it never once occurred to anyone to do such a ridiculous thing, even though many Venezuelans would have celebrated it. . . . If such a plan had existed, there were plenty of opportunities during which he could easily have been executed.[18]

Chávez has insisted, however, that his transfer to the naval base at Turiamo was part of an assassination plot:

> When I got out of the helicopter and I began to walk, I noticed there was a conflict among the military officers guarding me. Two of them were there to kill me, but the others, no, the others were constitutionalists. At the moment they are about to carry out the order, and I am standing there, one of these mercenaries turns me around and gets behind me and I am thinking: This man is going to give it to me in the back. I turn around and look him in the face: "Look at what you're about to do," I tell him, and at that moment a young officer jumps over to me and says, "If they kill my president, all of us are dead here." That neutralized the two mercenaries and saved my life.[19]

In a videotape of the deposed president in captivity at Turiamo, however, Chávez seems animated, chatting with his guards, even cracking a few jokes and waving hello when he realizes he is being filmed. At no point does he mention this assassination attempt, and at one point he even says, "These boys have treated me wonderfully since the minute I arrived, they are tremendous soldiers, human beings who have even shared some conversation with me."[20]

At Turiamo, the president wrote a brief proclamation on a slip of paper and then dropped it into a trash can, where it was later retrieved and used as proof of what was going on. On that piece of paper, Hugo Chávez wrote the following: "I, Hugo Chávez Frías, Venezuelan, president of the Bolivarian Republic of Venezuela, declare: I have not given up the legitimate power the nation gave me . . . forever!!!"[21] Not even at those darkest moments did his communicative abilities fail him. Just like his "for now" of February 4, 1992, he quickly coined a phrase capable of inspiring the same feeling: "Forever!"

The afternoon of April 13 was a shipwreck for the conspirators. Carmona attempted to save face and revoked the decision to dissolve the National Assembly. But progovernment leaders had already begun to congregate out on the streets, calling for people to join in. The armed forces had regrouped, and the coup leaders were now a minority whose endeavor had failed. In one last attempt to elicit his resignation, Chávez's captors took him to La Orchila. In a private biplane, Cardinal Ignacio Velasco and Colonel Julio Rodríguez joined him on the island. The book *El acertijo de abril* describes it as "an eleventh-hour effort that attempted to stave off the imminent fall of the transitional government. The High Military Command had accepted his request to leave the country, but Chávez changed his argument. Now he was thinking about his resignation. Chávez began to draft a document in which he committed to dismissing his vice president, Diosdado Cabello, and he agreed to sign the document once it had been transcribed onto a computer. But he never had time to do it."[22]

As more and more people filled the streets in protest and the criticism of the new regime grew louder and louder, the private television stations kept busy by trying to hide what was going on, abruptly canceling their news shows and occupying their screens with children's cartoons or foreign films. At this point, however, there was no way to stop the process that was now under way. At 10 P.M., Pedro Carmona tendered his resignation and relinquished the presidency of the Republic. Just before midnight, General Baduel dispatched three helicopters to La Orchila to bring the president back.

Exactly what Hugo Chávez and Ignacio Velasco discussed that night at the water's edge remains a mystery. The death of the archbishop, who succumbed to cancer in June 2003, adds another patch of darkness to this historic moment. There they were: one of the conspiracy's most crucial political operators, a man of the cloth who believed that the "Bolivarian" president was trying to impose a kind of "Castrocommunism" in Venezuela, and his victim—a victim who would no longer be a victim in a few short hours. What did they say to each other? What did they talk about? According to Velasco, Chávez mulled over a lot of things and asked to be forgiven for his mistakes. The president confirmed this version of the story but on another occasion claimed that he had harshly rebuked the priest for his direct participation in the coup and for the Church's unwarranted involvement in the political conspiracy. Velasco's signature appeared, along with several others, in support of the Carmona government's constitution. Some time later, the cardinal stated that he had not known what it was about and that he had signed a blank sheet of paper. Anyone familiar with the maze of characters and anecdotes behind the events of April 11 might find new significance in Hugo Chávez's first words that early morning when he addressed the nation after being reinstated as president: "To God what belongs to God, to Caesar what belongs to Caesar, and to the people what belongs to the people."

Once order was restored, Chávez acknowledged his mistakes, admitted the need for a national dialogue, and took measures such as changing the members of his cabinet and starting a new negotiation process with the executive board of PDVSA to demonstrate an intention to rectify his ways. He also assured the nation that there would be no political or personal interference when it came time to judge the facts. And although the Supreme Court of Justice accepted the

claim of the "power vacuum" and ruled in favor of the military officers who had tried to overthrow Chávez, the events of April 11 were
not so quickly forgotten. Two years later, the justice system went
after the generals who had supposedly "betrayed" Chávez. In 2004,
the attorney general's office also opened an investigation to press
charges against all those who had signed the Act of Constitution of
Pedro Carmona's short-lived government.

In the end, the coup attempt actually strengthened the government and gave it new motivation, new drive, greater international
legitimacy, and a political argument with which to discredit the opposition, by accusing them of plotting coups and using violent
methods to seize power. It also served to good advantage inside governmental institutions. As Maripili Hernández points out, "April 11
did us a great favor because it forced a necessary purge that got rid
of the traitors." After lengthy question-and-answer sessions in the
National Assembly, the Supreme Court of Justice ruled in favor of
the power vacuum theory. This, however, in no way hampered the
major purge that took place later on inside the armed forces. In the
civilian realm, some of the people who had participated in the coup
fled the country. Pedro Carmona, who spent a few days under house
arrest, left Venezuela in May and sought asylum in Colombia, where
he presently lives. When Monsignor Velasco died a year later, the
government announced a three-day mourning period, but during
the funeral near the Caracas cathedral, a group of Chávez sympathizers celebrated his death.

The country may have made it past the military and political crises
of those dark days, but the subject of human rights, deaths, and
abuses—both on April 11, and afterward under Carmona's fleeting
government—remains an open wound for the Venezuelan people.
Néstor Francia believes that "one of the most remarkable aspects of
the April 11 coup was the massive manipulation that took place afterward, orchestrated by the major media organizations and aimed at
distorting the facts, blocking the quest for truth, and condemning sectors of society without [the benefit of] any serious or credible investi-

gation."[23] Most especially, he is referring to the video that showed members of the progovernment party firing guns from a bridge. In addition to this videotape, which traveled the globe, other videos and photographs have also surfaced, with images of Metropolitan Police agents, who reported to the opposition mayor Alfredo Peña, firing away as well.

Though all the versions of what happened that day seem to accept the hypothesis that there were indeed sharpshooters positioned on the top floors of certain buildings, the opinions diverge when it comes time to lay blame, and both sides accuse each other of having been responsible for the sharpshooters. More than one analyst has also found it strange that the administration—one with a majority in the National Assembly, to boot—would block the creation of a neutral Truth Commission with international representation that would have investigated the events of April 11 and shed real light on the issue. General Raúl Salazar, Chávez's first minister of defense and later on his ambassador in Spain, resigned from his job over this, and stated, "The Commission was not allowed to function because a number of truths were coming out that would lead to the indictment of people in the government."

Perhaps, for a large part of the population, the most tragic thing of all is that both sides may be right, that when both sides accuse each other, neither is lying. That the inexplicable violence and deaths of those days are dangerously interwoven between the two groups. Perhaps the saddest thing of all is that in the end, neither side wants the truth to come out.

CHAPTER 13

The Showman of Miraflores

"CHÁVEZ DEFINITELY PICKED THE WRONG PROFESSION. HE WOULD have been a first-rate performer. Here in the world of television, movies, there's nobody like him." This is the opinion of Alberto Müller Rojas, his chief campaign coordinator for the 1998 elections. Many people would agree. Allies and adversaries, observers, simple witnesses—nobody can deny Hugo Chávez's communicative talents. The trust and affection he is able to inspire in people never cease to amaze. It is by far his greatest asset as a politician. In fact, the failed insurrection of February 4, 1992, was essentially a media coup. That day, Chávez failed in his military endeavor, but in terms of audience it was his first great triumph. It was his first encounter with the god of television ratings.

At first glance, there isn't very much in his personal history to suggest that this skill would eventually become one of his great assets. At the military academy he enjoyed public speaking, organized cultural events, and participated in plays. When the military assigned him to the town of Elorza, he became a kind of cultural and athletic promoter, an emcee at the town's festivals. These anecdotes, however, seem a rather faint foreshadowing of the tremendous media power that he would come to wield. In fact, many friends from his earlier years remember him for being somewhat withdrawn. According to them he was almost shy, something that is all but impossible to imagine now.

Hugo Chávez is the first Venezuelan president born in the age of television. One of his childhood friends recalls with absolute clarity the moment that television came into their lives; "The first television in Sabaneta belonged to Francisco Contreras, who was the father of one of the most prosperous families in town, earned with a lot of honest work. That was in 1964." At that time, little Hugo was around nine or ten. Efrén Jiménez, another friend from these days, describes their experience of the projected image: "The only entertainment we had was the movies, which cost one real. What did we see? Mexican movies and, every so often, westerns."

The Venezuela of those days was another country entirely. Chávez belongs to what is probably the first generation of Venezuelans who have grown up with and feel connected to the media, the industry of the masses. His confession to the Chilean magazine *Qué Pasa* in 1999 underscores this: "Instead of Superman, my hero was Bolívar."[1] The point of comparison here was a comic strip character who, when Chávez was a child, was featured in a television series as a slightly pudgy black-and-white superhero whose claim to fame was entirely dependent on some very rudimentary special effects.

Yet, while the media certainly existed as a circumstance in people's lives, at the very least as a harbinger of things to come, Chávez did not seem very interested in procuring a connection to that world, neither as a boy nor as a teenager. The remotest instance of any kind of nascent showmanship dates back to his school days, to a ceremony in honor of the first bishop of Barinas, Monsignor Rafael Angel González.

"I was in sixth grade, and they called on me to say a few things using a little microphone," Chávez recalls.[2] And although later on he was always willing to spice up parties and read and sing in public, nobody remembers him especially as a showman in the making. If anything, he was far more entranced by the dream of becoming a professional baseball player than of honing his communications skills as an announcer or emcee. One classmate from secondary school says that "Hugo was always very theatrical, very humorous, affectionate, and talking came very easily to him," but she also recalls that among his fellow students "he was absolutely anonymous." The Ruiz brothers and Jesús Pérez, Chávez's friends during those years, also recall his dramatic streak, his good humor, and his aplomb. Without a doubt, these characteristics would come together with a vengeance on February 4, 1992, as he entered the annals of history with those two words—"for now"—which quickly became a national motto.

Chávez's first television appearance was not a starring role but rather that of an extra, one of many soldiers who participated in the inaugural parade of the newly elected president of Venezuela in 1974. For the young Hugo Chávez, however, the moment was terribly meaningful. On March 13, he wrote in his diary, "At night, after turning out the lights, I went to watch the parade on TV and studied very closely how I walked past the stage. Did they see me at home?"[3] Years later, in the city of Maracaibo, a rather unusual occurrence took place during one of the marathon Saturday variety shows. Part of the show included a beauty pageant that at the very end featured a paratrooper who swooped down from the sky and handed a flower to the winner. Gilberto Correa was the emcee of the show, and years later Hugo Chávez would be the one to remind Correa that he had been the soldier who descended from the heavens to greet the newly crowned beauty queen. The announcement left more than a few people stunned that this man, someone capable of conspiring to overthrow the government, who had read Marx and idolized Che Guevara, had also been willing to lend himself out to one of the most classic productions of Latin American commercial television.

Beyond personal desires, however, Hugo Chávez has had no choice but to think seriously about the power of the media. He has lived with them at very close range and knows their intricacies well. In a personal, immediate sense, he is intimately familiar with the dazzling effects of media attention. Before February 4, being promoted to general was about as far as Hugo Chávez could expect to go in life. Right after the failed coup, he could easily have been handed a lengthy prison sentence or forbidden from entering politics for the rest of his life. A number of factors, however, interceded on Chávez's behalf, and the magical enchantment of the media was one of them. The military officer who appeared on television, assuming the responsibility for the coup and its failure, occupied the space of a performance that many Venezuelans had long been anticipating. Suddenly, there he was, the perfect incarnation of antipolitics, the face that perhaps represented the sentiments of a great majority of Venezuelans who were desperate and fed up with an elite that was no longer capable of understanding what was going on in the country.

At carnival time in February 1992, little children dressed up as Chávez strolled through the parks. Along with Zorro and all the other typical superheroes, a new kind of outfit found its way into the context of children's costumes that year: the field uniform of the military officer and the red beret of the paratrooper. Chávez's arrival on the scene on February 4 marked a sea change. That was when he began to tease out his real temperament and character. The journalist and former guerrilla Angela Zago, who wrote the first apologia for the 4F conspirators[4] and now opposes Chávez, remembers the early days: "When I went to the jail, I didn't go to meet Hugo Chávez, I went to meet all of them. But who was the most talkative, the most spontaneous, the nicest one of all? Chávez. I remember how he walked into the room where we were all waiting, and from far away—that's how good he is—he said to me, 'What an honor! I can't believe it!' He came over to me and said, 'It is such an honor for me to meet you, I have read you all my life,' and I don't know how many other things." Clearly, Chávez is a fast learner. He knows how to flatter his interlocutors, how to court them, how to make them feel close to him. At that very same prison, as representatives of different sectors of civil society began to visit the conspirators, Chávez began to hone what would become an extraordinary talent for seducing anyone he so desired. It was around this time, too, that he began to forge a personal relationship with the news media.

This process created some friction within the group. Jesús Urdaneta explains this with a story from those days behind bars at the San Carlos barracks: "We had a public telephone that was ours for two hours, and we would generally use it to call our wives and kids.

Chávez, though, used it to make statements to the press for half an hour, an hour. After a while they took the phone away from us, and I had it out with him. 'Great, now they've taken the phone away from us, all because of you and your needs,' I said to him. He already had plans of his own. I didn't. I was thinking about my family." Soon enough, this dynamic began to weaken the group, and Chávez grew stronger and stronger on his own, coming off as the absolute symbol of the movement. Beyond the typical arguments and internal debates that would naturally have erupted among the conspirators, an external factor had suddenly come between them, and it would be a decisive factor in the days and years to come: the popularity of Hugo Chávez.

The media frenzy generated by his release from jail was so great that he would not relive anything like it until 1998, when he threw his hat into the ring and ran for president. There were times when Chávez would lash out at the media, claiming that they were running a censorship campaign against him. William Izarra, who was working with Chávez at the time, acknowledges that in those days, "almost all the national media outlets attacked us and refused to give us any space."[5] On one hand, the media may not have been very interested in promoting him, but on the other hand, his popularity did take a dip as he refused to abandon his radical discourse against democracy and the electoral process. The essential change occurred in 1998. From this moment on, his relationship with the media would remain forever fluid and ever more intense. Sometimes they were in agreement, other times at loggerheads, but from this point on there was always some sort of relationship between them.

"HE CAN MAKE YOU cry just by looking at you." These are the sentiments of Maripili Hernández. Beyond whatever devotion she might feel for her leader, her comment reveals an important communicative trait: Chávez is a natural on television. He is friendly and amusing and inspires sympathy with ease. His brand of charisma is highly valued within the advertising and entertainment industry. It produces fervor, loyalty.

These emotions were reflected in the polls in 1998 as Chávez gathered more and more support, especially from the media. The most enthusiastic news source of them all was *El Nacional,* one of Venezuela's principal newspapers, and the Diego Cisneros Organization, owner of television's Channel Four. With the exception of a few isolated cases, all the media were on Chávez's side. The former army officer had clearly touched a chord with the media, which despised the country's traditional political parties and supported an antipolitical stance. In early 1999, when Chávez took office, his effervescent media presence was at an all-time high, and his administration reveled in its honeymoon with the press. The country was brimming over with giddy enthusiasm. Hope was in style again.

Winning an election, of course, is a lot easier than governing a country. It was not long before the relationship between Chávez and the media cooled off. Chávez, it turned out, was particularly sensitive to certain information the press brought to light and worked quickly to promote the creation of alternative media outlets and programs, of which he was the central focus and the guiding force. Thanks to these initiatives, he could personally offer his version of what was going on in the country. This was also the genesis of a project entitled *El Correo del Presidente,* an official newspaper aimed at reaching as broad an audience as possible. According to Humberto Jaimes, the newspaper's information director, the state has the right "to disseminate the information it deems strategic and important for public opinion; it has the right to publish its own version, just like any commercial media outlet does."[6]

On the state-run television channel, Chávez also began working on his first weekly television show. Maripili Hernández, who was in charge of the channel at the time, argued that it was part of "a communicational strategy that responds to a specific situation: at this moment, there is a need for a leader who can explain things to the country." Neither of these projects, however, achieved the desired re-

sult. Chávez has offered his perspective on this: "We started by putting out a newspaper, but it failed. . . . Then we did a weekly television show, *De Frente con el Presidente* [Face-to-Face with the President],
on live TV every Thursday night, with a studio full of people, and the
people would ask questions or call in by phone. It wasn't bad, but it
started to get boring and lost its audience."[7] Although these two experiences ended badly (the newspaper amid charges of corruption), the
Chávez government has continued to promote and support a variety
of communications projects with both logistics and financing. These
new endeavors include a new public television station, Vive TV; a new
government newspaper entitled *Vea,* edited by Guillermo García
Ponce, president of the so-called Political Headquarters of the Bolivarian Revolution; and even a magazine, *Question,* which is associated
with Ignacio Ramonet and *Le Monde Diplomatique.* Through the Ministry of Culture, the government also supports a wide variety of community initiatives and websites, all of which emphatically endorse the
Bolivarian Revolution.

Nevertheless, it was with *Aló, Presidente* that Chávez found both
the format and the results he was after. *Aló, Presidente* airs live every
Sunday morning. It usually kicks off at around eleven, and nobody
ever knows when it will wrap up. Audience participation takes the
form of screened telephone calls, and in general, the callers sing the
praises of the star. The show always has guests, either Venezuelans or
foreigners, who serve as a kind of panel that listens to the president,
intervening only when spoken to. Members of the cabinet are always
on hand as well, and their on-air nods and smiles offer unconditional
support of all the chief executive might say. As for the show's length,
this is what the president has to say: "I like it that way. I know that
other people don't like it so much. I have made an effort to reduce it,
but the trend—which I impose, after all—[*chuckles*] has been to make
it longer."[8] Show number 100, aired on March 17, 2002, took the
record at seven hours and thirty-five minutes. The show is completely
unscripted, relying solely on whatever Chávez decides to improvise:
he may talk about the government's activity that week, but he might

just as easily tell stories about his grandson, recount a few anecdotes from his personal life, sing, comment on the week's news articles, or summarize the projects his administration is planning to undertake. He has proudly asserted that his program is always number one in the ratings, despite the fact that the weekly reports of AGB, a media research group that measures television audience ratings, are not quite so flattering.

Even so, there is no doubt that Chávez has managed to make *Aló, Presidente* a focus of attention for other sectors of society. Thanks to the unpredictable quality of both the show and the president, journalists are always on high alert. On more than one occasion, for example, the head of state has surprised the country with exclusive on-air announcements, as he did on January 23, 2000, when he named Isaías Rodríguez his first vice president. Another time, in April 2002, he fired the majority of the management team at Petróleos de Venezuela with a cry of *"Fuera!"*—in other words, "Get out!"

"That was one of the biggest mistakes I ever made, and I did it with a whistle on top of it," he said with a titter to journalist Marta Harnecker.[9] "That was abusive of me, I'll never do that again." On the program that aired Sunday, August 22, 2004, a week after winning the recall referendum that allowed him to remain in the presidency, he announced that he would be appointing two new ministers in key posts: Interior Relations and Information.

All these things, combined with his own gift for television, his sense of humor, his anecdotes, and the colorful touches he adds to the program, only fan the flames of his intense relationship with the media. The psychiatrist Edmundo Chirinos states, "His show, *Aló, Presidente,* has become real working material for every journalist in the country. Everyone waits around for Monday, to see what the journalists have to say about the program. It makes me wonder what they would do if Chávez were to disappear." The opposition parties, however, say that the spectacle costs the country a great deal of money, given the logistics, the guests, and the audience members it needs. Carlos Berrizbeitia, an opposition congressman from 2000 to 2005, reported that as of May 23, 2004, the grand total for all the president's television programs was in the vicinity of $37 million. The government, however, did not seem to take the hint. In fact, its media aspirations have only grown, as Chávez is now promoting the idea of a continental television network for all of Latin America, plus a weekly hourlong radio show that people from Chicago to Patagonia can tune in to.

As early as the first *Aló, Presidente,* on May 23, 1999, Chávez was already talking about the media: "Even here, in Venezuela, sometimes people abuse, denigrate, lie, some people launch defamation campaigns through certain media of communication . . . this is a battle for Venezuela, for the future of our children, for the future of the homeland, and what I am trying to do here is fulfill a responsibility, so you see, my friends, we are here in the middle of a battle for freedom of expression." It was the prelude to a battle that had only just begun.

The journalist Rafael Poleo, an opponent of the Chávez government, believes that many important media outlets "fooled themselves into believing that they would be able to manage Chávez just as they had always managed politicians of humble backgrounds before him— some more, some less. The owners of the television stations, newspapers, and radio stations created their own personal fantasies, fed by a combination of fear, ambition, and greed. Chávez read them and used them, waiting for the moment when he would confront them, motivated by the real thing that determines his relationships with media: power."[10] The journalist and Chávez ally Vladimir Villegas, who was president of the state-run television station in 2004, believes that in the beginning "the media in general found themselves obligated to accept the harsh reality of Hugo Chávez Frías" but that after the honeymoon ended, confrontations began because of "the pervasive and mutual mistrust between the head of state and the owners of the communications corporations."[11]

Admittedly, some members of the media believed that they could interact with the new government exactly as they had done during the previous forty years. Early on in the Chávez administration, the

Diego Cisneros Organization, whose principal company in the country is Venevisión, tried to get someone close to the company appointed head of the National Telecommunications Commission. Chávez refused, and because of this the two sides became locked in a battle that raged on for years. In the end, his relations with magnate Gustavo Cisneros would be characterized by pragmatism. After Chávez met with Cisneros toward the middle of 2004, the old enemies seemed to have reached certain agreements. For the moment, the mutual aggression has ceased. Venevisión has softened its tone a notch by canceling a morning show that was sharply critical of the government and, according to sources close to Chávez, granting the Ministry of Information and Communication behind-the-scenes control over an interview show to be broadcast from six to six-thirty in the morning.

Alcides Rondón, vice minister for communications management in 2004, says that Chávez is not a man who gives in, that he "is frontal, and here with the media nobody was ever frontal, ever. And so, let's just say that this is balance." There are other perceptions. Angela Zago, an early government supporter who worked closely with the president, tells how she had a bitter argument with Chávez in late 1999 regarding the debate about whether or not to include the concept of "truthful information" in the new Constitution. During the Caldera government Chávez had fought against the use of this term, which he was now promoting. It was a delicate topic that led people to fear that freedom of expression might be threatened. Zago says she does not understand why the government could possibly have wanted to get mired in a confrontation with media corporations and journalists. The idea of regulating the media seemed misguided to her. When she brought this up with Chávez, the president replied, "Angela, that little battle is one that I want to fight." Zago was dumbfounded.

According to Zago, November 1999 was the beginning of a more or less permanent battle Chávez began to wage with the media.

Other incidents show signs of this tension. In September 1999, during an OPEC summit held in Caracas, Chávez accused CNN of "distorting" and "lying" in its coverage of the event. Earlier that month, some government employees had complained of an "international media conspiracy," and in protest, a small group of progovernment activists occupied the offices of the Associated Press. On another occasion, after Mario Vargas Llosa made some remarks about Chávez in an interview published in the newspaper *El Nacional*, Chávez's response was immediate and pointedly aggressive. On *Aló, Presidente* that week, he defended his sovereignty and criticized the opinions of the Peruvian writer, calling him "illiterate."

As his relationship with the media grew more and more confrontational, Hugo Chávez refused to visit the television studios, and he stopped giving interviews to the local press. His conflicts with the print media, especially the most influential newspapers, *El Nacional* and *El Universal*, were never-ending, and in speeches he would speak disparagingly of their owners. The only newspaper where he has not sown enemies is *Ultimas Noticias*, a middle-class newspaper edited by the well-known journalist and academic Eleazar Díaz Rangel, a man with close ties to the government. And if Chávez's relationship with the national media was bumpy, his relationship with the international media was a roller-coaster ride. Whenever favorable pieces were published, he would brandish them on *Aló, Presidente* like trophies. One day, for example, he waved an article from *The Wall Street Journal* in front of his audience. But when a newspaper published a critical editorial or a piece that touched on negative aspects of his administration, the president would declare that they were all part of an international media plot, that the big money was against his government, and that it was all a conspiracy hatched by the neoliberals of the world.

For a long time after the crisis of April 2002, the president praised the U.S. news channel CNN as a paradigm of objectivity and good journalism for having been the first media source to tell the world that he had not resigned. The Venezuelan president's attitude would change radically a few years later, thanks to a little news item about a quadruped, a short but colorful news piece that showed a skinny cow named Mariposa living in a commercial district of Caracas and its owner, a *chavista* militant, preparing to turn her into barbecue meat. The president's displeasure hit the ceiling. Why on earth, many people wondered, would he get so angry over a saucy little cartoon?

"Because it summed up the way things were. It wasn't that cow itself, it just summarized the [media's] treatment of the Venezuelan situation and our hope, after the coup, that we might be viewed with more objectivity by the international news channels like CNN," explains Alcides Rondón.

From mid-2000 onward, another factor further complicated his already acrimonious relationship with the media: the Organic Telecommunications Law. Among other things, Article 209 granted the executive branch the power to suspend transmission of whatever medium of communication it deemed necessary in order to protect the interests of the nation. One year later, the general framework was announced for a Law of Social Responsibility, also known as a Law of Contents, which was intended to regulate all aspects of the communications media. The opposition quickly called it a "gag law." Despite widespread protests and criticism leveled by trade groups and other organizations around the world, the law was approved in 2005. The television stations have the most to lose with this legal instrument, which regulates programming and establishes standards for the prohibition of certain content.

Of even more concern to analysts was the relationship between the new law and another aspect of the country's legal framework: the reform of the penal code. According to political analysts, this reform bill was an attempt to control news reports, information programs, and opinion shows. The idea was to open a very broad and ambiguous margin for sanctioning possible incitements to violence and conspiracy. According to the reform, approved in 2005, if a guest on a participatory television show were to slander or insult someone, the show's presenter and possibly even the TV station would bear responsibility for the guest's comments. Of the eleven commission members evaluating and judging television content, seven are selected directly by the executive. Some people maintain that this represents the end of a cycle that Chávez himself started. With the failed military coup of April 2002, the Chávez team purged the armed forces. The strikes in December 2002 and January 2003 allowed the government to take control of the oil industry. The recall referendum in August 2004 consolidated Chávez's political authority. And finally, the Law of Content has empowered the government to regulate and control the media while promoting self-censorship, a mechanism that is more subtle but also more effective.

Another disturbing element about Chávez's relationship with the media is the issue of the "chains," as they are called—those moments when the Ministry of Information and Communication orders all the commercial television and radio stations in the country to cede their space to the government's signal and carry out a joint transmission, effectively "chaining" themselves to what the administration chooses to air. Since his first year in office, Chávez has used the chains frequently and at random, subjecting the country to an unprecedented phenomenon. In 1999, the "chains" occupied 62 hours and 27 minutes of air time. In 2000, they took up almost 108 hours. In 2001, 116 hours and 58 minutes. In 2002, the number went down to 73 hours, but in 2003 it shot back up to 165 hours and 35 minutes. As of July 24, 2004, the sum total of "chain time" was 25 days and 8 hours, with no interruptions.

In short, this is a national policy designed and directed by the president himself. On many occasions, public events like diplomatic greetings, microcredit grants, military award ceremonies, law enactments, musical performances, and provincial tours are "chained" and the entire spectacle occurs in front of Chávez's audience as if it were something spontaneous. Suddenly, someone will begin to yell, "Ca-de-na! Ca-de-na!" and the public will shout back the same word. Then Chávez smiles and asks a nearby aide, "Can we?" Of course they can, they always can. In any event, most times it has been planned in advance.

"There is a team that draws up and makes recommendations regarding the pros and cons, the strengths and weaknesses of each type of broadcast. The work is systematic, and [Chávez] really does listen. But the person who makes the final decision is the president. The decision regarding the chain comes from the president," says Alcides Rondón, who attests to the fact that it is not easy to work closely with the president, a demanding boss who stays on top of the smallest details, especially when they have anything to do with the media. During his first six years in office, he changed his information chief nine times.

Many government supporters, even when they admit that the addresses have been excessive, insist that they are waging a "war," a "battle" for information, and that all the commercial media outlets produce subjective and biased information that tends to attack the government. In this sense, they say, the commercial stations operate their own "chains" and the government is only defending itself against the siege of the commercial media. Chávez's supporters say that he uses his "chains" only to tell the country the truth about what is going on. Maripili Hernández, for example, recognizes that "there have been too many chains, and they have gone on for too long, to the point that they go on at noon and then are rerun at night, for no reason at all. That could have been avoided." But she also accuses the privately owned media of outrageously manipulating its information segments, with absolutely political goals. "It should never have come to either of the two extremes: Chávez should not have used the chains so much, and the media should not have broadcast one single news report urging Chávez's removal."

Marcelino Bisbal, a university professor specializing in communications studies, has baptized this odd relationship as a "media schizophrenia" in which "an extremely antigovernment sector and a government sector, also very extreme, believe that all the country's problems may be resolved in the space offered by the media."[12] Bisbal's comment reflects an almost palpable sensation that permeates the day-to-day life of most Venezuelans. It is a country that is intoxicated, overinformed, saturated by the manner in which one single story is told over and over again, subjected to the most endless and exhausting media diatribes. In the middle of this cross fire, the everyday citizen ends up in the worst position of all. The role of the media, independent of political affiliation, becomes blurry. Boundaries begin to fade. On several occasions, the media associated with the opposition have made the mistake of disseminating information that was later discovered to be false and of reporting controversial statements that, in the end, had no factual basis.

The state-run media, on the other hand, have become veritable propaganda brigades that seem willing to stop at nothing in their defense of the president. Venezolana de Televisión (channel 8) has gone so far as to broadcast taped telephone conversations between opponents of the government, which is illegal and expressly prohibited by the Constitution. On one occasion, channel 8 aired an exclusive interview that belonged to the news channel Globovisión: the material was robbed and aired before Globovisión, the channel that actually produced and owned the material, was able to use it. In the middle of this media war, the government has employed another old tactic, that of refusing to grant government advertising to anti-Chávez stations. At the same time, the government reproaches these stations, calling them coup plotters, fascists, terrorists, and "horsemen of the apocalypse."

According to the annual report issued by Reporters Without Borders, in 2003 "at least 72 journalists were harassed," two were arrested while on the job and jailed for short periods of time, and three media employees were threatened in Venezuela. The report also included a separate section listing the pressures and obstacles threatening the exercise of journalism in Venezuela. This part of the report included information on all sorts of practices such as robbery and/or burning of equipment, intimidation through protest groups, damage to the facilities of certain TV stations, and even personal aggression.

Vladimir Villegas, a journalist who has held various positions in the Chávez government, points out the following: "Just as generalizations are never a good thing, paradoxically, personalizations are also not entirely advisable, because to a large degree—this is undeniable—the harassment sustained by certain social communicators whether or not they engaged in reprehensible practices, was provoked by certain expressions of the president, but that does not imply that this was the head of state's objective."[13] In the other corner, however, are those people who insist that all of this is yet another part of the same plan to destroy or suppress the existing structures. These people believe that Chávez's authoritarian program will bring on the demise of freedom of expression and paint the media into a very tight corner.

On July 28, 2004, Chávez chained all the radio and television channels in the country one more time. The images that flashed across the screen featured a delighted head of state at a hacienda in the plains surrounded by his family. The reason for this official message to the nation was a party: the celebration of Hugo Rafael Chávez Frías's fiftieth birthday.

Once, while serving as the general manager of the Central Information Office, Juan Barreto was asked about Chávez's affinity for appearing in the news. He replied, "He likes it, but that isn't a sin. I understand that Madonna likes it, too—that's why she attracts the media."[14] Barreto's flippant answer, however, offers a glimmer of truth about the industry and its effects: few people are immune to the charms of the media. The glow of the spotlight may be more powerful than any other charm. Beyond strategies, beyond political machinations, vanity tends to be an uncontrollable force, which begs the question: Is the historically minded Chávez capable of governing his own fascination with the media-minded Chávez? Which of the two is closer to the real man?

CHAPTER 14

Bush the *Pendejo* and Fidel the Brother

WASHINGTON HAS ALWAYS TENDED TO MISREAD LATIN AMERICA. AND Hugo Chávez is no exception, for he is a rare specimen who eludes easy categorization. Is he a Communist? A revolutionary? A neoliberal? For the U.S. State Department, Hugo Chávez is the latest headache in the region. But Chávez has not always been the enfant terrible. His first public statement regarding the United States was issued with delicacy, just a few days after he had emerged from relative anonymity. With these words he assured the world, "Our struggle is not against the United States. Our struggle is against corruption and against this government. . . . We believe that the United States would not interfere with our project because it is not openly at odds with [U.S.] foreign policy."[1] Moreover, during one of his first interviews in prison, he clarified that his endeavor espoused "no anti-imperialist or anti-*yanqui* discourse, which, in any event, went out of fashion in the era of the 1960s."[2]

Six years later, however, in light of the incendiary campaign rhetoric with which Chávez promised to pulverize forty years of Venezuela's past and demolish the establishment, Democrat Bill Clinton forgot about that early declaration of goodwill. As Chávez got ready to travel to Miami to participate in a televised forum with his rivals, he was denied a visa on the grounds of his conspiratorial past, despite being the clear front-runner in the presidential elections. This was surely a tough blow, and the candidate would likely remember the brush-off for a long time. Perhaps he was thinking about it on December 6, when former U.S. president Jimmy Carter called his overwhelming victory "a peaceful revolution." Soon enough, Washington would serve him his revenge on a silver platter.

His incredible leap into the political realm awakened a good deal of curiosity among international circles. On his first European tour in 1999, Chávez was on top of the world—that is, until something happened at a dinner with a group of Spanish business leaders in Madrid. The president-elect of Venezuela was sailing through an improvised bit of chitchat when he was suddenly interrupted by an urgent phone call. Chávez took the cell phone that was handed to him, listened for a few minutes, and responded, "These things are not discussed through these channels." Then he hung up. The following day he traveled to Paris and was received by President Jacques Chirac. During their meetings, the two leaders warmed up to each other, and Chávez told him about the previous evening in Spain.

"He told him that he had received a phone call from Peter Romero, assistant secretary of state for Latin American affairs. 'President Chirac,' he said, 'look at how clumsy the Americans can be sometimes when it comes to foreign policy, especially in Cuba. They have really made a mistake with us. Did you know, President, that I do not have a visa to go to the United States? And Peter Romero told me that President Clinton could receive me, that I didn't have problems anymore with the visa, but that they were worried because on this trip I have a last stop in Cuba. That they were concerned about me going to Cuba before going to the United States. I am not going to tolerate any kind of U.S. interference in Venezuela's foreign policy. I don't talk about these things with Romero, or anyone else. That's why I hung up on Peter Romero,' " Hiram Gaviria, the former coordinator for the Patriotic Pole recalls Chávez saying to Chirac. "That was the first unequivocal indicator of where Hugo Chávez was headed with respect to foreign policy. He was not the traditional president who would make concessions in order to be received by the president of the United States. Instead, he stuck by what he believed."

Hugo Chávez's first visit to Washington was postponed twice. The first time, he changed his plans when he found out that Clinton would not be in the U.S. capital on the days he was planning to visit. The second time, he had to cancel his trip due to a case of colitis. When the meeting finally happened, on January 27, it was not a momentous occasion. The appointment was not accorded the status of an official visit, and the U.S. president granted Chávez only fifteen minutes of his time in the office of the national security advisor, Sandy Berger. Five months later, when the Venezuelan president returned to the United States after his inauguration, he did not stop in Washington at all. Clinton and Chávez would meet again, for the second and last time, during the U.N. General Assembly. At the U.S. Mission to the U.N., the two leaders spent an hour talking about drug trafficking, Venezuela's constitutional reform process, and the Colombian conflict. Chávez, who at the time objected to Plan Colombia, a U.S.-designed program to control the drug trafficking trade, did not want to allow U.S. antidrug planes to fly over Venezuelan territory, a stance that was annoying—though not surprising—to Washington.

By the end of the year, Washington-Caracas relations had soured even more, thanks to the incident following the Vargas mudslide, when Venezuela requested assistance from the United States and then refused it when it was already on its way. Peter Romero now adopted a threatening pose. In an interview with the conservative Spanish newspaper *ABC,* he questioned the Chávez administration's inconsistent behavior: "In Venezuela, you don't see a government in charge . . . but we gringos are not exactly known for our patience." From that point on, President Chávez would become, steadily and implacably, more and more hostile when referring to the Clinton government, and he would continue doing so in earnest with Clinton's successor.

At that time, the person who came closest to deciphering Chávez's behavior and attitude was John Maisto, the first U.S. ambassador who had to interface with him. According to Maisto, Chávez was to be judged not by his words but by his actions. "Look at his hands, not his mouth," was Maisto's advice, which the State Department would heed only rarely. Ambassador Maisto was replaced in 2000 by Donna

Hrinak, a strong character who was perhaps the most openly combative U.S. official the Chávez administration faced.

The ever-strengthening bond between Caracas and Havana, as well as certain inflammatory statements made by Fidel Castro, also caused some serious consternation in the most conservative sectors. *The New York Times* took sides by publishing an editorial that criticized the Chávez-Castro alliance, calling Chávez "demagogic" and saying that he "clearly means to be an influential symbol of resistance to American influence, not just in Latin America but around the world."[3] It was decided that for the duration of the Chávez administration, Romero would play the bad cop, and he would be joined by other tough guys later on, including Otto Reich,[4] the White House's special envoy to Latin America, and Roger Noriega,[5] assistant secretary of state for Western Hemisphere affairs. At the bottom of it all, though, the ex-*comandante* seems to enjoy it: he loves to be defiant, he loves to be newsworthy, and he does whatever he can to be at the center of controversy and confuse everyone. Chávez has claimed that his political adversaries were conspiring to provoke a serious conflict with the United States but ultimately promised that "relations with Washington are doomed to be good."

By the time Republican George W. Bush assumed the presidency of the United States in January 2001, more than one dart against American imperialism had shot out of the mouth of the Venezuelan president, which earned him the sympathies of many in the European and Latin American left. Chávez was delighted to see his popularity cross borders. The job shuffle in the State Department would pave the way for more public confrontations and scathing attacks. In the end, Clinton's secretary of state, Madeleine Albright, would turn out to be moderate next to her successor, Colin Powell, a man of few words who toughened the U.S. stance toward Caracas. One month later, when the pro-Chávez congressman Rafael Simón Jiménez, then the vice president of the National Assembly, visited Washington with a parliamentary delegation, former ambassador Maisto would say to him in the White House, "Chávez always said to me, when he would talk about the topic of [the friction with] the United States, 'Don't worry, ambassador, I know where the red line is. And I'm not going to cross that line, I just go up to that little edge.' "

In response, Jiménez replied, "You see how he pushes it, pushes it, pushes it, but then when [things] reach a breaking point, he eases up."

Chávez later described his informal meeting with Bush during the Third Summit of the Americas, held in Canada that April: "He said he wanted to be my friend, and I said to him, 'I want to be your friend, too.' We said our hellos, but there was no agreement, no commitment, no bilateral meeting, that hopefully we can hold sometime in the near future."[6]

Chávez's wishes were not to be granted. Mired in an eternal dispute, the two presidents seem ages away from arriving at any kind of understanding, much less friendship. In formal diplomatic terms, their relations grew worse, though never to the point of no return. With respect to trade, things would always be rosy. The United States, buying approximately 72 percent of Venezuela's oil exports,[7] continued to be Venezuela's number one commercial partner, and Venezuela continued to be a reliable provider that did not create problems for the U.S.-based multinationals keen on investing in the country. George W. Bush is one thing, but Chevron-Texaco is something else entirely, and in fact, Alí Moshiri, Chevron-Texaco's representative for Latin America, was received by Hugo Chávez with open arms.

The World Trade Center attack on September 11, 2001, gave rise to a whole new set of troubles. One month later, with the superpower still in shock from the discovery that it was vulnerable, Hugo Chávez grazed the edge of that red line. On television, Chávez pointed his finger at a photo of dead Afghani children. "They are not to blame for the terrorism of Osama bin Laden or anyone else," he said. Then he asked Washington to stop bombing Afghanistan and to end "the massacre of the innocents. Terrorism cannot be fought with terrorism."[8] His last words weighed heavier than his first words, which condemned the terrorist attacks. The United States responded by saying that it was "surprised and deeply disappointed" and promptly recalled Ambassador

Hrinak for a consultation. After a week, Chávez let up a bit, expressing regret that his statements might have been misinterpreted. Venezuela and the United States were partners, he stated, and "the revolutionary government has neither the slightest desire nor intention to damage these relations."[9]

But it didn't seem to be enough. In early 2002, Chávez's most complicated year in terms of domestic issues, Colin Powell communicated the Bush government's attitude toward Chávez. In addition to questioning the level of democracy of Chávez's government, Powell also blasted the president for visiting government leaders openly hostile to the United States, such as Saddam Hussein and Muammar Gaddafi: "We have expressed our disagreement on some of his policies directly to him, and he understands that he has been a serious irritant in our relationship." Ambassador Hrinak said good-bye to Venezuela when the constant tension became another source of strain in and of itself. In her farewell, she did not mince words. She left the country concerned, she said, by what she felt was Chávez's sympathy for the Colombian guerrillas and did not hide that she was bitterly disappointed. "I hoped to see a real revolution in Venezuela. Real changes. A more efficient public administration, less corruption, more economic development, more opportunities for people. And I have not seen those things."[10] She was replaced by Charles Shapiro, a man with a perennial nervous smile who stepped into a carefully spun spiderweb. The new ambassador's first meeting with president Chávez occurred scarcely a week before the April 11 crisis.

The day after the coup attempt, when the Venezuelan populace believed that Chávez had resigned, the White House suggested that Chávez himself had caused the situation that culminated in his removal from office and asked Carmona's provisional government to organize elections as soon as possible. The fact that Washington did not categorically condemn the coup generated a serious controversy both inside and outside the United States. On April 12, Shapiro met with Pedro Carmona. As he explained it a week later, he had gone to Miraflores first thing in the morning "to suggest two things: first the importance of reestablishing the National Assembly and second, to welcome the OAS mission."[11] Once Chávez was back in the presidency, after bouncing back from the coup and countercoup, the Chávez machine began to accuse Washington of having encouraged the group that tried to overthrow him. From Condoleezza Rice, then the powerful national security adviser, all the way down the line, U.S. government officials flatly denied this. Perhaps taking a leaf from the tone of contrition and reconciliation that Chávez adopted during those delicate days, President Bush said he hoped Chávez had "learned the lesson" and Powell also chimed in, saying "We hope that the most recent turn of events in that country foretell a president much more cognizant of the demands of democracy."[12]

Many people felt certain that the United States had been involved in the coup to get rid of this very inconvenient president, and their suspicions were amply documented and analyzed by the news media both in and out of Venezuela, though Washington strenuously denied these accusations. President Chávez, however, did not complain until two months later, when, on one of his Sunday broadcasts, he asked Washington to explain its lukewarm reaction to the events of April 11, and claimed to have evidence that U.S. military officers had met with Venezuelan officials at the military base of Fort Tiuna and that a U.S. ship had been in Venezuelan waters during the thirty-six hours he had been held in custody. Washington denied everything. A U.S. congressional investigation concluded in July that Bush had not supported unconstitutional activity in Venezuela. Despite this, however, the issue would always remain something of a mystery. The suspicions regarding U.S. participation in the coup were never fully cleared, and Chávez's evidence was never aired in public.

It is possible that U.S. officials were present at Fort Tiuna. In fact, the U.S. military mission operated out of Fort Tiuna, headquarters of the Venezuelan Defense Ministry, on the basis of an agreement signed in 1951. Ever since the beginning of the Chávez administration, Venezuela had been asking Washington to move the base somewhere else, but because of negotiations that were not made public, the issue was always postponed. It wasn't until May 2004, two years after the coup, that the U.S. mission finally abandoned the base. What happened in the aftermath of April 11 was a kind of escalating tug-of-war in which Chávez and his officials would make almost daily statements against the United States and then a dozen or so U.S. officials[13] would take turns at bat, questioning the democratic commitment of the ex-*comandante*. Even former president George Bush—a close friend and fishing buddy of the magnate Gustavo Cisneros—intervened at one point, stating that a very vague "we" did not much like what Chávez was doing in Venezuela.

In 2004, the Venezuelan president reacted with irritation to Washington's requests that he behave democratically during the process leading up to the recall referendum regarding his presidency. Chávez called Condoleezza Rice "illiterate" because she was, according to him, incapable of reading Venezuelan reality. With Bush he was a good deal harsher. During a progovernment rally in March, Chávez yelled out that the American president was a *pendejo* (which the U.S. newspapers translated as "asshole") for presuming he had no popular support the day he had been briefly overthrown. He also accused Bush of having reached the White House fraudulently and challenged him: "From here, I would like to place a bet with Mr. Bush to see who lasts longer, him in the White House or me here in Miraflores." He also threatened to suspend oil sales to the United States and added that he would not accept any interfering with his country's domestic issues. "We've got enough balls here to run the country, dammit!"[14]

After that, Chávez, who later said that Bush should be in jail for having started the war against Iraq, made Bush his favorite topic during the campaign leading up to the recall referendum, which ultimately confirmed his legitimacy as president of Venezuela on August 15, 2004. This fit of passion did not alter the course of U.S.-Venezuelan relations. The White House, it seems, learned its own lesson and pretended not to hear.

Still, while Chávez was busy insulting the U.S. president and using him as a leitmotif in his campaign rhetoric to win popular support, the Venezuelan government was paying $1.2 million to Patton Boggs, LLC, one of the most important lobbying firms in the United States, to improve its image in Washington. This was nothing new. During its first year in power, the Bolivarian government spent "a record $15,363,398" on lobbying, according to the magazine *Latin Trade*, which placed Venezuela at the top of its list of Latin American governments that spent money racking up connections and influence in the United States. Venezuela even opened up its own Bolivarian lobbying office in Washington, the Venezuelan Information Office.

In Washington, after more than five years of verbal attacks, people realize that Hugo Chávez is not as evil as he seems. And they do bear in mind Maisto's advice: "Don't pay attention to what he says, pay attention to what he does."

Venezuela has kept its commitment to deliver oil on time as the fourth largest exporter of oil to the United States, after Canada, Saudi Arabia, and Mexico. Venezuela also does plenty of business with U.S. oil companies, without any anti-imperialist vexations. A good portion of the exploration of the Deltana Platform, a massive project of five oil fields some 150 miles from the Orinoco delta, has been granted to Chevron-Texaco. When Chávez threatened to suspend the oil shipments, Alí Moshiri, Chevron's president for Latin America, calmly said, "Politics is separate from business, and until now we have never had any hiccups in our projects. . . . In the Orinoco we are improving things, and that means lots of money."[15] At a press conference a few days before the recall referendum that would decide his fate as president, Hugo Chávez showed off the analyses of the most important U.S. financial publications, which predicted that businessmen would enjoy more stability and less uncertainty with Chávez. No longer was there even a trace of the rudimentary language of the oversimplified left, nor did anyone hear any impassioned invectives against imperialism and savage neoliberalism this time around. When it comes to statistics, the deaths in Iraq and U.S. interventionism don't seem to matter so much. When it comes to the oil business, Chávez does not scream, "Yankee go home!"

While Chávez's relationship with President Bush is as strident as a heavy metal concert, his relationship with Fidel is as smooth as a *guaracha*. And that is how it has always been. A few months after his release from prison in late 1994, Chávez received a signal from Havana. According to Luis Miquilena, Germán Sánchez Otero, the Cuban ambassador in Caracas, personally extended an invitation to Chávez. Miquilena recalls, "We didn't know if Fidel would receive him because [the invitation] was for him to give a talk at the Casa de las Americas. Naturally, it was Fidel's way of retaliating against President Caldera. The prominent Cuban exile [Jorge] Mas Canosa had come here to visit Caldera, who received him like a king. And so Fidel said, 'All right, now I'm going to invite that lunatic.' It was just to wave a red flag at Caldera. That's how Fidel is, he's another one who likes to provoke. Hugo's trip was planned. Well, well, Fidel not only went to receive him, he was waiting at the door to the plane! He gave him a welcome that was fit for a head of state. At midnight they went out to get some food at the Venezuelan Embassy, and had to go to the guesthouse to make the food. You know, with that kind of camaraderie . . . that's Fidel. He stayed with him from the minute he arrived until he said good-bye to him at the door to the plane. And of course, he won him over."

During his visit to Cuba, a brief lecture was arranged for Chávez at the University of Havana. "Cuba is a bastion of Latin American dignity, and that is how she should be seen, that is how she should be nurtured," he stated in the opening lines of his speech. To gain the sympathy of his audience, he went on to say, "and we are honored as rebel soldiers by the fact that we are not allowed to enter North American territory." He also stated that "We do not rule out the path of weapons in Venezuela" and promised that the Cuban people "have a great deal to offer" his project, "a project with a horizon that stretches from twenty to forty years."[16]

According to Miquilena, that was the first link, "but Chávez never considered the idea of a Fidel-style revolution, not at all. Never," which is contrary to what many people in Venezuela believe, largely because of the almost filial relationship the two leaders have forged. The two men did not cross paths again until January 1999, when Chávez visited Havana as president-elect. His Colombian counterpart, Andrés Pastrana, was also in Havana then, and the two men discussed the Colombian conflict. With Chávez was Marisabel, who had brought along three sick children who were to be treated on the island in what would be something of a dress rehearsal for a medical program that was later developed between Venezuela and Cuba. And on February 2, 1999, a contented Castro found himself in the front row among the group of fifteen presidents that attended Chávez's swearing-in ceremony. As always, the bearded Cuban leader was the darling of the local and international press.

The two men next met toward the end of the year, when an exalted phrase that escaped Chávez's lips caused serious consternation among the Venezuelan opposition. This time, he had gone to Cuba to attend an Iberoamerican summit. Chávez had such a good time that he decided to stay an extra three days, playing an unforgettable game of baseball with Fidel—who had also been a pitcher in his younger years—in the Latinoamericano Stadium, the bleachers overflowing with some 50,000 excited fans. According to Chávez, Castro played "one of those jokes he likes so much" by having the nation's Olympic baseball team come onto the field dressed up like old men. When the joke became clear to Chávez, whose team was beaten to a pulp, he abandoned his competitive spirit and laughed, saying, "I had noticed those bearded men, they looked like they'd just come down from the Sierra [Maestra]." Afterward, in one of his speeches, Chávez expressed his solidarity for his colleague, noting that there were people "who come here to ask of Cuba the path of democracy, false democracy." Immediately thereafter, he underscored that his movement in Venezuela "is going in the same direction, toward the same sea where the Cuban nation is going, the sea of happiness, of true social justice, peace."[17]

Chávez is well aware of the effect his words have. His adversaries in Venezuela, and even those who were not yet his adversaries, must have felt their hair stand on end as they envisioned that "sea." But Chávez was too busy having fun. The visible empathy between Castro and Chávez, however, is more than a passing detail—people all across the Americas scrutinize the Castro-Chávez encounters, for a variety of reasons. The Venezuelan ambassador in Washington, Alfredo Toro Hardy, told the *Washington Times* in May 1999 that "Mr. Chávez and Mr. Castro may have personal affinities. They are both strong, charismatic leaders from the Caribbean, but there is no ideological affinity." Around that same time, the Brazilian weekly *Veja* stated that "the awe he feels for the Cuban leader is so shameless that in diplomatic circles people readily believe that Chávez gave his presidential inauguration speech to Fidel for a once-over."[18] Speculations of all sorts (a "Caracas-Havana" axis has even been mentioned) sprout forth every time the Venezuelan president defends Cuba at international forums, asks for its reinstatement in the Organization of American States, or calls for the end of the "brutal sanctions on the brotherhood of Cuban people."

Chávez's friendship with Fidel, twenty-eight years his senior, has always served as a kind of buttress for Chávez's sense of self, making him feel more independent, more sovereign, more revolutionary. He demonstrated his gratitude by signing an oil agreement with Cuba that the executive branch neglected to submit to Venezuela's parliament for approval. According to the agreement, starting in late 2000 Venezuela would provide Cuba with 53,000 barrels of oil per day— a third of Cuba's oil consumption—under extremely preferential conditions. In exchange, Cuba would pay part of the bill with generic drugs, vaccines, and medical equipment and treatment. Within one year Venezuela would almost double its trade with Cuba,[19] edging out Spain as the island nation's number one commercial partner.

This prompted a wave of paranoia in Venezuela, but Castro averted trouble by promising the nation that Chávez was not a socialist and claimed that he had never heard Chávez utter "a single word" related to the idea of establishing socialism in Venezuela. During an eleven-hour press conference with Venezuelan journalists visiting Cuba,

Castro went out of his way to state that Chávez's thinking is "not based on the philosophy of socialism and Marxism." He then recalled his affinity for Chávez, which grew out of the military insurrection of February 4, 1992, but promised that "Chávez is not a man of violence . . . like Bolívar and Washington, he is a revolutionary."[20] This, of course, was the older revolutionary's way of giving the younger revolutionary his bona fide seal of approval.

Shortly after this, an advance party of ninety Cubans—baseball players, artists, technical experts, parliamentarians, students, and precocious child thespians—visited Venezuela in what was a prelude to a visit from Castro. For five days, Venezuelan officialdom would revolve entirely around the Cuban leader, with all the government ministers vying to get their photograph taken with him. On this, his seventh visit to Venezuela, Fidel kicked things off by giving the country some lessons in anti-imperialism. Upon arriving at Maiquetía airport, he stated, "Your country is much bigger than ours. This is a continent, and if that little island managed to resist, there is no way that the continent of Bolívar, the land of so many great statesmen, cannot resist as well. I have no doubt about this. How can it not resist when it has men like Chávez?"[21] With the exception of four medical doctors who spoiled the party by defecting and requesting asylum in Venezuela, it was smooth sailing all the way. Chávez ordered his men to remove Bolívar's sword from the vaults of the Central Bank and deliver it to the National Pantheon, the eternal resting spot of his idiosyncratic god, to show his guest.

"Chávez and Fidel have the power," chanted a chorus of children and admirers from abroad. Next the party headed over to the place where Chávez had been held prisoner, the nearby San Carlos military barracks, which was now a museum.

The following day, in his speech before the National Assembly, Fidel Castro indulged in another lesson, which left more than a few orthodox parliamentarians grumbling. "The revolution is possible in a market system," he claimed, irritating the opposition whose hands he had shaken when they had been in power, as he criticized the forty years of Venezuelan history to which they belonged. Between the Cuban leader and the Venezuelan president, however, it was all smiles and mutual praise. The legendary *comandante* of the Sierra Maestra then boarded his own plane and paid a visit to the plains region, becoming the first foreign leader to visit Sabaneta de Barinas, the small town where Hugo Chávez was born. He was awarded the keys to the town and was duly declared an "illustrious son" of Sabaneta. Castro accepted the honor by declaring that Chávez "should be multiplied by a thousand, by five thousand, by ten thousand, by twenty thousand." The entire visit transpired in a cloud of mutual adoration. In his usual ebullient way, Chávez did little to hide his admiration and counted, quite literally, the days that had gone by since they had first met: "So, just as I said to you in Havana on a night of farewells and hugs, when I met you five years, ten months, and twelve days ago: I want to see you in Venezuela and receive you as you deserve to be received. And in Sabaneta I repeat: We have received you as you deserve to be received, with the nation's people in the streets."[22]

Castro's trip, of course, wasn't complete without a visit to the stadium for another baseball game or an appearance on *Aló, Presidente.*[23] Encouraged by Chávez and the oil agreement they would be signing the next day,[24] Fidel joined the Venezuelan president in a rousing rendition of the song "Venezuela," a sugar-coated, modernized version of the song *"Alma llanera."* The image was more than a bit ludicrous, given that Fidel was familiar with neither the lyrics nor the music of the song in question. Wearing a pair of headphones, trying to read the song lyrics off a piece of paper, Fidel attempted to hit the right notes but only managed to come off looking rather tacky and tuneless.

Castro then went on to ask Chávez to be more careful about his safety, a comment that likely caused the *comandante* to break out into a cold sweat, since being assassinated has always been one of his greatest fears—so much so that his security system is far more elaborate than that of any other Venezuelan president before him. Even in 1998, he won renown for being the most bodyguarded candidate of the lot. Months before his visit to Sabaneta, Castro had warned the Venezuelan leader on two separate occasions that the Cuban intelligence service had detected plans to assassinate him in December 1999 and July 2000. Fear of magnicide is a recurring topic for the president, as are the accusations of presumed conspiracies to wipe him off the map of Venezuela. According to official sources, Chávez has others besides the anti-Castro groups who are after him: the Colombian paramilitaries, the Venezuelan far right, and his purported number one enemy, Carlos Andrés Pérez. Not one of these conspiracies, however, has ever been proven.

Hugo Chávez advised those people who were purportedly out to kill him. "Don't even think of it! Not for my sake, but for the sake of Venezuela and what could happen here," he said, ominously alluding to what occurred in Colombia following the murder of the legendary politician Jorge Eliécer Gaitán in 1948: civil war. After the April coup, Miraflores became a real-life bunker and would stay that way for several months: the palace was surrounded with sandbags and barbed wire, there were tanks on every corner, and vehicles were forbidden to enter the premises. At one point later on, it was said that the political police had intercepted a plot to shoot down the presidential plane, with Chávez inside, just as it was about to land. A rocket launcher was produced as evidence, and the president assured the nation that they already had photographs of the suspects and that they were on their trail. After that, however, the public would never hear another word about the case, which simply faded away among so many others. In January 2001, Chávez swore that he had proof of international plots to murder him: "The day may come when I am forced to report specific things, with first and last names, and plans that might well complicate diplomatic relations on this continent."[25] He has not done so to date. As of September 2004, that day of first and last names was still unknown—with the exception, of course, of the oft-mentioned name of George W. Bush.

—

FIDEL CASTRO'S VISIT TO Venezuela came to an end, and on a rainy night at Maiquetía, Chávez said good-bye to the Cuban leader. The farewell was jointly broadcast by all the TV channels, thanks to a presidential order to that effect. For one fleeting moment, the cameras captured the boy from Sabaneta: with a nostalgic look in his eyes, Hugo gazed at the plane and blew kisses as it took off. This effusive, almost theatrical scene surprised and shocked more than a few of his television viewers. In less than a year, on August 13, 2001, the Cuban leader would return to celebrate his seventy-fifth birthday in Venezuela, where Chávez escorted him on an excursion to Canaima National Park, in the southern part of the country. At the Plaza Bolívar in Ciudad Bolívar, he announced to an audience filled with impatient, needy souls, "Let us forget about woes, papers, and requests. Today, just today, let us concentrate on Fidel with heart and soul."

Between 1999 and 2004, the two "revolutionaries" would see each other on at least fifteen occasions. Their closeness inspired some very mixed feelings both in and out of Venezuela. Chávez and Castro speak regularly. In Venezuela, some people claim that the two men have held secret meetings in Cuba, three hours by plane from Caracas, and on the Venezuelan island of La Orchila, where access is restricted to members of the military.

"Hugo Chávez has a direct line to Fidel Castro, and every time something important and unflattering to Chávez hit the news, Chávez would turn to Fidel. It was automatic. At a certain point it became something of a joke to us. Something unpleasant would come to pass, and we knew that we'd either have to start planning Chávez's trip or else get ready for a visit from Fidel," Juan Díaz Castillo, a former presidential pilot, told the newspaper *El Nacional* in early 2003.

Chávez defends Fidel, and Fidel, who denies any involvement in Venezuelan politics, not only defends Chávez but harshly criticizes the opposition. Among the Venezuelan populace, this has resulted in an unprecedented wave of polarization regarding the country's relationship to Cuba. After Chávez himself, of course, Castro is the man most reviled by the extremely radical elements of Chávez's opposition—even more reviled than Chávez's cabinet. This reality came into bold relief when a group of people launched an attack—purportedly spontaneous—against the Cuban Embassy, when it was believed that Chávez had resigned during the 2002 coup. According to Luis Miquilena, "I am one of the people who feel that the preeminence of this relationship has done a bit of damage to Cuba. They have taken things too far. They talk about North American intervention, but the Cuban ambassador is everywhere: on *Aló, Presidente,* when land is being handed over . . . I don't care one way or the other about it, but from the perspective of appearances, it creates problems. With respect to Cuba, a country that has always been well liked in Venezuela, a great deal of antipathy has emerged—so much that when this [Chávez's government] is all over, a lot will have to be done to keep Cuba from being called into question."

In Venezuela, anything related to Cuba is scrutinized. Once the newspapers published screaming headlines stating that Cuba was not paying for the oil it received. In 2003, Energy Minister Rafael Ramírez was forced to admit that, in fact, Havana owed the country some $190 million. For Fidel Castro, Hugo Chávez is the perfect ally who arrived just in the nick of time, when sugar prices took a nosedive and oil prices went through the roof. And the Venezuelan leader, who admires Fidel to such a degree that he himself admits he can't decide whether to call him father or brother, feels proud to come to the aid of the Cuban leader. In Venezuela, many people have been extremely skeptical of the sudden influx of thousands of Cubans whom the Venezuelan government has put to work on literacy campaigns, health care, and athletic training. The Chávez government justifies the program by arguing that Venezuelan professionals do not make themselves available to perform the jobs undertaken by their Cuban counterparts, who set up camp in poor areas with high violence rates. The official government tally places the number of Cuban professionals and technical experts in the country at more than 20,000, which has given rise to speculations regarding the possible "infiltration" of security agents working for Castro's G2. There are those who believe that Castro's agents have come to Venezuela to perform special services for President Chávez, to carry out intelligence-gathering activities for the Venezuelan government, and to help train a pro-Chávez militia. These suspicions have not been confirmed, though there are people who swear they have heard the unmistakable island accent inside the ranks of the military.

Certain sectors of the opposition and some analysts insist that Fidel's authority in Venezuela is overwhelming. According to them, Chávez's actions are simply those of someone following a script that is written, day in and day out, in Havana. What seems evident is that Fidel Castro has been granted an unprecedented level of privilege by the Venezuelan president, who is thrilled when people liken him to the old revolutionary turned dictator who boasts the longest period in power of any Latin American leader. It is no secret that Hugo Chávez admires Castro's feat of staying power, for he himself has admitted his intention to remain in the presidency of Venezuela for a very long time. Perhaps that wish is what led him, on one occasion, to call himself "a second Fidel."

HUGO CHÁVEZ'S FOREIGN POLICY is a pendulum that swings perfectly in time with his leftist tendencies and his repudiation of the U.S. government, as the Venezuelan president is known for establishing either warm relations or icy distances based on ideological questions. His verbal warfare knows no bounds: he proffers flowery praise for his allies and relentless tongue-lashings for those outsiders he believes to be enemies of his Bolivarian Revolution. Ever since he assumed the presidency in 1999, Venezuela has had diplomatic run-ins with almost a dozen other Latin American countries, including Colombia, Bolivia, Chile, Peru, the Dominican Republic, Ecuador, Costa Rica, Panama, and Mexico.

The Venezuelan president has grown fond of rewarding presidents who employ leftist policies with which he agrees, such as Luiz Inacio Lula da Silva of Brazil, Néstor Kirchner of Argentina, and Evo Morales in Bolivia, whom many consider a Chávez disciple. These rewards are generally granted in the form of favorable trade agreements and oil supply treaties, and in some cases the discrimination is abundantly evident: in Nicaragua, Venezuela decided to supply oil only to townships governed by Sandinistas, and the Chávez government very openly endorsed the return of Daniel Ortega to the Nicaraguan presidency—which is exactly what happened in 2006.

There are, in fact, a number of cases in which diplomatic disputes have erupted because of the Venezuelan leader's clear support of certain presidential candidates. Several presidents in the region have protested what they feel is interference in their internal affairs. The most emblematic examples of this are Mexico and Peru, two countries with which Venezuela's bilateral relations are currently in limbo. The case of Mexico came to a head when, at the November 2005 Summit of the Americas, the United States proposed a Free Trade Area of the Americas (FTAA). Former Mexican president Vicente Fox endorsed the proposal, and an angry Chávez declared him "the puppy dog of the empire" for doing so. As a result, both countries recalled their ambassadors and diplomatic relations were frozen. Later on, left-wing presidential candidate Manuel López Obrador's perceived closeness with Chávez was used to frighten the Mexican electorate, and when the Mexican courts proclaimed Felipe Calderón the winner, the Venezuelan government refused to recognize his victory.

Then, in May 2006, Chávez publicly prayed that Alan García, whom he called "corrupt" and "Bush's lap dog," would lose the Peruvian presidential elections. He went on to promise that if García won, he would sever diplomatic relations between the two countries, and because of this, Peru recalled its ambassador from Caracas. Chávez's favorite was the former military officer Ollanta Humala; according to some analysts, Chávez's attitude offended so many Peruvians that it in fact ended up tipping the scales in favor of García. In late 2006, despite the mediation efforts of various countries, Caracas still refused to restore diplomatic relations with Lima.

The oil boom has become such an important tool of Venezuelan diplomacy that a new word, "petrodiplomacy," was coined to define the manner in which Chávez uses his influence in the region. For certain countries that receive oil under favorable terms, Chávez represents relief from economic woes; for others, he is a noisy and irksome neighbor.

In 2005 and the first quarter of 2006, the *ex-comandante* decided, without parliamentary consultation, to allocate at least $4 billion (10 percent of Venezuela's 2006 budget) for foreign expenditures, which would include donations to social welfare projects, solidarity-based investments such as the purchase of Argentinian debt bonds, the construction of bridges, the paving of highways, and the injection of capital to develop projects in foreign countries.[26] As for the program of low-cost heating oil for poor Americans, the Spanish language daily *El Diario/La Prensa* of New York placed on its front page a retouched photo of Chávez dressed up as Santa Claus. In Venezuela, people began to call him Don Regalón (Mr. Gift-Bearer).

The winds have blown in his favor. Ever since he reached the presidency, there have been substantial changes on the chessboard of Latin American politics. Thanks to the failure of neoliberal economic policies and the increasing inequality they brought about, the twenty-first century has kicked off with a spate of left-wing governments in the proverbial "backyard" of the United States. As 2006 came to a close, there was no longer any doubt that Hugo Chávez was the most influential head of state in Latin America.

CHAPTER 15

The Ugly Duckling

Mothers tend to be less than enthusiastic about the romantic fate of their sons. With a healthy Freudian spirit, which varies depending on the case in question, they are wont to bemoan the sentimental injustices that, far too often, are dealt their offspring, who never seem to find that ideal woman they deserve. Elena Frías de Chávez is no exception to this rule. Of her son, she has said, "God can never give a person everything. God has blessed him, God does bless him, but he has had very bad luck with women. There has never been an ideal woman for him."

One can assume that she is referring to the three most stable of the president's acknowledged partners: Nancy Colmenares, his first wife, with whom he had three children; Herma Marksman, his lover of nine years; and his second wife, Marisabel Rodríguez, the mother of his youngest daughter, Rosinés. Aside from them, there is quite a legend about Chávez the seducer and womanizer, a man who some say has quite an insatiable appetite.

There is little information to suggest that Hugo Chávez was a ladies' man in his younger years. His secondary school classmates recall him as a sweet, easygoing kid, not much more. According to one of his female classmates from the early days, his physical appearance was a strike against him: "Hugo was really ugly, so skinny."

Jesús Pérez, the current Venezuelan foreign minister and a friend of Chávez from those days, underscores that "he got around a lot . . . he was charming, not because of his physical appearance, because I don't think he responds to the canons of what might be called a good-looking man. Before, Venezuelan women wanted a man with hair, tall," he says, laughing, and goes on to mention some of the classic soap opera actors of the day: "José Bardina, for example, or Raúl Amundaray."

It is an image that bears little resemblance to the sex symbol he would become, specifically after he rose to fame following the 1992 coup attempt. There may well be more than one melodrama, more than one lustful affair between the postcardlike images we know of his childhood and the myth described by Luis Pineda Castellanos, his security chief in 1998: "My God! The furor that man unleashed was about as conclusive evidence as you could ask for, unbelievable: girls, young, middle-aged, old women, single, married, divorced . . . they all wanted to touch him, see him, stroke him, have his baby."[1]

It is without a doubt an intoxicating experience to become the object of such intense desire overnight. Not even Chávez himself was prepared for it. His upbringing, with respect to women, was characterized by the very straitlaced standards of his mother, Elena.

"At home there were never many girlfriends. I did not accept my sons' girlfriends. If they had them, they had them outside. And still . . . I will accept a woman who is a wife, or with whom [a son of mine] may live, or if they already have a child; in that case, yes, they can come here. But just because they have a little fling, they're going to bring her over here? No, no, no. Not then, and not now." Even after fulfilling these formal requirements, it does not seem easy to earn the approval of the mother of the Chávez Frías boys. And the first wife of the Venezuelan president was not very lucky in this sense.

"That one, I met her before, I don't like to even talk about that," mutters Elena, ending the discussion abruptly.

Nancy Colmenares became Hugo Chávez's first wife when she was twenty-three. She is also the mother of his three eldest children. Curiously, Nancy has managed to live in a strange and difficult kind of anonymity. Some people attribute this to the fact that by the time Chávez became a public figure, their relationship was already somewhat nonexistent, or at least had deteriorated significantly. Others believe that this anonymity is attributable to Nancy's personal style, for she is known as a modest, reserved woman. There are others still who feel that she is a woman who started her life over, who shares her life with another man now, and as such has made a conscious effort to keep away from the more dramatic parts of this story. Even today, not much is known about her. Apparently among those who know her she is *la negra*—the black lady. In Venezuela almost every family has a *negro* or a *negra*—terms that, despite their remotely racist origins, are widely accepted in Latin America as expressions of endearment and affection.

One incontrovertible fact is that Nancy does not give interviews. The photographs of her that have circulated in the media are few and far between. The image of her that lingers in many people's minds is one that dates back to 1992, when she was the overwrought wife going to jail to visit her husband, after he was imprisoned for his attempt to overthrow the government. Those who know her or knew her in some way—even those who have since distanced themselves from Chávez and joined the opposition—speak well of her. Nedo Paniz is a good example: "I know for a fact that at one point they tried to persuade her to make it seem that Chávez beat her. Nancy was not willing to do that, which says a lot about her," he said, referring to a political group that was known for its efforts to demonize Chávez during his presidential campaign.

All those who were close to the couple say the same thing when it comes to Nancy's qualities as a human being. A good friend of Nancy's recalls the wedding: "It was a very simple wedding. *La negra* was a very simple woman, a very good person. Just like him, very humble. . . . She didn't go to school. She was the kind of woman who stayed at home." Carmen Tirado seconds this opinion, saying that Nancy was "a very nice girl, very humble, a great woman." Hugo and Nancy became husband and wife in 1977. They had a daughter, Rosa Virginia. Next came María Gabriela and then Hugo Rafael, known as Huguito. During those years, the official reports on his itineraries, political and geographical, never mention his wife and children. Nancy and the family remained in the shadows, drawing little attention to themselves. And Chávez, nowadays so inclined to talk about his family in public, has almost never spoken of that early family experience.

Francisco Arias, the number two conspirator of the 1992 plot, says he thinks that "Nancy was a woman who was a lot like all the other *llanera* women, the kind that belong to their husbands, they got married, and they cook the food, they keep things together, take care of him, take care of their kids—a very elemental kind of thing, you know? But I think that he loved Nancy in all the right ways, and that he respected her, too." Despite all this, Arias makes a point of mentioning a quality that Hugo possessed even back in those days, one that quickly became the stuff of legend: "He had a good relationship with Nancy, but since he has a way of falling for women easily . . ." From very early on, there were rumors regarding Hugo Chávez's womanizing ways. According to his friend at the time Jesús Urdaneta, "He had started to separate from Nancy when he was a captain— meaning, from the first half of the 1980s. He had problems with her. 'Try to keep your home together,' I told him, but we never talked more about it after that. Later on at some point he mentioned they were separating. . . . Then everything that happened happened, and Nancy would come and visit him in jail. She was a marvelous woman, very humble, very noble, simple, hardworking. She is in Barinas. I think she eventually married her first boyfriend."

THE DYNAMICS OF THE military lifestyle made certain things easier for Hugo Chávez. It was in this environment that he met Herma Marksman, with whom he was romantically attached for almost a decade. It began in 1984, in Caracas, by chance. A historian and the divorced mother of two children, Herma was trying to get herself a job transfer to Caracas. When she met Chávez, she was living temporarily in a house where her sister Cristina lived. The owner of the apartment, Elizabeth Sánchez, knew Hugo Chávez. A chance encounter and that mysterious thing called "chemistry" took care of everything else. By September 1984, five months after they first met, they were lovers.

"When I first met him," Herma recalls, "he had a reputation for being a womanizer. Around then he was going out with someone, a psychologist, I think. . . . I don't know if he kept on womanizing during those years, when he was with me. I don't think so. Although he is a very affectionate man, always tossing out compliments." Five months after they met, "he appeared with flowers" on her birthday. His sincerity was very disarming: right away he told her how much he liked her, and then he went on to explain his situation.

"He never deceived me—he did that later, when he was in jail. From the very first moment, when he wanted our relationship to become more serious, he was very clear with me—and now I'm not going to say that he's a slime, a degenerate," says Marksman, now an open adversary of her former lover's governing style.

Herma also comes from a humble family. Her father had been quite closely linked to social causes, particularly the workers' struggle in the region of Guayana. He was a man of nationalist devotions and Bolivarian passions. Because of this, the relationship between Marksman and Chávez grew deeper on other levels as well. Marksman soon found herself joining Chávez in his conspiratorial pursuits. From the very start, Chávez told her that he was married and that he was plotting to overthrow the government. He would later apologize to her, however, for having had her secretly followed and investigated. He had had to take care of himself, he must have said. It was no easy task: between war and love, he was already leading more than a double life.

During this period, at least in the romantic and marital sense, Hugo Chávez proved that he was cut from more or less the same cloth as many Venezuelan men of his day and age. His lifestyle, moreover, was quite typical of men in the military. He operated on two fronts: there were "headquarters" and a "branch office." The distances probably helped. The two women in his life lived in different cities, and, at least during the early years, Chávez managed to make sure that neither of his two houses caught on fire. He saw Herma frequently, and together they created a kind of everyday life, to the extent that this was possible. She still remembers Chávez as a loving, affectionate man: "He would write such pretty things for me, and I remember him as the man who brought me chocolates, who would come by to serenade me, who would sing me *rancheras;* the man who always remembered my birthday, the man who brought me flowers." Herma had just come out of a very traumatic divorce and at the time was not especially keen on formalizing their relationship in any way. Even so, their life as a couple grew more and more stable and solid and was filled with all the rituals that mark the life of a couple.

"I don't think he is such a *machista,*" says Herma. "But he is jealous. My mother always told me to be careful because he was jealous. And he would write to me and say so himself."

Her whole family knew him. "Yes, my mother, my children always knew, I felt I had to be honest with them about these things." And she was honest with them not only about the relationship but about the conspiracy, though some of them didn't take it very seriously.

"My daughter says she never thought they would actually pull off the uprising." Despite the fact that Herma's mother was never very thrilled that her daughter's boyfriend was a married military officer, her house in the city of Valencia, some two hours from Caracas, occasionally served as a meeting place for the conspirators. In fact, the last time Hugo Chávez and Francisco Arias saw each other before the 1992 insurrection was on her spacious terrace.

Herma's sister, Cristina Marksman, who also supported Hugo in the coup, became so close to her sister's boyfriend that he called her *hermana* (sister). He also had another connection to her: superstitious, as many people say he is, Chávez would ask her to predict his future.

"My sister would read his palm, and sometimes she got things right. He would ask her to read his cards, he liked that a lot. He really believed the things she said." He would ask Cristina, who died some years later, to banish the bad spirits "because he is a tormented man," as Herma puts it, underscoring another trait of her former lover. "He could be in one room, very bothered by something, and then if you came by for a visit, he would come out as if nothing at all was on his mind. He had that ability to change his expression. He could be laughing right now and then turn around to face someone else, and start crying . . . but with feeling! Yes, I believe he really is an excellent actor," Herma remarks.

The relationship went on without any major hitches until the end of the 1980s. Herma describes what happened: "In 1988, he made the decision that we had to formalize our relationship. . . . One day he called me and said, 'Herma, have you ever thought about the possibility of us getting married? I want to marry you, would you marry me?' And I said to him, 'My friend, you have to get a divorce first if you want to marry me.' Hugo assured me, 'If you say yes, I will get a divorce so that we can get married.' " As often happens in life and soap operas, obstacles began to pop up. Herma knows that Hugo tried: that he went to Barinas, talked to Nancy, and tried to leave her. She also knows that the Chávez family was against it. In the end, the marriage plans never made it past the first step: Hugo's divorce. Slowly, their relationship waned: "I think it was in March of 1989 that he came to me and said his children were still small," Herma remarks. With that comment, the chapter of the impossible wedding ended.

In 1990, Herma recalls, Chávez proposed that they have a child together. "He began to say that we needed to have a child. 'But why should we have a child with this hectic life we have? At this stage?' And he replied, 'I just feel that everything is happening so fast, that everything is on top of us all of a sudden. And this will be like a bond between us, a link. We couldn't get married, but our child will keep us together.' "[2] Herma says that during 1991, they tried to have a baby, and she managed to get pregnant but had a miscarriage during the most stressful days leading up the conspiracy. That, Herma thinks, is the reason she lost the baby.

In all likelihood, Herma Marksman would never have guessed that the failed coup would turn out to be a success—a personal success, a leap to fame for the person who was, as they say, the man of her life. From inside the jail, her lover became a public figure. And much more. "There were people who would go there to touch him, to see if he was real . . . that was how the myth was born, and he believed it." During his time in prison, rumors circulated about his affairs with other women, a situation that only escalated when Chávez was released. In the words of one of his companions from those days, "He was like that, he was very promiscuous with women. With the aura and the fame, that quality of his only grew more pronounced." The list of women who had apparently enjoyed intimate relations with him grew longer and longer. He would later call upon some of them to work in his administration.

Marksman endured all of this with patience, but it was not easy. Angela Zago, however, a journalist who became a close friend of both Hugo and Herma during those years, suggests why. "The first serious separation happened because, while he was still in prison, he was once asked on a radio show about his wife, Nancy. 'How did she manage when you [and your co-conspirators] were plotting [the coup]?' His response was 'If it had not been for my wife and everything she did, and the support she gave me, I don't know how I would have put the movement together.' Well, Herma didn't just up and die that day, by coincidence. She risked her home and her children, everything, allowing military officers who were conspiring against the government into her home. For years, she was the one who safeguarded their papers, she was the one who had the plan for the 1992 uprising. She risked her life, her economic stability, her social stability, her personal stability, all for him."

It is probable that this was the detonating factor, but there were plenty of other things bubbling beneath the surface as well. Herma herself has admitted how uncomfortable she was with Hugo's popularity and the ensuing media frenzy, neither of which showed any signs of abating. It was not just a political problem: it had become something that affected her personally, as well. Perhaps that was when she began to feel that Hugo Chávez had started to slip away from her. She recalls, in particular, one very tense discussion between them at the jail. " 'Do you realize what this is like?' she said to him. 'I'm out here, but I'm as trapped as you are, the only difference being that you are in there safe and sound, but I'm trapped out here on the street, because they follow me, they take photographs of me, they even put my children at risk, and the minimum I should be able to expect from you is fidelity, loyalty.' "

Herma left Chávez in June 1993, while he was still in prison. She simply could not bear their relationship any longer—she didn't like what was going on inside the prison, in both the political and the personal sense. It seemed that Hugo had slowly turned into someone else, someone she no longer knew. According to her, he turned into the "Chávez on the pedestal. I always said, 'What a shame things had to happen the way they did.' He was my ideal companion, and maybe that's why I've never had another relationship since him. The man I lived with is dead. Yes, I am a widow. And I hold on to my memories. As for me, that thing out there, I don't know who he is. He has no connection whatsoever to me, or to the man with whom I shared so much. . . . I feel that he betrayed the dream that the two of us tried to build for years. He threw everything out the window."

They have not seen each other since then. And since he became president, they have spoken on only one occasion, in 1999, when he called her to offer his condolences after her mother died.

Of that intense relationship, there remains something of a "bequest" that Herma Marksman, history professor, has been meticulous about preserving, as if she knew that one day it might be of interest to the general public. The cache includes diaries that young Hugo Chávez kept while at the military academy, some letters he wrote to her, her grandmother, and her family, other letters that he received from them, several photographs, and the first lock of hair that his grandmother Mamá Inés clipped from his head back in Sabaneta.

Chávez has never made any explicit or public statement regarding Marksman or their relationship. Herma, on the other hand, began to speak in public in 2002, when a journalist friend convinced her to participate in a television program commemorating the ten-year anniversary of the 1992 coup attempt. She has appeared on numerous radio and TV programs and has cooperated with journalists and researchers. Laughing at herself a bit, she recalls one on-air incident: "One day, a woman called in to one of those call-in radio shows and asked me, 'How can it be that you, being such an accomplished woman, could have gotten into bed with the devil?' And I said to her, 'Well, the heart has its reasons that reason cannot understand.' "

IT WASN'T UNTIL after he was released from jail and began to live his new and very public existence, that Hugo Chávez's love life took off. Between 1994 and 1997, when he was divorcing Nancy, until Marisabel Rodríguez entered his life much later on, there was a period that might best be summed up by a song that could easily have served as background music to his life and times: "Livin' la Vida Loca."

Nedo Paniz, who is now affiliated with one of the most radical sectors of the opposition, gave Chávez a place to live after he was released from jail. "Nancy never came to visit him. Just the children. We really looked after Huguito and the girls. They were a very fractured family unit, no question. Sometimes we brought the girls or Huguito on the trips we made." By the time he got his divorce, Paniz says, Chávez was already involved romantically with a journalist. Their relationship had been rumored since he had been in jail. The affair was short-lived, and conflicts erupted. Nedo Paniz recounts, "One of his bodyguards told me something that made my hair stand on end. Chávez ordered them to throw her out of the car when they were in the middle of some road on Margarita [Island]. And they did." A friend of the journalist confirms the incident, adding that it had been prompted by a private dispute between the two.

As far as Luis Pineda Castellanos is concerned, this woman was one in an almost endless list of women who had some kind of intimate relationship with Chávez during those years. The group includes women who have held positions in the Chávez administration. Many of them have repeatedly denied any relationship with Chávez, whereas others among them simply refuse to discuss the topic or say nothing.

Describing their days as they crisscrossed Venezuela promoting and stumping for Chávez, Luis Pineda tells of an effervescent playboy at the top of his game who carried a first-aid kit everywhere he went, "with merthiolate and Band-Aids, because the girls would scratch Chávez's hands at the rallies." According to Pineda, women went wild over Chávez. And he was not one to spurn the lustful impulses he inspired.

"He loved all of them. Really, I never was able to figure out what his ideal type was," says Pineda.

In every town or village they passed through, there was always some woman—sometimes more than one—who wanted to spend the night with Chávez. According to Pineda, they even had a selection method worked out between them. "Every time, as we would step up to the platform, he would survey the female talent, and there were always a few stunners, you could always pick them out, so in the middle of an event he would look at me and indicate in one direction, he would make a little gesture with his mouth, and I would make my way over to the lady in question, the pick of the evening, until I finally got over to her and he would nod his head."[3] Later that same evening, Pineda would discreetly arrange the encounter, and he would remain on alert back at the hotel to make sure that the women who had not been selected that evening, or some spontaneous admirer, would not try to surprise the *comandante* in the middle of the night.

There are plenty of other stories like this one, and Pineda seems unconcerned about maintaining any kind of decorum on behalf of his old friend. In fact, he admits that when he finally realized that it would be impossible to control his friend's romantic merry-go-round, "I went out and bought a sofa bed and stuck it in the office we used as our campaign headquarters. . . . And I told Hugo that this was his new method for receiving lady friends." The system would come in handy sometime later, when Chávez and Marisabel Rodríguez began to see each other seriously, for it served as a kind of security routine that they baptized the "anti-Marisabel" and kept him from being discovered with his hands in the proverbial cookie jar. During this period, however, one woman seems to have touched the heart of Hugo Chávez in a deeper sense. A singer of folkloric music, she was not very well known, at least not in Caracas. Her nom de guerre was Aguamiel, and her true identity remains a secret, though some say she was married.

"She must have been twenty-seven, twenty-eight, about fourteen years younger than him," Pineda recalls. "She was very pale, with brown hair, very stylish and discreet. Once he invited her to El Castillo de la Fantasía in San Cristóbal [a love motel], but she didn't show up." Not much more is known about her, but various people concur that Chávez fell deeply in love with this woman.

"The only time I ever saw Hugo cry was when he told me about her, in Gran Sabana," says Nedo Paniz. Pineda similarly recalls how Chávez once broke down in tears over Aguamiel in his presence.

"He got tied down because Marisabel got pregnant and he had to marry her because he was running for president . . . he was in love with the girl, a singer and a cousin of a friend of ours, a general." Nevertheless, no one can swear this is true. What is true is that Hugo Chávez was already a legend by the time his love story with Marisabel began.

MARISABEL RODRÍGUEZ FIRST SAW Hugo Chávez up close at a plaza in Carora, a city that sizzled beneath the relentless sun in the central-west region of Venezuela. By that time she had fallen under the spell of this new leader, who had already attempted to seize power as an armed insurgent and who invoked Bolívar and traveled the country preaching his new message. That day, amid the crowds of people waiting to see him, with her tiny son in her arms, Marisabel managed to make it over to Chávez and passed him a short note she had written: "*Comandante,* our homeland deserves everything, without reservations, and I am with you in heart and soul. When you need me for your struggle, please call me."[4] She included her name and telephone number at the end. But this message never found its way to Hugo Chávez.

They met for the first time in January 1996. As she recalls it, the encounter consisted of a handshake and a brief exchange of words, after a radio announcer in the city of Barquisimeto introduced them. That was their first direct contact, and it was followed by messages, greetings, and more telephone calls. Marisabel maintains that Chávez's intelligence was what captivated her, that he was a great strategist in the game of courtship. Their incipient relationship became more official on January 14, 1997, the day of the Divine Shepherdess, the patroness of the region. According to Marisabel, that was the day they became a couple. During an interview the couple granted in 1998,[5] a few mischievous sparks flew through the air when they reminisced about that evening. It was something of an ambiguous moment, a few smiles and a meaningful pause, giving the impression that Hugo and Marisabel, caught in the throes of passion, had sex that night. The surrender, it seems, took place inside an automobile and left Marisabel pregnant on their first night together. In a later interview, Marisabel neither confirmed nor denied anything beyond the fact that the pregnancy was indeed unexpected: "It happened our first time together, we were completely innocent and without any kind of preparation, neither he nor I was at all promiscuous."[6]

The wedding of Hugo Chávez and Marisabel Rodríguez, at Christmastime in 1997, when their daughter was two months old, would be remembered for the very recent birth of their baby. While a pregnancy in the middle of a love story is certainly momentous, a pregnancy in the middle of a presidential campaign can be transcendental. The journalist Angela Zago, close to Chávez and a good friend of Herma at the time, has her own theory. "I even said to him, 'Come on, what is that? She's a thirty-six-year-old woman.' If she slept with him, it was because she wanted it. We're not talking about a man who slept with a young girl and got her pregnant. But then people

began to gossip, saying that it was a marriage of political convenience." There are those who believe that the matter went beyond
questions of morality or of having to protect the image of a potential
president by presenting him as a responsible father, a family man.
Marisabel, some say, was a very big publicity boost.

She was an enterprising, modern, self-made woman. She also had
several other attractive qualities that could help dispel the aggressive
image the opposition had painted of Chávez: she was young, white,
blue-eyed, blond. She was aware of this proposition, and consciously
lent herself to it: "I was there to lower my husband's rejection rate in
the polls, and to win over a segment of the population that was totally unwilling [to support him]."[7]

The strategy was an incredible success. Marisabel soon became an
independent figure, a trademark in her own right with a political profile all her own. Months after the presidential elections, she threw her
hat into the ring as a candidate in the popular election for the representatives of the Constituent Assembly, and won. She had forever
changed the country's perception of the role of first lady. She wasn't
content to just be Mrs. Chávez, the president's wife.

Beyond this image, however, family life in the Chávez-Rodríguez
household was not easy. Marisabel did not have the best relationship
with her mother-in-law. The first lady herself described it: "She was
never a bonbon with me, you know, sweet. But she also never did anything to me that I couldn't bear, that any other mother-in-law would
do to any daughter-in-law. . . . Obviously, from the beginning she
never cared for me, and maybe it would have been better if she had
interacted more with me, to get to know me better."[8] Angela Zago,
unconcerned with such considerations, is a bit more specific when
she describes the day Hugo won the election. Everyone had gone over
to Venevisión, the channel owned by Gustavo Cisneros, where Hugo
and Marisabel were participating in a TV program. "Elena sat down
next to me," says Zago, "and when she heard what Marisabel was saying, she said to me, 'She's a phony, she's real two-faced.' She never
liked Marisabel."

Luis Miquilena, who let Chávez stay in his apartment until he married Marisabel, doesn't believe that it was a marriage of convenience.

"No. She was a good girl, a pretty girl, and he was divorced. He thought it would be a good idea to try her out, but things didn't go his way." And with respect to family unpleasantness, far more vexing than her mother-in-law's frostiness were Chávez's three children and her problems with them. According to Luis Miquilena, "That marriage was a really troubled one, very problematic from the very beginning. . . . His children were the problem, they had conflicts with her, and he is a very good father to his first wife's children. Those kids and Marisabel never saw eye to eye, and that was the beginning of some very serious differences. And those differences only grew deeper and, well, you know how those things are." On several occasions Miquilena served as a mediator between the two when they would fight: "Our friendship ran so deep that whenever he had some kind of domestic problem, I would be the first to know about it, after him and his wife. And sometimes we would air it among the three of us. That was the kind of relationship we had, Hugo would tell me about his problems with Marisabel, and then I would go and look for Chirinos [Chávez's friend and onetime psychiatrist]."

The most difficult moment probably came the night that, according to Pineda Castellanos, Hugo came home to the building where they lived, in a housing complex in southeast Caracas, and found his son, Huguito, fourteen at the time, sobbing. Marisabel had thrown him out of the apartment. The situation was so difficult that, shortly before Hugo became president, his three oldest children had to be moved to an apartment that one of his supporters in the Jewish community lent him. The day after his electoral victory, he moved to La Viñeta, an official residence inside Fort Tiuna, but his daughters Rosa Virginia and María Gabriela "did not go because Marisabel didn't want them there."

Nedo Paniz is more categorical: "Marisabel was very difficult. Full of problems. Dealing with her was a real drama. . . . Chávez had a

very complicated relationship with her. It was always very strained."
The majority of the time he spent with them was during the campaign. He remembers one occasion when Marisabel insisted on joining them on the road, bringing along their newborn baby and a nanny. She seems to have had a way of turning their plans upside down in the space of a few seconds. Once in a plane, as they were taxiing down the runway for takeoff, she suddenly decided that the plane had to be stopped, because she had a feeling that it was going to crash and that they would all die. She also had a recurring fear that Chávez would be assassinated. She developed a reputation for being insecure and paranoid, an image that has stayed with her to this day. Bodyguards did not like looking after her, privately calling her "Lalo," shorthand for *la loca*—the crazy lady.

Although she never said as much, clearly there was something else she was afraid of: that Chávez would get involved with another woman. Many people agree that Marisabel was an extremely jealous wife, forever trying to keep tabs on the president—making sure she knew where he was, what he was doing, and who he was with at all times. And people say she caught him by surprise on more than one occasion. "Once Chávez was confirmed as president-elect, he went off on a tour of Europe. During a stop in Madrid, Marisabel suddenly turned up and caught him in the middle of the act, with the daughter of some small-time boss in the revolutionary government . . . a major scene broke out on account of that," Pineda Castellanos recalls.[9] All of this, however, remains in the murky terrain of speculation. Nothing ever escalated to the point of becoming a public scandal.

Eventually, Marisabel toned down her high profile. As time went by she seemed increasingly less like her old self and more like Chávez's wife. It is common knowledge that many people within Chávez's inner circle were not fond of her and began pushing her away from the political sphere, away from any kind of role in the public eye. She, on the other hand, suggests an explanation for this: "I noticed, among many of the people who were close to my husband, a hunger and a desire for power, for money. My mistake—and perhaps this was not very intelligent of me—was that I confronted them. And I did this very early on, without any shield or protection for myself. Immediately, they all turned into my enemies."[10] Another theory maintains that Chávez himself was the one who decided that his wife's high profile was not good for the revolution and that he pressured her to move out of the limelight. In 1999, amid ambiguous claims regarding personal health and conflicts with some sector of the pro-Chávez party, Marisabel resigned from the National Constituent Assembly. Even so, after the constitutional reform process was over, the polls continued to rate her the second most popular figure in the country, right after her husband. Political offers poured in from every direction. There was even a group of people who, based on the polls, wanted to present her as the candidate for governor of the state of Miranda in the 2000 elections, but her husband, who was also the head of his political party, deemed it inconvenient and chose to present another candidate, who went on to lose the election.

There are also those who say that the couple had an air of the Peróns about them, which generated a certain degree of alarm. At one point, when Marisabel updated her appearance, people began to perceive a symbolic likeness to the Argentine heroine: for many people, one particular variation in her hairstyle seemed to reproduce the image of Eva Perón. And whether or not this dynamic actually existed, the relationship between Hugo and Marisabel was rocky at best. In January 2001, Marisabel emerged from the low profile she had been maintaining by granting an interview to the newspaper *El Nacional,* which infuriated Chávez. The interview quoted her as criticizing the parliament ("the National Assembly is wasting its time")[11] and featured a photograph of her in shorts, thirty pounds lighter, during a spinning session at La Casona with her personal trainer. The following day, she had been planning to join her husband on a trip to Puerto Rico, but as she boarded the plane Chávez had her removed and condemned her to a long period of silence. At that point she vanished from the headlines and did not reappear until more than a year later, on the day of the coup against Chávez, April 11, 2002.

By 2002 the situation must have been intolerable, given the judicial order issued on February 27, which granted her permission to abandon the official residence with her two children, Raúl (from an earlier relationship with a tennis instructor) and Rosinés, eleven and four years old, respectively. Though at first her departure was attributed to the constant presence of opposition protesters outside La Casona, she later stated, "I could not continue to subject my children to the stress of living in a place we had already fled three times before, practically with a bag of clothes slung over our shoulders. That is no kind of life for anyone." Most people viewed that step as confirmation of the rampant rumors regarding an imminent separation. Marisabel returned to live in Barquisimeto.

In any event, the relationship seemed to keep going, ups and downs notwithstanding, as Marisabel frequently turned up in Caracas, even though she never really warmed up to the capital city. It was there that the April 11 coup caught her by surprise. That night, before General Lucas Rincón publicly announced Chávez's resignation, she boarded a plane bound for Barquisimeto in the middle of a military operation. Nobody in the government or Chávez's party seemed terribly concerned about her fate. During those chaotic and confusing days, she nonetheless demonstrated the loyalty that her husband clearly needed from her. On April 13, via CNN, Marisabel stated, "My husband has not resigned and is being held incommunicado, and his life is in danger." There she was, the first lady of Venezuela, confirming for all the world that a coup d'état had indeed taken place. Chávez's return to power, however, would not signify a return to stability for the couple.

Two months later, in an interview granted to the newspaper *El Universal* and held at La Casona, Marisabel expressed herself in no uncertain terms:

> I said it two years ago, that I would never carry on my shoulders the role of a wife of convenience, a wife of appearances. I prayed to God that this moment would never come, because

nobody wants their family to come apart, especially someone who believes that it is the cell of society and its vital impulse. But I think that by now, it is no secret to anyone that the situation of the president and the first lady is now in a process of separation that has gone from personal to legal, and it is time to let the country know. I imagine everyone was expecting this. It is no surprise to anyone. Now we just have to wait for the president to officially initiate the legal proceedings.[12]

During this interview, she also denied the rumor spread by the opposition that her husband had abused her physically:

"No, there has been no act of violence in any way." She did, however, qualify this statement by saying, "Two years ago I stated that, for me, perhaps because I am hypersensitive, there are other kinds of violence, like, for example, when you are not listened to."[13]

Given the general polarization and confusion that were wrought by the events of April, one question posed by the journalist seemed especially pertinent: "Are you also getting a divorce from the Bolivarian Revolution?"

Marisabel's response was equally categorical, and it was every bit a definition of her personality and her perspective of the entire process that she had lived through. "Where have you ever heard that I am married to the Bolivarian Revolution? I am married to the leader of the Bolivarian Revolution. When I made my commitment to Hugo, I did so with a normal man, with the father of a daughter, and everything else is [a series of] circumstances that have occurred around us."[14]

The next day, her confessor, Jesús Gazo, a Jesuit priest, could not keep from expressing his opinion and publicly sided with Hugo Chávez, offering an ideologized explanation for their separation: "Marisabel could not accept that Hugo Chávez is married to his countrymen. . . . She did not understand the political process, she did not understand the revolution, she did not understand what he could do

THE UGLY DUCKLING | 243

with the immense potential he had."[15] That last sentence would re-main in the air for posterity, like a bit of unfinished, tricky, difficult business. The priest, who saw them regularly, also felt that "they did not know each other, and they were both unable to accept certain things about each other's personality. They have very different charac-ters, different expectations, different life plans. That is the essence of their problems, problems that existed before they moved into La Casona and that have nothing to do with the current political situa-tion. I have spoken with both of them before, to try to see if they might be able to forgive each other for many things."

A month went by before Marisabel appeared in public again, and when she did, it was to participate in an evangelical music concert entitled "Sana Nuestra Tierra" (Heal Our Land), the purpose of which was to pray and intercede before God on behalf of the coun-try and its political leaders. Toward the end of the year, during the turmoil of the national strike between December 2002 and January 2003, as the country reeled from the impact of almost twenty thou-sand oil workers who had gone out on strike, the first lady made a brief appearance in the media, surrounded by her children. The message she sent over the television airwaves was terse: "President: Listen to your people." The government resisted the sentimental message of the former first lady and crushed the opposition's new effort to undermine it. This may well have been the incident that de-finitively buried Marisabel as a public persona. After that, nothing more was heard from her.

In the middle of 2003, Marisabel refused to be interviewed, saying, "I don't want to know anything about that man. I cannot work the miracle of extricating myself from the life of the man. I do not want to make any comment, neither positive nor negative. I do not want to have anything to do with his life." The courts would soon grant this wish, as their divorce became final in January 2004.

——

THE WOMEN WHO HAVE stood at Chávez's side at different points in his life are certainly quite different from one another, but one might also venture to say that the man himself has also transformed over time. The Chávezes who were with each of those women were very different men. After his second divorce, Chávez's love life seemed to slip beneath the mysterious cloak of power. There has been no dearth of easy jokes, hallway gossip, and wild speculations. It was rumored that he had a twenty-three-year-old girlfriend, the daughter of a good friend and a general; that he had a fling with a foreign correspondent; even that he was going to marry a former Venezuelan beauty queen. Chávez seemed quite amused by this last story, though he very flatly denied it.

"How do they come up with these things? Me, get married? . . . My own mother actually called me up to ask me how I could get married and not invite her. Well, I am here to make it clear that it is completely untrue." Chávez later promised that he would not celebrate his third nuptials until 2021 at the earliest, the year he vows to retire from political life. In the meantime, the sentimental life of the Venezuelan president remains an enigma.

The only foreseeable change in this vein is related to his image, and his family—specifically, his two oldest daughters, with whom he often appears in public. Ever since 2003, the private universe of Hugo Chávez has became a symbol and reflection of the myth that has been built around him, revolving around the notion that his one true love is the Venezuelan nation. From that point on, it seems, his private life became the stuff of mystery, his intimacy practically a state secret.

Now, more than ever, it seems that his mother's declaration has managed to turn this entire saga into a *bolero*: "He has had very bad luck with women. His perfect woman has not appeared."

If that is in fact the case, one might argue that more than a few women could reply by saying that plenty of women have had equally bad luck with him. Perhaps it is part of a process that happens to many people. Love affairs, at least as we conceive of them, are never easy to navigate. Perhaps, in this case, it has something to do with the manner in which Hugo Chávez perceives himself—or others. On two separate occasions when Hugo Chávez found himself mired in depression, both Nedo Paniz and Herma Marksman recall how he used the exact same words when lamenting his romantic miscalculations: "I destroy everything I touch."

CHAPTER 16

La Chavera

THE VENEZUELANS WHO FOUND THEMSELVES SITTING IN FRONT OF the television that evening, idly watching a soap opera or waiting for the ten o'clock news, were suddenly jolted out of their reverie by a sudden change of protagonist and programming. Yet again, President Hugo Chávez had interrupted the television broadcast of the hour so that the Venezuelan people might see him, hear him, feel his presence. The date: July 28, 2004. That evening, he had a very important message for the nation: it was his fiftieth birthday. And he wanted everyone to know about it.

The camera focused on the supreme leader of the Bolivarian Revolution, dressed in black denims, tennis sneakers, and a red shirt, sitting on a pristine white fence. Perched atop that slender fence with a book in his hands, Chávez appeared rather uncomfortable as he struggled to keep his balance. What was this about? At first, his perplexed viewers didn't have the slightest idea. What did he want now? With the intonations of a television announcer, the head of state solemnly read the first paragraph of *One Hundred Years of Solitude*. You see, he explained to his nation, he had just received the novel as a gift. This was his way of announcing, loud and clear, "Venezuela, it's my birthday today! And, coming up next, you can forget about the soap opera you were watching."

Up next was a personal evaluation of half a century on earth, another kind of soap opera entirely.

In the background, a group of magnificent stallions promenaded through the fields, as if to prove that this was not some studio in the back lot of Venezolana de Televisión—this was a real-life hacienda. The head of state was just a few days away from the country's evaluation of his performance as president of the Republic. The polls were on his side, but he still had no way of knowing for sure whether or not this would be his last birthday in power. That evening, Hugo Chávez looked visibly emotional, and even slightly nervous. Still, he had full command of the scene and gazed directly into the camera as he stepped down from the fence and walked over to a group of people standing in front of a large house. Equally emotional and jittery, the Chávez Frías family, convened for an extraordinary session, awaited the president.

In the foreground, quite appropriately, stood his parents, Hugo de los Reyes Chávez and Elena Frías de Chávez. Married for fifty-two years and with six grown sons, they seemed on top of the world there on television, but in the past they had had to weather many an economic crisis as an emotional crisis or two, which had been a cause of concern for their son Hugo during his years at the military academy. His father, seventy-two years old, had first earned a living as a rural schoolteacher in the 1950s. That was how he had met Elena, in the tiny village of San Hipólito.

"He was nineteen years old, I was sixteen. A girl," recalls Elena, who was born and bred in San Hipólito and raised by her grandmother, a very typical custom in the rural Venezuela of those years. Elena, by all accounts a peasant girl who dreamed of going to school one day, says, "I wanted to be a professional, I liked education a lot, probably because that was what I saw in San Hipólito. . . . I saw the school, the teacher, and the idea began to take root in my mind that I wanted to be a teacher because the teacher was so well dressed, so pretty, and so I said, 'When I start studying, I want to be a teacher so I can get dressed up.' " But she was never able to study because she started having children in rapid succession, one after the other, seven in all: Adán, Hugo, Narciso, Argenis, Aníbal, and Adelis, and Enzo, who died at six months.

During their first years as a married couple, and despite the family's meager economy, all of Elena's time and energy were dedicated to caring for her little boys, though her mother-in-law, Rosa Chávez, did help out by taking in and raising her two eldest, Adán and Hugo. According to two family friends, after they had moved to the city of Barinas so that her sons could go to secondary school, she was finally able to work and held a job purchasing food and supplies for the public school, though this information does not appear anywhere in Elena's official résumé.

In the year 2004, when a sitting room was dedicated to the educators of Barinas, some local schoolteachers were shocked to see Elena Frías de Chávez's name on the list of "illustrious educators." Her official résumé describes her as a retired teacher with twenty-five years of experience. She herself has said that occasionally she helped out at school, filling in for absent teachers.

"I was in adult education. I didn't really like working with children. I would go with the group where my husband was the director. I always went, at least, to cover someone on three-month maternity leave, or on vacation. . . . And that was extra money coming in," states the president's mother in her new home for the past six years— the Barinas state governor's residence.

Her husband, Hugo de los Reyes, had been able to advance professionally with the courses offered by the education ministry and for twenty years was a teacher at the Julián Pino school, the only one in Sabaneta. Some of his former students remember him as a marvelous teacher, "a very serious, responsible person, with a great deal of discipline, always very quick to give someone a rap on the head with his knuckles as punishment for bad behavior. He was strict, though never arbitrary. . . . At home, it was the father who imposed the discipline, the studies, the concern for doing better, the need to move to Barinas."

In addition to and independent of his work at the Julián Pino school, Hugo de los Reyes had spent twenty-two years as an activist for the Christian Democrat party, COPEI, and was eventually named director of education for the state of Barinas during the administration of Luis Herrera Campins (1979–84). That, however, was as far as his political aspirations went, or so it seemed. After thirty years of work, he had finally retired, to devote himself to his small farm, La Chavera, on the outskirts of Barinas, when his son changed the course of his—and Elena's—life by convincing him that he had a chance to become the supreme authority of his native state if he so desired. And so, riding high on his son's popularity and motivated by his insistence, Hugo de los Reyes threw himself into a campaign to become governor of Barinas state on the Fifth Republic Movement ticket. And one month before Hugo Chávez became president, his father won the governorship of Barinas state with a three-thousand-vote victory over his rival.

BARINAS IS A CITY of suffocating heat and charms that are mostly found in the haciendas and landscapes that surround it. Aside from the Ezequiel Zamora University of Los Llanos and a couple of McDonald's, almost every street corner seems trapped in the early 1970s. The same is true of the city's two spiffiest hotels, which presumably rate three stars each. It is a city that seems to look inward, focusing on itself, its music, its food, and the rhythms of its residents, who wake up early and vanish when the midday sun emerges. The Chávez family, known as "the royal family" among locals, is an inescapable topic here. It is not unusual to hear the inhabitants of Barinas say things like "The person in charge at the governor's house is not Maestro Chávez, it's Elena." In response, the governor's wife, accustomed as she is to running the show at home, says with a smile, "I wouldn't exactly call that a lie."

The president's mother, who is the head of the local chapter of the Children's Foundation, is a woman from the countryside: she is friendly and expressive and has a strong character. She also says that her son takes after her in many ways. "His character is a lot like mine. He is direct, when he doesn't like something, he says so." He can also be imprudent at times. "Sometimes he says things he shouldn't say.

Afterward he regrets it, but what's said is said." She adds that from his father, Hugo Chávez inherited "his sensitivity. My husband is very humane, very sensitive, very easy to get along with."

Her husband is also a man who should avoid stress. Less than a year after becoming the governor of Barinas, he had to be rushed to a hospital in Caracas, where he was diagnosed with "arterial hypertension crisis with neurological ramifications, manifested by a localized, moderate cerebrovascular hemorrhagic accident." After a few days in intensive care, the elder Chávez was released from the hospital under treatment for hypertension. In a few weeks' time, he returned to Barinas to fulfill his gubernatorial obligations and even went on to run for reelection in the regional elections in 2000, which he won with 58 percent of the vote.

The mother of the president looks quite a bit lovelier today than she did twelve years ago, when her photograph was snapped and splashed across newspapers and on TV for the first time, when visiting her son in jail. Back then there was no makeup to hide her anguish, no adornments of any sort, no beauty salon coiffures. Her appearance is carefully tended nowadays—a reflection of her journey from the humble life to an existence at the highest levels of power.

Ever since the elder Chávez became governor, the president's family life has become a rich source of local gossip in Barinas. The opposition swears that the Chávez family has dipped into state funds to finance the nouveau riche lifestyle they have grown accustomed to and that they have used their influence inappropriately to benefit family and friends. In 2000, the endless speculations led the local parliament to open an investigation to determine whether or not the direct family of the head of state had managed to accumulate more than 8,600 acres of farmland in Barinas state. La Chavera was among the properties under particular scrutiny, due to the opposition's claim that it had grown from about 200 to nearly 800 acres in the space of five years and had been subsequently revalued at upward of $700,000. The salary of a governor in Venezuela is approximately $1,500 per month.

The elder Chávez, who has emphatically denied all rumors of embezzlement in his administration, has also come across resistance within the ranks of his son's political party. One stretch of graffiti in Barinas reads, "Enough, old man, retire already! Signed: Fifth Republic Movement." In March 2004, polls carried out by the Fifth Republic Movement in anticipation of the regional elections in October of the same year did not predict favorable results for Hugo de los Reyes. The possibility of his reelection did not seem to inspire much enthusiasm within his party either, which led to an internal dispute. In the region there were Fifth Republic militants who had been trying to branch out beyond the Chávez family. Months before the elections, the dissenting faction went to Caracas to garner support for an "internal consultation" to select the gubernatorial candidate, but the matter was quickly snuffed out by the president of Venezuela, who also happens to be the president of the party. Hugo Chávez took care of it personally, deciding that his father would be the party's candidate. No ifs, ands, or buts.

Elena claims that she wasn't very keen on the idea: "If it were up to me, Hugo would not have been candidate this year, because what I wanted was for us to fulfill our duties and leave with our heads held high, to go calmly, so that we could rest already. So that when we wanted to go to Caracas to see my son, we could do it without worrying about having to work or going to a meeting. That was what I wanted. But no, things got so ugly around there that they said, 'No, let the teacher stay.' " Ultimately the elder Chávez won the election, garnering 76 percent of the vote.

IN THE TELEVISED PORTRAIT of Hugo Chávez's family, the second row offers a lineup of the Chávez brothers: Adán, Argenis, Aníbal, Narciso, and Adelis. The youngest, Adelis, a regional manager of the banking group Sofitasa, is the only one of them who has nothing to do with politics. The other four traded in their old lives when their brother assumed the presidency. Before then, only Adán had ever shown an interest in politics: during his years as a student at the

University of the Andes in Mérida, he had been an active member of the Party for the Venezuelan Revolution. As for Argenis and Narciso, as soon as their father won his election, they abandoned their previous activities and went to work for the governor's office.

Many have confirmed that Argenis Chávez Frías, who previously worked as an electrical engineer, is the person who really runs things in Barinas. His job title is secretary of state, a position that does not exist in any other governorship and was invented exclusively for him.

In early 2001, four of Argenis Chávez's fellow party members accused him of "extorting certain Barinas government contractors"[1] and demanded that the party strip him of his position as state coordinator of the Fifth Republic Movement in Barinas. It is believed that the president intervened in the matter and ordered his party's National Tactical Command to halt the conflict, a turn of events that was leaked to the press. In the end, it was decided to expel the claimants from the party and withdraw Argenis from the regional coordination of the Chávez party movement.

Another Chávez brother, Narciso, nicknamed "Nacho," also set tongues wagging in the governor's office, where he began to work after he failed to get himself elected mayor in the town of Bolívar, also in the state of Barinas. In 1999, the press offered a summary of the various accusations against him, all of them involving presumed insider dealings. Narciso, who trained as an English teacher and lived in Ohio for five years, had recommended that certain government contracts be awarded to certain individuals. When asked about it on one occasion, he replied, "To avoid getting stuck with the *adecos* [Social Democrats], we recommended our own candidates for the contracts."[2]

The scandal caused friction between Narciso and Hugo Chávez's old friend Vladimir Ruiz, who had assumed the role of acting governor when Hugo de los Reyes had been temporarily unable to fulfill his duties. Ruiz, who would later run for governor on an independent ticket in the 2000 elections, stated, "What's happening is that in Barinas there has been confusion regarding the difference between governor, party, and family. And Professor Chávez is not aware of those limits."[3] Narciso, the "uncomfortable" brother, left the limelight when the president decided to send him to Canada to fill a position at the Venezuelan Embassy there. Not long ago he was transferred to Cuba, where he holds the position of commercial attaché at the Venezuelan Embassy, where he looks after bilateral cooperation agreements.

Aníbal Chávez Frías, who has a degree in education, has also been unable to resist the charms of power. In 2004 he presented his candidacy for mayor of Sabaneta, his family's hometown, on the ticket of the Fifth Republic Movement and won the election. But the person who wields the most power and influence in the Chávez administration is Adán, Hugo's oldest and favorite brother. Given that they grew up together under the care of their grandmother, it is hardly surprising that the two brothers are extremely close. Adán, in fact, was the person who first put Hugo in touch with the ex-guerrillas from the Party for the Venezuelan Revolution when Hugo began to conspire against the government. Adán, who studied physics with middling results at the University of the Andes in Mérida, knew about the 1992 insurrection while it was being planned.

Hugo Chávez has acknowledged that his older brother "was one of the people who had the most influence in my political inclinations. He is very modest, and would never say so himself, but he was very much responsible for my education."[4] Previously a physics professor at the Ezequiel Zamora University of Los Llanos, Adán has been at the president's side ever since Chávez took office in 1999, first serving as a delegate in the Constituent Assembly, later on as the director of the National Land Institute, and after that as a private secretary. In 2004 Hugo Chávez sent him to Cuba as ambassador, a position of paramount importance to the government. In 2006, the president asked him to return and subsequently named him minister of the secretary of the presidency.

Once, when Elena was asked, "What is nepotism for you?" she replied, "I don't like it at all. First, because we are not politicians. We are a very honest, sincere family with a deep desire to keep helping the country."[5]

When Maripili Hernández, the journalist who has been a key figure in the campaigns for the Fifth Republic Movement, was asked whether she thought there might be some nepotism in the government, she replied, "You have to make a distinction between Adán, who has held posts designated by the president, and the position held by the president's father, which is [awarded] through popular election. In other words, Chávez does not determine those positions, it was the people. . . . Well, he has to have some kind of leadership. . . . If they are through popular election, to me that doesn't seem like nepotism. It wasn't Chávez, it was the people of Barinas who cast their votes. They could have voted for someone else."

Beyond all definitions, one thing is clear: never before, at least since 1958, has a president's quest for power been quite so contagious among his family. After an entire lifetime without ambitions, the Chávez Frías family has discovered a true passion for politics.

THE YOUNGEST PEOPLE in the 2004 televised family portrait were the head of state's children: Rosa Virginia, María Gabriela, and Hugo Chávez Colmenares, from his first marriage, and Rosinés Chávez Rodríguez, the youngest, from his second marriage. The older children have always shunned the spotlight and remain relatively unknown to the public. Though the president did have his two older daughters join him on the campaign trail leading up to the 1998 elections, Chávez's children generally maintain a low profile that the Venezuelan press, by and large, has respected. There are neither paparazzi racing after the young women nor impertinent reporters dogging their every step.

Rosa and María, twenty-six and twenty-four, respectively, at the time of the television event, have often stepped in to fill the void left behind by former first lady Marisabel Rodríguez at certain official events, such as the Independence Day parade. They dress and behave discreetly, and their voices are a mystery to most. They never make statements of any sort. Each has given her father a grandchild: María has a young daughter and Rosa, a little boy. The girls have clearly enjoyed certain privileges but in general seem to lead relatively normal lives. This, however, is likely part of a strategy. It is never easy for the press to gain access to the private world of a nation's president. There is always someone who looks after public relations. Certain security procedures are put into place in order to ensure the family's privacy as much as possible.

The greatest enigma in the family, however, is Hugo Chávez Colmenares, born in 1981. Unlike his two sisters, the president's only son has been conspicuously absent from public events. Until mid-2004, when he appeared at the window of Miraflores next to his father, celebrating the victory of the recall referendum, few Venezuelans would even have recognized him. Some people say that Huguito, as he is known, is a troubled young man whom the president has not managed to control. Unlike his sisters, Huguito is rarely mentioned in public by his father. People once close to the president—Luis Miquilena, Nedo Paniz, and Luis Pineda Castellanos—indicate as much.

"The boy had behavioral problems, he has had some problems with the boy. And, I can give you every assurance, [Chávez] is taking care of him," Miquilena states. It is known that the young man lived in Madrid and spent a period of time in Cuba.

These three children have lived through some very difficult times. First, their father's military career kept him away from home for long stretches, as did his conspiratorial project. By the end of the 1980s, his marriage to Nancy was already in bad shape. When Hugo Chávez staged his coup in 1992, his children were just approaching adolescence, at thirteen, eleven, and eight years old.

During his first few years in power, Chávez's preference for his youngest daughter, Rosinés, was overwhelmingly obvious, to the point that the head of state appeared on his official Christmas cards accompanied only by Marisabel and Rosinés. On *Aló, Presidente,* his endless remarks about his little girl and the amusing things she says and does contrast starkly with what little he has to say about his older children. After Chávez and Marisabel separated in mid-2002, Marisabel moved to Barquisimeto, five hours away from Caracas, and Chávez has not been able to see his daughter as frequently as before.

"Unfortunately, she almost never sees her father, and me, even less," Elena says with a heavy heart.

As president, Hugo Chávez has proven himself to be ferocious with his political adversaries. And though they have often retaliated in equal measure, his enemies have never crossed the line with his children. There seems to be a tacit code of nonengagement surrounding them: the president does all he can to keep his children away from the public eye, from the power it holds and embodies. Perhaps he wants to protect them from the battlefield that is his own life. Those who oppose him, it must be said, have never gone searching for scandals by sniffing around his family life, nor have they tried to turn it into a space for confrontation.

On that birthday night, however, all those bits of reality suddenly became terribly fragile. Through the television and radio waves, Chávez had effectively chained the country to his birthday celebration, and everyone in Venezuela found themselves almost forced to witness that very private moment. Beyond the need for exposure, it was clear that in the Chávez realm there was a deep confusion regarding what was supposed to be public and what was private. The absence of boundaries between those two spaces is probably what would make a president decide that his birthday celebration was an affair of state as well as a family affair.

CHAPTER 17

2021: Looking Ahead

The year was 1999. Jesús Urdaneta was still heading up the Directorate for Intelligence and Prevention Services when President Chávez called him up on the phone and said, "I'm sick of that old bum, always going after me. Take care of it, will you?" He was referring to the Argentinian sociologist Norberto Ceresole, who at that moment had forty-eight hours to leave the country. The reason: interference in internal affairs. There is no question that Ceresole was not a simple person. He had served as adviser to the Peruvian president Juan Velasco Alvarado from 1968 to 1975 before being exiled to Europe in 1976. When he returned, according to press reports, he established connections with right-wing military groups such as the *carapintadas*. He also lived and worked in the Soviet Union. He has also been linked to the military dictatorships of Argentina and various Arab governments.

He and Chávez met in Buenos Aires in the winter of 1994. The good feelings were mutual, and toward the end of 1994, they toured the Venezuelan interior together, traveling around in a beat-up old van. Of those days, Norberto Ceresole is believed to be the person who inculcated the ex-conspirator with a theory.

Ceresole's formula, which was officially published in Madrid in 2000, states that the caudillo guarantees power through a civilian-military party that acts as an intermediary between the will of the leader and the masses. Among other things, this so-called post-democratic model defends the importance of maintaining one unified and centralized source of power.

Venezuelan history is fertile terrain for this type of paradigm: 67 percent of Venezuelan governments between 1830 and 1999 were led or overseen by people linked to the world of the military, of the caudillo.[1] The specific case of Hugo Chávez offered an ideal backdrop for this structure, which legitimized the personalist *caudillismo* and military hegemony as the only hope, the great political solution.

Chávez has never let go of that military symbolism. When he took his oath of office as the country's new president, he was also instantly given, as the Constitution established, the position of commander in chief of the national armed forces. For a citizen who had risen to the presidency from civilian life, this would not have been quite as transcendent as it was for Hugo Chávez. Democracy brought him back to the military—in fact, it was almost a shortcut for his meteoric rise in the military.

This fact became clear when he stepped up to the presidency: from the execution of social plans that were administrated and managed by various divisions of the armed forces to his use of the military uniform for certain official speeches or events. This military focus is also evident in his constant references to military history and life and in his decision to make premilitary education a mandatory course for secondary school students. A quick glance at the Chávez team reveals the preeminence of the military in Venezuela's public life.

At the beginning of 2002, the vice president was a military officer, just like the head of the agricultural projects in Sur del Lago. The Ministry of Infrastructure, the Central Budget Office, the Venezuelan Corporation of Guayana, the National Agricultural Institute, the Urban Development Fund, PDVSA [Petróleos de Venezuela, the national oil company], CITGO [a refinery and network of 14,000 gas stations in the United States], the Seniat customs office, the People's Bank, the Industrial Bank of Venezuela, and the Centralized Social Fund were all in the hands of military officers. The economic power.

They also controlled state transportation and communications and the Caracas Metro, the airport of Maiquetía, Avensa [airline], and Setra [Autonomous Transportation Service], Conatel [National Telecommunications Commission], Venpres [State News Agency], Venezolana de Televisión, and the Ministry of the Secretariat. They also controlled national security: the Division for Military Intelligence, the DISIP [Directorate for Intelligence and Prevention Services], the Directorate of Foreigners, and the Vice Ministry of Citizens' Security of the Interior Ministry. They were governors of the states of Táchira, Mérida, Trujillo, Cojedes, Lara, Vargas, and Bolívar. Naturally, in the Foreign Ministry they occupied positions of minister, vice minister, several directors general, and many ambassadors, those of Peru, Bolivia, Ecuador, Brazil, El Salvador, Spain, Malaysia. . . . Many military personnel have also been congressmen, the secretary general of organization for MVR [Fifth Republic Movement], the president of Inager [National Geriatrics Institute], the INCE [National Institute for Training and Education], and the headquarters of the National Sports Institute.[2]

The process of militarizing areas that were traditionally civilian has not abated. According to the newspaper El Universal, more than one hundred men in uniform, most on active duty, occupy po-sitions of leadership in state-run corporations, autonomous and national services and institutes, governmental funds, foundations, and special commissions. For the regional elections in October 2004, fourteen of the twenty-two candidates on the Chávez party ticket, who had been handpicked by Chávez, were from the military realm.

Now, more than ever, Venezuelan society has more direct contact with the world of the military. Elements from life in the barracks even pop up in the popular lexicon. During his campaigns, Chávez would organize his followers in what he called "patrols" that were to awaken "at reveille" to enter "battle" and "defeat the enemy" at the polls.

During one of his national chains, on November 28, 2002, he warned the country, "When I talk about armed revolution, I am not speaking metaphorically; armed means rifles, tanks, planes, and thousands of men ready to defend the revolution."

This was not empty rhetoric. By 2001, Venezuela had more generals and admirals than Mexico and Argentina combined. By 2004, in violation of the Constitution, 120 civilians had been tried in military courts.[3] More than one political observer has sensed Norberto Ceresole behind all of this: the notion of the armed forces transformed into a political party, governing the people, protagonist of the society.

ON OCCASION, PEOPLE who speak directly to Chávez in public refer to him as *"mi comandante"* or *"mi comandante en jefe"*—my commander, my commander in chief. Early on in his administration, people transformed this greeting into a cruel joke by accentuating the first two syllables of *"mi comandante"* so that it sounded like *"mico mandante,"* which means "monkey in charge." The idea of associating the president with a monkey is a reflection of the racism and classism of Venezuelan society, which labels the poor as vulgar, crude people who are closer to the jungle than the civilized world.

This type of "joke" has special significance in the context of late-twentieth-century Venezuela. There is a sector of society that has insistently accused Hugo Chávez of encouraging class conflict and hatred among Venezuelans, stoking the flames of social resentment, and dividing the country. Government allies defend themselves by saying that the nation had previously been living under the false illusion of harmony and that far from inventing these differences Chávez simply revealed them for what they were. As is often the case, both sides probably have a point.

Venezuelans have always perceived themselves as possessing a degree of egalitarianism, a multiclass diversity that—thanks to the succession of oil bonanzas—produced a fluid, frictionless social fabric.

This image, however, eludes another reality: the massive and ever-growing level of poverty and the resentment of those who feel excluded from the country's immense natural wealth. At a press conference on August 13, 2004, just before the recall referendum, Vice President José Vicente Rangel stated, "What divides Venezuela is poverty. Poverty is what polarized the country."

This is true. But also true is the fact that Chávez's verbal temperature rapidly became a highly combustible detonating force. His fierce rhetoric, without a doubt, was highly effective on the electoral battleground. Not only was the country ready for him, he was ready for the country, too. According to Teodoro Petkoff, "When Chávez entered the picture as forcefully as he did and began to speak as forcefully as he did, nobody hesitated, not for a second. He was the perfect avenger, tailor-made for the disenchantment and frustration of the Venezuelan people."[4]

When it came time to govern, however, that forcefulness quickly became a wellspring of conflicts. Chávez would accuse, discredit, and insult people far too readily, decreeing the law according to the maxim "He who is not with me is against me." That, at least, is how Luis Miquilena sees it: "When he started to fight with people, I said to him, 'Listen, kid, you have confused the logical and natural combativeness of elections with the exercise of power, and they are two very different things.' " His behavior was a strategy, a confrontational way of being that, for more than one political observer, pertained to the military realm. Raúl Salazar maintains that "Chávez has a problem that all men in the military have: he plays the politician, but he doesn't learn how to negotiate; he just learns how to give orders."

At one of his last rallies before winning the presidential elections in 1998, he called out to the crowd, "On December 6 [election day], we, you and I, are going to wrap the *adecos* [Social Democrats] up in a giant ball of"—he paused for a moment—"I can't say that because it would be vulgar." It didn't matter. The multitude, in euphoric unison, screamed out, "Of shiiiit!" That is how Herma Marksman recalls the scene, appalled.

"For me," says Marksman, "it was too much." This was not the Hugo she knew. And she was not the only one to register surprise. This aggressive, contentious, even crude image was very disturbing for those who had known Chávez at other periods in his life. Some believe that this was simply a communications strategy. Others say that the popularity and power had transformed him. And others feel that both are true.

Alcides Rondón, his friend since military school, adds a bit of nuance to this facet of Chávez's character: "His emotions are always stirred when he finds himself in front of a crowd. To have a mass of people respond that way to you would be an emotional experience for anyone. Certain reactions are a direct result of that. But when we are talking for real about politics, of a change in discourse, and a shift toward an open and even aggressive offensive tactic, I am convinced that it is the product of a reflection and an objective. He has an objective; this isn't spontaneous." This comment, of course, directly contradicts the image Chávez has created for himself, that of a leader who easily breaks protocol, subverting the solemn agendas of power, improvising rather than reading his speeches, appearing to speak his mind with neither reservations nor fear. This is the image he himself has cultivated and promoted all over the planet. It is the image he reasserts whenever he tells the country about some new plan of action that occurred to him at two in the morning. Nevertheless, it is a fabricated kind of spontaneity. Former vice president José Vicente Rangel also confirms that "Chávez is viewed as impulsive, but he is an extremely deliberate person. Everything he does is the result of planning." This supports the theory of those who believe that the president's verbal fury is almost a discipline, a well-designed method, a military strategy based on provocation and constant confrontation.

"If Christ were here, among us, do not doubt that Christ would cast his vote in the Constituent [Assembly], he would cast his vote for the revolution," Chávez declared in 1999. That same year, one month later, he became embroiled in a conflict with a group of bishops who were not one hundred percent in agreement with the revolution:

"What they need is an exorcism, so that the devil that got into them will come out from under their robes."

He has displayed this kind of attitude toward various other sectors of Venezuelan society as well. Far too quickly, Chávez began to wage far too many battles. His aide Maripili Hernández sees things from a different perspective: "Of what use is a president who cannot stand up and speak his mind about what he feels is unjust? That doesn't bother me. I am not going to tell you that there haven't been moments when I have thought that something [he said] wasn't exactly political or diplomatic, but on the other hand I love the fact that the president of my country has the courage to say those things."

This controversial position resulted in a rather paradoxical perception of the head of state: on one hand, Chávez was clearly the leader of his own government, yet he spoke and acted as though he were the leader of the opposition. Luis Miquilena was very close to the president during this period, and in addition to his role as minister of the interior, he was also Chávez's political mentor at the time. When the president began to lock horns with Venezuelan business leaders, the Church, the media, and other sectors of the country, Miquilena said to him, "In the exercise of power, that style of managing social relations is not acceptable." In retrospect, Miquilena adds, "He thought that the belligerent, confrontational attitude of our electoral campaign was something we could reproduce once he was in power, when in fact power requires a man with understanding, someone able to manage the state as a kind of national arbitrator."

For anyone who visited the country before the presidential referendum took place, there was an almost palpable feeling that Venezuela was on the brink of civil war. And the issue at hand was not an ideological problem or a need to drastically change existing political programs. The one and only debate in the country revolved around a single person whom people either fervently supported or opposed. There is something infectious about the character of Hugo Chávez: you either love him or despise him. One or the other. And the discourse from the seat of power was handled in such a way that no other option was possible. People close to the president acknowledge this. "Sometimes I wish he weren't so direct, I wish he weren't so tough. I suffer a lot with his speeches," admits Alcides Rondón.

The notion of Chávez as a victim has been successfully promoted whenever the president has had to explain the shortcomings of his government or the excesses of his own leadership. Chávez portrays himself as the victim of the opposition, of the past, of the power elite—of the evils of his own government, even. From this perspective, the virulence of his discourse becomes a reaction to the invective of his adversaries.

The American journalist Jon Lee Anderson, who wrote a profile of the leader in 2001, does point out that a number of Chávez's personality traits foment divisiveness among Venezuelans, but Anderson also criticizes a certain coterie of political and business leaders opposed to the president, observing that they have not done anything one would expect of people with their education and resources—they either took their money out of the country or spent their time plotting, telling journalists that the military was restless, spreading tension everywhere, fearing and despising Chávez, calling him a monkey. According to Anderson, the level of political discussion in Venezuela is dismal.[5]

Beyond the schism between the government and the traditional political-economic elite, the polarization that has come about because of Chávez has not divided the country in a simple, neat manner. On the contrary: more than one family has found itself divided on the issue. It is not unusual for government aides to run into problems with family and friends because of their political preferences. In one family you may find chavistas and anti-chavistas, and you may also find a mix of supporters and opponents in a neighborhood of a uniform socioeconomic level. It is an extremely peculiar phenomenon that has not been sufficiently analyzed or recognized by foreign observers.

Testimonies suggest that even in his closest circles Chávez is combative, often grossly insulting those who work with him. As Angela Zago tells it, "He is a person of violent reactions. I saw him insult

Aristóbulo Istúriz [currently the minister of education] at the beginning of his administration. It was because of something Aristóbulo had done and he insulted him in front of all of us. He said all sorts of things to him." Luis Miquilena recalls that after Chávez became president there was a tremendous shift and says that he became "a despotic man with his subordinates . . . an autocrat, authoritarian, brutal with his aides. The way he treated his ministers was degrading. What he did to Diosdado Cabello, for example, I don't know if I would have accepted that from my own father."

What some people see as strength and gravity, others call authoritarian; what some call leadership, others describe as messianic fervor, unbridled populism. Where some people see responsibility, others find only egocentric personalism. Nobody, however, on either side of the matter, can fail to recognize the charisma of Hugo Chávez, the magic he has created with the poorest people in the country. For them, the idea that there is a public Chávez and a private Chávez is an unthinkable hypothesis. For them, Chávez is a deep, unquestionable sentiment, an emotion that has long since become faith.

THE ROOT OF CHÁVEZ'S power resides in the religious and emotional bond he has forged with the popular sectors of the country. It is what the theorist Peter Wiles has called the "mystical contact with the masses,"[6] of Latin American populism. Chávez is a symbol that has not been devoured by the protocol of power. He always breaks through the ostensible solemnity of the events he attends and will halt pomp and circumstance to hug a little old lady calling out to him or to sweep a child up in his arms. Wherever he goes, there are always throngs of humble people holding little slips of paper, pleas for help that he or his bodyguards collect. Chávez touches people. He asks their names, he asks them about their lives. He always seems genuinely interested in his fellow man. Chávez speaks from their position, suggesting that he is one of them. Even after six years in the presidency, with more than thirty pounds of extra weight, wearing designer clothes and Cartier watches, he maintains the bond with remarkable intensity.

On occasion, he presents himself as a victim of his own luxuries, as he did when he commanded his people to stop ordering him suits. And in fact, he does seem far more seduced by vanity than the enjoyment of material pleasures. Some of his adversaries admit that they see very little ambition for worldly goods combined with a very real social sensibility. But there, yet again, they seem to confuse the personal Chávez with the public Chávez. Frequently he tells people that he has nothing and claims that there is nothing he wishes for, nothing he needs, even though he uses massive amounts of resources to promote himself and retain his power.

His is an empathetic discourse that moves people, generating trust and loyalty. He touches hidden feelings like fear and resentment, invoking differences, experiences of rejection and injustice. From there he builds his voice, a plural of which he is the protagonist. "They don't love *us.*" "The oligarchy scorns *us.*" "They have always laughed at *us.*" "*We* disgust them." Much of his rhetoric unfolds with an emphasis similar to the preachers of the so-called electronic churches. He speaks with simplicity, explaining things with anecdotes and a masterful command of popular codes of speech. In the realm of the spoken word, he always sabotages the official solemnity, disdaining all that is formal. He acts spontaneous. Popularly spontaneous. According to Maripili Hernández, "He believes very deeply in the ideal he preaches. He lives it, he suffers with it, and he works on it every day. Unlike what many people think and say, that he is a charlatan, honestly I don't believe it. He believes every word he says, down to the letter, and I believe he will die to do everything within his ability to achieve the things he says."

Nedo Paniz offers a very different version of things when he talks about how, before Hugo Chávez became president, the two of them traveled together to Colombia. They had been invited to an event at the Quinta de Bolívar, the Liberator's onetime home in Bogotá, where Chávez was to give a speech. Paniz suggested that he bring a gift for the president of the Bolivarian Society. "And so Chávez grabbed a fistful of earth from the courtyard, close to the hotel, and stuck it in a box. Once we got there, he gave an impassioned speech. And at some point he took out the box and said that he had brought that earth especially from Campo de Carabobo [where Bolívar led the critical battle that liberated Venezuela from Spanish rule]. It was a farce, but people were deeply moved. Many people cried."

If there is one thing the president has most successfully communicated, it is that he cares about people, that he has true concern for the poor. As José Vicente Rangel puts it, "He is a man of simple language. That is the connection to the streets. Chávez abandoned the stereotype of the politician. He is not a shameless populist, he does not banalize language, he has succeeded in rescuing the popular lexicon and placing it at the center of the presidential discourse. He is one more among the people." Over and over again he reminds people of his past, his rural, humble origins. He does not speak English, and in public he has made a point of laughing at his dubious pronunciation of the language. He describes himself as an ugly man of the popular class, without property and without the background for high-handed affairs, with no other ambition than to offer affection and service to the neediest. His slogan during 2004 went beyond allusions and into the terrain of direct definition: "Chávez is the people."

In this light, his existence, his conquest, and the pleasure he derives from the power he wields are a triumph, a victory for many people.

The academic Patricia Márquez points out that "many people who felt excluded for many years now see themselves as part of a project for change, which they believe to represent, at the very least, a transformation of the rules of the political and social order."[7] For these people, Chávez is the symbolic and emotional guarantee of that change, the incarnation of the hope that they may one day break out of their poverty—despite the fact that poverty rose by 10.8 percent during his first six years in office, according to official statistics.[8] His figure serves as a sacred intermediary between the country's millions of oil dollars and the dreams of a majority population held captive by poverty.

Nevertheless, during the first four years of his administration, popular expectations did not seem to receive concrete answers. The majority of the changes implemented were in the area of political conquests, while the social welfare programs were inefficient. Indeed, they seemed a bit too similar to the previous government's programs—asphyxiated by cronyism, bureaucracy, and accusations of corruption. This landscape changed in 2003, when the government implemented the *misiones,* a compendium of social assistance plans and aid to the poor, which remain mired in controversy.

The first of these plans was called Barrio Adentro (Into the Neighborhood). Its principal goal was to manage health issues in the huge lower-middle-class urban neighborhoods all over the country. The protagonists of this plan were volunteer Cuban doctors who would move into these neighborhoods and, in small clinics, attend to the medical needs of their local community. There were two great advantages to implementing this project: First, it would enable on-site treatment for certain emergencies, stanching the flow of patients and alleviating the workload at the large public hospitals. And second, the project gave these communities a greater sense of security and ease in the event of a medical emergency. On the other hand, certain sectors of society were disturbed by the fact that the doctors were Cuban and perceived this as part of Hugo Chávez's "Castrocommunism" project. Matters were not helped by the government's implementation of this plan, which allowed the Cuban doctors to practice without legal consultation or supervision by the Venezuelan Medical Federation, or the appropriate academic associations.

A series of education programs followed this initiative: first was the Misión Robinson, a literacy program baptized with the pseudonym used by Simón Rodríguez, mentor of Simón Bolívar. After that came Misión Sucre and Misión Ribas, which focused on people who had been unable to study or who had been forced to leave school at the primary and secondary levels. The next initiative, Misión Vuelvan Caras ("About Face"), which took its name from a battle cry of the Venezuelan plainsman and independence hero José Antonio Páez, was designed to combat unemployment and foment self-management. Another program, Mercal, focused on food distribution and established a network of local markets. The Misión Miranda was more specific, granting benefits to all those who had once belonged to the national armed forces.

When there were no more social programs left to offer, Chávez coined a grandiloquent term to bring them all under the same umbrella. "We want to put an end to poverty, and power must be given to the poor. We are at the birth of a new power. It is a power that leaves behind the concept of oligarchy and plutocracy. Only this way can there be life,"[9] he claimed. He then went on to announce that on December 24, 2003, he would launch the Misión Cristo, which would serve as an umbrella for all the other missions. Its goal: to eradicate poverty by 2021.

Criticism of this project is centered on three fundamental points: it is populist, discretionary, and operated without the benefit of external control. According to sociologist Luis Pedro España, the *misiones* are just like the government's other social programs in that they seem designed more to help Chávez retain power than to combat poverty in Venezuela effectively. All the programs function by remitting salary grants to the participants, according to a system of partisan affiliations and loyalty to the government. Moreover, none of these programs is audited. For this reason, there is no way to know how many people participate in these programs, how much is invested in them, or what kind of results they obtain. The only possible source for this information is the government itself. On top of this, certain analyses show that a parallel state has been created on top of the one that already exists. Instead of solving the country's dire problems of education and public health, the government has created new structures, generating another administration and another budget, in an unequal and uncontrolled manner. Sooner or later, some believe, both entities will cease to be viable. The most effective aspect of these programs, it seems, is in the electoral sense.

The launch of these initiatives coincided with a downward trend in Hugo Chávez's popularity ratings. The upturn was immediate. A few months later, Chávez's approval rating rose to 46 percent, highlighting the hopeful effect of the government's projects: though only 15 percent of those polled stated that they had actually benefited from the projects, 85 percent felt hopeful that, at some point, they would see some of that "distribution of resources" the government often talked about. Even with this very high approval rating, there is something here that jibes with Norberto Ceresole's theories. "The middle and upper classes despise populism because that implies distribution. But those of us who come from the lower class say, 'Long live populism! It dignifies us . . . every dollar we give the people is a dollar that we will not give the International Monetary Fund. And so, long live populism. There is no other form of revolution in Latin America."[10]

For many, Chávez's victory in the 2004 recall referendum was inextricably linked to the distribution of money and hope through the *misiones*. The president even admitted to this on one occasion: "In 2003, they gave me a news bomb: if the referendum were held today, you would lose. . . . That was when we started to work with the *misiones* and I began to ask Fidel for help. He said to me, 'If there's one thing I know, it's about that kind of thing.' And we started to invent the *misiones*." After an intense campaign for which, according to the opposition, the president availed himself of state funds and indulged in electoral opportunism, 5.6 million Venezuelans[11] (59.06 percent of the voters) decided on August 15 that Hugo Chávez would stay in power.

The controversial victory, however, was sullied by accusations of fraud both inside and outside Venezuela. On one hand, it is true that the majority of the National Electoral Council was sympathetic to the Chávez government (three out of five in the executive committee) and that in the very process of activating the constitutional recourse of the recall referendum, the Council seemed determined to complicate rather than facilitate the work of the citizens who had petitioned for the recall referendum. But it is also true that the opposition has not produced any conclusive evidence of the purported electronic fraud. And in a highly questionable move, some opposition members accused César Gaviria and Jimmy Carter, observers and guarantors of the referendum process, of sealing an agreement with the government and participating in what they termed as fraudulent proceedings.

SOME STUDIES[12] INDICATE a difference between the notion of the caudillo, the classic Latin American strongman, and that of the "populist leader." The first figure evolves in a rural environment and concentrates its power through the exercise of direct personal relationships, whereas the second figure engages in the dynamic of the big city and exercises its power through the political party. Hugo Chávez is right in the middle of these two paradigms. Galloping over classifications, he represents a kind of leadership that, for those who legitimize him as well as those who question him, is difficult to define.

According to the academic Alfredo Ramos Jiménez, Chávez's case falls into a category that might be termed "neopopulism," which "includes elements of domination and manipulation of the popular classes, combining them with participatory experiences that include a high level of identification. In such circumstances, the leader will always be unique and irreplaceable, entirely necessary. His power is not delegated except in unusual circumstances, and his charisma represents a threat to democracy."[13]

The philosopher Alberto Arvelo Ramos states that "Chávez is a nineteenth-century military caudillo. And not just any caudillo: a reactionary nineteenth-century caudillo." Arvelo Ramos also acknowledges the ideas of Chávez's old Argentinian adviser: "Ceresole convinced him that he was the second Simón Bolívar, he filled him up with that megalomania of the universal, historic man. . . . Chávez does not believe in plural democracy, where the social and political forces balance each other out and control each other. It is a complete dictatorship of one single person." Among other things, Arvelo Ramos mentions the absence of balance. In Venezuela, all power is fused to the executive branch. The parliament, dominated by the Chávez party, has not distanced itself one inch from the Miraflores mandate, and the same is true of the institutions designed to control the presidency. The Comptroller's Office and the attorney general, which were decisive in the impeachment of Carlos Andrés Pérez, for example, are in the hands of Chávez acolytes. In fact, the attorney general of the Republic was his first vice president. Moreover, there is a fear that, thanks to a 2004 legal reform, the Supreme Court will soon be dominated by pro-Chávez magistrates. In this structure, the president will be bulletproof. No claim against him—there are already a dozen or so languishing in the attorney general's office—can constitute a threat to his power. Hugo Chávez is the Venezuelan president with the greatest accumulation of power since 1958.

No analysis is complete without taking Chávez's personal attributes into account. The leader's individualistic idiosyncratic style is a key factor. At a rally in his native Barinas, during the campaigns leading up to the regional elections of October 2004, he declared, "To be a *chavista,* you have to be like me!"

In campaign posters, all the pro-Chávez candidates were shown anointed by the president. Chávez traveled all over the country raising the arms of his candidates, adding fire to their rallies, and guaranteeing them an audience that, on their own, they probably wouldn't have attracted.

Within the Latin American caudillo and populist tradition, the Chávez movement may well have added a new twist. After all, the situation of the oil-rich Venezuela on the map of a globalized world at the dawn of the twenty-first century is a new twist in and of itself. But while the previous administration was forced to adhere to a maximum price of $16 per barrel, the Bolivarian revolution has navigated through a market that has driven the price of crude oil to over $50 per barrel by 2006. In a country like Honduras or Peru, Hugo Chávez probably would not have made it through two assaults on his government. According to some analysts, the economic reality of the country's *plata dulce,* or "sweet cash," an oft-used term for describing boom periods in Latin America, offered a luxury that facilitated this "Bolivarian revolution." It is a situation that concentrates and reinforces the various elements that give Hugo Chávez the power—both symbolic and real—of being the protagonist of the process, the head of state and the star of the story.

"That man either changed or he didn't; maybe that was the real one, the one I didn't know," says Luis Miquilena with a twinge of melancholy. "There is a refrain that says, 'Give a man a bit of power and you will learn what kind of man he is.' I found out who my friends really were after I saw them in power. Power swallowed them up, carried them away. . . . What I mean is, the humble man I bought into turned out to be an autocrat, authoritarian, absolutely different."

Those in Chávez's circle, obviously, do not share this vision. Pedro Carreño has known Chávez since their days in the armed forces, when the president was his teacher. Carreño was also at Chávez's side in the early days of his political life, when they traveled around the country together, roughing it and making tremendous sacrifices. Carreño does not believe that power has affected him adversely. "He is the same Chávez, the same dreamer and tireless fighter he always was, with the same social sensibility and thirst for social justice. He is touched by poverty, by a little boy in school with an unemployed father. I don't see any change."

Others believe that the problem is the people who surround him. Yoel Acosta, who participated in the 1992 coup, maintains that "The president is almost a hostage. He doesn't make the decision to find people who are committed, because it seems that those bigwigs, that circle, has taken him hostage, they don't allow him to see beyond what they want him to see." Still, it seems highly unlikely that someone with a personality like Hugo Chávez would so easily submit to a circle of advisers. On the contrary, in fact: it is common knowledge that he does not tend to delegate, that he likes to have a hand in everything.

General Alberto Müller Rojas, who was his campaign chief in 1998 and is currently Chávez's military adviser, observed a particular personality trait that might explain certain people's ambivalence regarding Hugo Chávez: "People have to feign, at the very least, absolute submission to him, which reveals a total lack of self-confidence on his part. For me, this is one of the most negative things about him: he does not have faith in himself, because a person who has faith in himself has faith in other people and faith in his own ability to convince people of his leadership and the things he proposes. And so he is quite a voluble individual in that sense. He goes from one position to another very easily. He is an individual who has a tendency toward cyclothymia—mood swings that range from moments of extreme euphoria to moments of despondence."

As often occurs in this type of situation, Hugo Chávez and his purportedly mercurial personality have given rise to more than a few mysteries and legends. He has been said to suffer from periods of severe depression, panic attacks, and lithium imbalance, and some people claim that he is medicated. None of this has ever been confirmed. Edmundo Chirinos, who was once Chávez's psychiatrist, says that Chávez "has a need for recognition. In that he is not humble, he is arrogant. He needs to be listened to, paid attention to, admired, even idolized."

Chávez has abandoned a great many friends and allies on the road to power, starting with his comrades in arms, the other figures in the 1992 military uprising. Many others who stood by him during his first few years in office have also distanced themselves, joined the opposition, or disappeared from the political realm entirely. Chávez does not seem troubled by these separations. In this process, the leader's personalist quality always springs into action. Luis Miquilena, who distanced himself from Chávez and is now part of the opposition, refuses to say anything about his former friend's private life, but when asked about his personal defects, he is very direct: "He is a man who cannot resist flatterers, and that is a terrible weakness. He is an immensely vain man." Edmundo Chirinos, who does still feel close to

Chávez, points out, "Maybe my one criticism is that his vocation for power is so passionate. With this thing of feeling that he is a conqueror, plus the adulation and all the trappings, he would be capable of sacrificing everything, even his own life, for power." Francisco Arias Cárdenas, who was appointed as Venezuela's ambassador to the United Nations in 2006, believes that this is the key element that drives Hugo Chávez. "I think he lives in the clutches of a paranoia to preserve his power. The preservation of his power is his own personal hell, and that is why he is constantly at battle."

The image of the very powerful man who becomes a hostage to his own power, sooner or later, is one that paints every populist leader or caudillo into a corner. This notion has even become an integral part of the Latin American literary tradition, to the point that it is almost a cliché: the solitude of power.

"He has become a sad man," confesses Alcides Rondón, "a lonely man. For Chávez this must be very difficult. . . . He is a man who takes such pleasure in going to baseball games, but now he can't go. He is a man who lives to have good, clean fun with his friends, but he doesn't have time for that type of thing anymore. Definitely, like all powerful men, he is all alone. The court of a king does not always make the best company. That is an axiom of power."

IT IS A SOLITUDE that is compensated for, more and more, by power and the vertigo of omnipotence. Not only does Hugo Chávez feel confident that he will govern until 2013, as allowed by the Constitution that was designed under his guidance in 1999, he believes that he will project himself further beyond that date and continue to fuse his life with the history of Venezuela. In the early morning of August 16, after the National Electoral Council declared his victory in the recall referendum, Hugo Chávez appeared with his three eldest children on the "people's balcony" of Miraflores. On that occasion more than a few relatives and cabinet members wore red T-shirts with "2021"—the date that Chávez refers to as the year of his "retirement"—emblazoned in black. The president knows that there is no democratic way for him to remain in his position until 2021. Nevertheless, he has frequently repeated this intention: "I'm not leaving until 2021. So start getting used to it."[14]

In a similar way, from very early on in his presidency, Chávez began to attack the idea of alternation in Venezuelan political life. The very notion that "finally the revolution has become the government" began to introduce a new social sensibility, a perception that this was not just another administration but a different exercise entirely, with different aspirations. In fact, Chávez has suggested the possibility of reforming the Constitution to permit unlimited presidential reelection. With a majority in the assembly and control of all the public powers, the government's party may well be able to pull it off. According to the historian Elías Pino Iturrieta, "2021 is the denial of republican alternation, the denial of democracy, the denial of civility and disrespect for the people. . . . It is the denial of all civic cohabitation that we have enjoyed since 1945, or at least, without a doubt since 1958. Alternation and coexistence no longer boast the chronology they once did. The republican clock, the almanac, is entirely disrupted when it is decided that the fate of a society will be handed over to one single person until the year 2021."

Some have stated that this plan is in fact not new, that it does not represent a change in mentality or strategy, and that it is simply the result of the concupiscent indulgence in power. Nedo Paniz says he clearly remembers something Hugo Chávez once said to him several years ago: "If I get to Miraflores, nobody is going to take our power away." His comrade in arms Francisco Arias Cárdenas recalls an anecdote that is perhaps less categorical but certainly suggests intent: During the final event of the 1998 electoral campaign in Caracas, some voices began to chant Arias's nickname: "Pancho! Pancho!" they cried. Chávez had him climb up to the stage and brought him to his side. The two men, overcome with emotion, looked out at the crowds. As Arias Cárdenas recalls, "I said to him, 'Damn, Hugo, what a tremendous commitment, what change. From the days when the two of us were stuck under some tree in Paraguaipoa, waiting for those lieutenants who never showed up, to this mass of people that just make your heart leap, all these people so full of hope. What a huge responsibility!' " Arias Cárdenas then remembers how Chávez moved closer to him and whispered, "Pancho, ten years for me, ten years for you, and then we'll see how to keep it going until we've got this whole process wrapped up."

In Latin America, part of the enchantment of the word "revolution" has to do with the idea of staying in power. The example of Fidel Castro is perhaps too close. In this regard, once again we see a combination of populism, or neopopulism, and the military ingredient, part of a foundational saga in Venezuelan history, a mythology in which men of action are the people who make history.

"The last representation of this myth," states Pino Iturrieta, "is Chávez and the helmets and military boots that surround him. Chávez is a moving military fortress that is very attractive for the element of Venezuelan society that is not a republic, that does not depend on civic citizenry but on the arrival of a messiah. And if that messiah uses a military uniform and a combat tank, then that part of society will feel more secure." At the bottom of it all, it seems that the issue has reopened an old and very complex debate that many thought was long since settled: the difficult, belligerent coexistence between the civilian, republican culture and the caudillo, praetorian, military culture. It is from that juxtaposition that Hugo Chávez Frías has emerged.

The writer Ibsen Martínez has repeatedly pointed out that the opposition has failed every time it has tried to ponder, judge, and react to the Chávez movement by viewing it and acting as if it were an old-style dictatorial, fascist government. To quote the American Mark Lilla, there are presently "few functioning democracies, only a variety of mixed regimes and tyrannies that pose new challenges to our understanding and our policies. From Zimbabwe to Libya, from Algeria to Iraq, from the Central Asian republics to Burma, from Pakistan to Venezuela, we discover nations that are neither totalitarian nor democratic, nations where the prospects of building durable democracies in the near future are limited or nil."[15]

Hugo Chávez has created a country where everything is legal but inadmissible. A country where, in the year 2004, the president cried out at a public rally that the opposition would never return to power, "no matter what." There is a massive sector of the country that had been waiting for someone like Chávez for a long time. These people appear happy to believe that Bolívar has been resuscitated, that history is an exercise in salvation, and that Hugo Chávez is an emissary sent to complete a job that the Father of the Nation left unfinished. And it is no coincidence that the president selected 2021 as the year of his supposed retirement: it marks the bicentennial of the Battle of Carabobo, the decisive event in the war of independence against Spain. Perhaps, in his own version of Venezuelan history, Chávez sees himself in that same vein, as part of that same saga begun by the Liberator, a saga that would reach its climax two centuries later, with him.

Who is Hugo Chávez, really? Where is he going, that little boy who was raised by his grandmother in a hut with a dirt floor and a roof made of palm leaves? Is he a true revolutionary or a pragmatic neopopulist? How deep is his social conscience, and how great is his vanity? Is he a democrat trying to build a country where certain people will no longer be excluded and marginalized, or is he an authoritarian caudillo holding his country and its institutions hostage? Is he, perhaps, both things at the same time? Who is this man who waves a crucifix in the air as he quotes Che Guevara and Mao Tse-tung? When is he truly himself? Of all the men we know Hugo Chávez to be, which is the most genuine? It is very hard to tell. What does seem evident is that they all have something in common. It is a desire, a craving, that drives him and keeps him awake at night. An obsession that, like all obsessions, is self-evident, impossible to hide. No matter which Chávez he is, he will always, obsessively, seek power. More power.

THIS BIOGRAPHY WAS ORIGINALLY COMPLETED IN AUGUST 2004. HUGO
Chávez's victory in the recall referendum seemed like an exceptional
opportunity to end a book that ran the risk of doggedly following a
process that is far from finished. Two years later, it seems important
to offer, even if only superficially, a general account of what happened between August 2004 and December 2006.

During this time, Hugo Chávez consolidated his power inside
Venezuela and through a broad international agenda fashioned himself as an enemy of George W. Bush. He also began in earnest to
develop an ideological definition, summoning the world to a war
against neoliberalism and a crusade in support of a new "twenty-first-
century socialism." As for his more personal plans, his political future
seems to be looming larger than ever.

Hugo Chávez is another man now, one who is edging closer and
closer to the myth. His image is reproduced on posters and photographs that adorn government offices, it has been sculpted into small
busts and statues that are popular altars; there is even a little doll
with batteries that was one of the more memorable toys sold during
the 2005 Christmas season. But the more his presence is felt in the
public life of Venezuela, the more remote his private life seems. It is
known that on one of the upper patios of Miraflores Palace there are
a hammock and a desk, a personal space to which he retreats when
he wants to read, visit with close friends, or play with his grandchildren. His romantic life is always something of a whisper. They say he
is involved with a famous soap opera actress, although both have denied this claim. Publicly he declares that he is wedded to his homeland, and the rings of security only seem to grow in number and
breadth.

For local journalists who do not work for pro-Chávez media

groups, it is impossible to get an interview with the president. For the majority of foreign correspondents, it would take a miracle. In public, he continues to be charismatic and unpredictable. One minute he might insult the president of Mexico, and the next minute he will head out to a rally wearing a charro hat and singing the ranchera song "*Sigo siendo el rey*" (I Am Still the King) with a backup mariachi band. Nevertheless, one thing does seem to have changed. He is in another league now. He has different challenges. He sees himself with a different destiny.

"Our task," he said on August 15, 2006, "is to save the world, planet Earth. Our task is much greater than the one Bolívar took on, the commitment is much greater."[1]

HE TOOK HIS TRIUMPH in the recall referendum as a great boost to the Bolivarian project, a turning point that would allow the process to continue evolving. Beneath the slogan "The Revolution Within the Revolution," on November 13 and 14, 2004, in a military fortress in Caracas, Chávez gathered together all the government leaders in his party. The upper echelons of Venezuelan officialdom were summoned behind closed doors to participate in a workshop in which they were divided into working groups with the goal of designing a "New Strategic Map." This plan, colloquially known as "the great leap forward," is fueled by the president's demand to hasten and radicalize the process that Venezuela is presently living through.

This is not a hidden agenda. The web page of the Ministry of Communication and Information offers plenty of news about this workshop. It is based on a series of proposals aimed at building a new societal model, with different modes of economic production that transcend capitalism and establish new social and political relations. The idea is to create a system governed by a new set of laws and institutions, a system that will wield greater control over communications, develop a new kind of educational and cultural fabric, and foment the civilian-military union.

"We have a new map in front of us," Chávez announced a month later. "The actions that we articulate can be summed up in a verb: accelerate."[2]

Accelerate, yes. It is an "offensive" action, as Chávez himself has put it. On the legal front, the Land Law was approved in 2001 and has been implemented, and a number of large tracts of privately held land have been expropriated. Other laws that came into effect include the much-disputed Law of Social Responsibility, which controls and regulates the media, and the equally controversial penal code,[3] which severely sanctions defamation. But perhaps the most momentous reform of all is the political reengineering operation that Chávez has designed so that he may direct the Supreme Court of Justice. It was expanded from twenty to thirty-two magistrates, thus packing a court favorable to the president.

One of the first jobs of this court was to revoke the sentence that, using the "power vacuum" argument, absolved the military officers implicated in the 2002 coup d'état that briefly expelled Hugo Chávez from the presidency.

The government has achieved an even more hegemonic level of authority within the National Electoral Council. Not only does Chávez enjoy tremendous popularity, but it is becoming clear that he also has quite an advantage among the electoral authorities. Four of the five members of the new electoral board are Chávez sympathizers.

A few months after the recall referendum, the president openly promoted his candidates for the regional elections, without even a sidelong glance from the National Electoral Council. On October 31, 2004, the Venezuelan map would turn red as Chávez continued winning elections and cornering the opposition. Of the 22 governorships at stake, the pro-Chávez candidates secured 20. Almost half of the new governors, all handpicked by Chávez himself, were military officers. Of 335 mayoral posts, the Chávez party took 231.[4]

In the 2005 parliamentary elections, an almost serendipitous turn of events validated the demand for impartial electoral observers and gave the opposition leadership the reason it needed to withdraw from the election entirely. OAS observers, while inspecting the voting machines, determined that the ballots would not be cast anonymously and that it was possible to determine exactly how each voter had cast his or her ballot. In light of this, the opposition candidates decided to withdraw from the parliamentary elections. The withdrawal surprised the country barely a week before the elections were to take place.

The ensuing political crisis left the government reeling, but not for long. An incensed Hugo Chávez attributed the political maneuver to "another one of the U.S. government's destabilization schemes." Rangel swore that "the American Embassy is behind all of this" and finished off by saying, "They can go to hell!"

The *chavista* candidates were left without rivals. And on December 4, 2005, they went alone to a boring election with more than predictable results: the parliament that would legislate for the following five years would be *chavista* through and through.

This "triumph" was clouded over by an extremely high abstention rate: 74 percent.[5] The president attributed the low turnout to internal failings: "lack of debate, triumphalism, electoral campaigns based on dancing, fighting, and grandstanding; and partisanship, which is always harmful."

During this period, both in and out of the country, Chávez did nothing to hide his rotten mood. In the middle of a Mercosur summit on December 9 in Uruguay, he aired his displeasure with the OAS and EU observers' reports on the parliamentary elections. Both delegations had come to the conclusion that broad sectors of Venezuelan society did not have faith in the electoral process or the administration behind it.

One week after the elections, Hugo Chávez still thundered. "For the No [the presidential recall referendum of 2004], almost six million of us voted. Now we are barely three million. Where are all those people? What happened? Well, governors, mayors, people in the [pro-government] parties, I warn you: I do not accept excuses from anyone! In one year we will have to stick ten million votes in the mouth of the opposition," he warned on *Aló, Presidente.*[6]

FOR MANY PEOPLE, the so-called Tascón list is a metaphor for the Venezuelan experience of late and probably for the days to come as well. In 2003, the *chavista* congressman Luis Tascón posted on his website the names of all those citizens who had signed petitions soliciting the recall referendum that would decide Chávez's future as president, exercising a right that was granted them by the Constitution. The opposition denounced the posting and suggested that certain members of the National Electoral Council had been involved. Tascón and the government officials in question defended their actions by claiming that the opposition had padded the list with forged signatures of people who were in fact government supporters. By publishing this list, said the parliament, it was simply uncovering a ruse. In any event, the confidentiality of the effort was compromised, and the path was cleared for future violations of the right to an anonymous vote.

After the referendum, Tascón's list became a political instrument, and complaints began to pour in: from public employees who had been fired from their jobs and from people who claimed that public assistance programs had engaged in discrimination when allotting state-assigned benefits. The motive was always the same: they had signed the petition. In the pages of his afternoon paper *Tal Cual,* the leftist politician Teodoro Petkoff launched a campaign of personal testimonies from the victims of what he considered to be Venezuelan-style "McCarthyism."[7] Shortly thereafter, another list was discovered, called "Maisanta," with detailed information as to how the Venezuelan people had voted in the plebiscite.

Statements also poured in from people who had been excluded from all kinds of state services and benefits, such as national identity cards, jobs in the public administration, loans for state-subsidized housing, and government contracts. The opposition began to speak of a "Bolivarian apartheid," and the complaints continued to appear in the press until the president finally felt obliged to address the matter. On his Sunday television show, Chávez ordered that the Tascón list be filed and buried, saying that the "famous list certainly fulfilled an important role at a given moment, but that moment has passed."[8]

For a certain sector of society, it is not so easy to banish the ghost conjured up by the experience of living in a state that is capable of making citizens pay for exercising their political options. Along with the ever-increasing authority of state institutions; the escalating hostility toward the United States; an ideological definition that is, nominally at least, more and more specific; a military industry that has grown stronger; and the government's desire to militarize civilian life, one of the greatest fears associated with Hugo Chávez has been revived: the Cubanization of Venezuela.

In January 2005, at a gathering at the World Social Forum in Porto Alegre, the Venezuelan leader stated his conviction that "socialism is the path." Some months later in an interview, he confessed that "at one time I came to think about the Third Way. I was having problems interpreting the world. I was confused, I read the wrong things, I had some advisers that confused me even more. I actually proposed a forum in Venezuela on Tony Blair's Third Way. I spoke and wrote a lot about 'humane capitalism.' Today I am convinced that that is impossible."[9]

For some, this declaration was the confirmation of a foregone conclusion. What could one expect of a leader who called Cuba "a sea of happiness," declared himself a *fidelista,* and invoked Che Guevara? For others, however, the statement was the expression of a precise ideological definition that had been absent from the Bolivarian Revolution until that moment. But when Chávez was asked to offer some content to this "new" socialism, his response was vague: "In reality this is what it's about: solidarity with one's brother. The struggle against the demons sown by capitalism: individualism, egotism, hatred, privileges. I think that this is where it should begin. It is a daily effort, a long-term cultural and educational task."[10]

At first, this sounds like little more than an ethical pronouncement, a declaration of lofty principles. But Chávez himself believes in thinking on his feet, that theory is born from praxis, that twenty-first-century socialism has yet to be invented and, apparently, declared. Time and words feed off each other, they work in a dialogue. In mid-2005, at the World Festival of Students and Youth, held in Caracas, the president proclaimed, "After the referendum, we find ourselves in a transitional phase headed toward postcapitalism that might be called presocialism."[11]

More than one adviser pleaded with him to be prudent, warning him that this definition might affect his popularity. The word "socialism" may be an uncomfortable term for Venezuelans to digest, given that they tend to be highly aspirational people with a desire to improve their quality of life. Every time Chávez begins to wax Franciscan, he strikes an inevitably discordant note with his audience. In this sense, oil is not necessarily an advantage. Venezuelans are aware of their country's wealth, and they may understand *chavismo* to be a more fluid and democratic system for distributing the country's oil income. But they do not seem interested in taking it any further. Whenever Chávez proposes Cuba as a kind of model, he only aggravates the discord and disgruntlement.

On August 21, 2005, from Havana, the leader of the Bolivarian Revolution asserted that "Cuba is not a dictatorship, it is a revolutionary democracy." According to a survey by Hinterlaces, 91 percent of Venezuelans value equality of opportunity, but Oscar Shemel, the director of the firm, also points out that

> people disagree with social uniformity. They reject extreme wealth and extreme poverty, identifying the ideal political system as one that combines capitalism and socialism: a combination of private investment that generates employment and a society where justice prevails. From this, it may be inferred that an important sector of the population would not agree with the idea that there should be a shift from private to collective property in their country.[12]

Without a doubt, between the abundant oil income, with which Venezuelans have an unresolved relationship, and the religious overtones that occasionally creep into the Chávez discourse, there is something tenuous, a stumbling block of sorts: the person who triumphs because he has offered to redistribute the enormous wealth that belongs to everyone is the same person who now says that those who possess an excess of whatever product they work to produce are bound to give it away, donate it to charity. This is Chávez's message to the country: "Rich is bad."

AT THIS POINT it is no longer clear how many Venezuelans live in poverty. This has also generated controversy. At the end of 2004, 53.1 percent of Venezuelan households were at the poverty level, according to official figures from the National Statistics Institute. This indicates that poverty grew during the first six years of the present administration by more than 10.8 percent despite the considerable rise in oil revenue.[13]

But shortly after these statistics were published, Chávez questioned the National Statistics Institute: "I have no doubt that the instruments they are using to measure reality are not appropriate, they are measuring our reality as if this were a neoliberal country, a capitalist country, where no revolution was taking place."[14]

In fact, toward the end of the 1980s, a number of governments did suggest that the income indicator as a method for measuring poverty was limited. The United Nations, in response, developed another form of measurement based on the indicator of Basic Needs Unsatisfied and the Human Development Index. With the aid of these two instruments, the National Statistics Institute, prompted by Chávez's concerns, decided to develop new parameters that would incorporate access to the *misiones* and other state-run social welfare programs, as well as people's evaluation of their own "level of satisfaction." In 2005, using the evaluation methods suggested by the president, poverty appeared to have decreased by a surprising 15 percent in one year.

There are other areas in which the Venezuelan president has made progress that his more moderate opposition has questioned less and even broadly acknowledged, including the Misión Barrio Adentro, which provides basic medical attention, and the literacy campaign that led him to declare Venezuela, with the support of UNESCO, an illiteracy-free territory, in October 2005.[15]

DESPITE THE INTERNAL criticism that continues to flow, there was no doubt that by late 2006, Hugo Chávez was Latin America's most influential leader. A consummately newsworthy figure whose face graces the covers of countless magazines and the front pages of newspapers everywhere, it is hard to believe that ten years ago he was just a skinny former coup plotter, an unemployed nobody who received little or no attention from the Venezuelan media. The little boy who played baseball in Barinas is finally what he always wanted to be: an international celebrity.

When Fidel Castro became ill in mid-2006 and announced his temporary leave of absence from the presidency, many people began to make predictions about Hugo Chávez's potential role in Cuba. Many of his followers even went so far as to hypothesize that he was on his way to becoming the political successor of the Cuban revolutionary in Latin America.

A few weeks later, on August 13, 2006, the rumors of Castro's death suddenly came to a halt when the Venezuelan president made a trip to Havana. "This is the best trip of my life, better even than when I used to travel to see my first girlfriend," Chávez said jokingly after a conversation with Castro on the occasion of the Cuban leader's eightieth birthday, portions of which were broadcast on Cubavisión.

Chávez is clearly proud of his friendship with the most legendary Latin American politician of the twentieth century and tends to offer optimistic reports regarding his health. Observers note that Chávez's bond with Raúl Castro will never be as strong, but they also dismiss the idea that Fidel's death will have any impact on the close relations Venezuela and Cuba presently enjoy.

Controversial and magnetic in the media, Chávez has ensured that he will remain a fixture all across Latin America, far beyond the exposure that his friendship with Fidel Castro offers him. The Venezuelan president has a guaranteed stage wherever he goes, as well as sympathizers ready to applaud him and swoon from his charisma. A controversial supporter of efforts to aid the poor, whether they are Bolivarians from Potosí or gringos in the Bronx, Hugo Chávez is no longer a tropical curiosity, and hasn't been for a long time.

Chávez masterfully exploits the disenchantment of people who feel excluded for whatever reason, and he feeds on controversy whenever he can. A considerable amount of his fame stems from his anti-imperialist stance and his fierce antagonism for the man believed to be the most powerful in the world, George W. Bush, whom he has recently been calling "Mr. Danger."[16]

Chávez loves to measure himself up against the American president and never misses a chance to call Bush a murderer responsible for acts of genocide. For Chávez, Bush is both a tool and an obsession. The *comandante* has accused his opposition of obediently following the librettos of the CIA and has even gone so far as to attribute natural disasters and climate change to the American president's refusal to sign the Kyoto protocols.

But not everything is rhetoric. In the middle of 2005, the government decided to raise the tax paid by multinational oil companies operating in Venezuela, from 1 percent to 16 percent at first and to 30 percent by 2006. Local analysts considered the measure to be fair, given that when the 1 percent rate was established, crude oil was at $12 a barrel, whereas by January 2006 it had reached $60. Given the vast income derived from the oil business, the companies in question did not object.

Chávez has questioned the policies of the Bush administration from the very heart of the empire. In September 2005, while in New York to attend the U.N. General Assembly, he joined Jesse Jackson and Democratic congressman José Serrano on a visit to the Bronx, where he told local residents that he would invest a portion of Venezuela's petrodollars in health and environmental programs.[17]

The president walked through the Bronx neighborhood serenaded by the Latin rhythms provided by a local band. He gave hugs all around, evoking shades of Che Guevara with comments like "The present is a struggle, the future belongs to us" and stopping for a moment to dance and play the congas. He seemed magnanimous and very much in his element.

"We are going to save the world, not for us, we are fifty-one years old, but for you," the Venezuelan president said to a needy young woman who, he said, reminded him of his daughters.

Shortly afterward, the president established a humanitarian program to provide 25 million gallons of oil to heat the homes of the poorest residents of the northeastern United States, through the Venezuelan-owned CITGO.[18] The program was designed to help out some 100,000 families and, according to certain analysts, humiliate Bush on his own turf. The idea came from a group of Democratic senators who sent letters to the principal oil distributors in the country, asking them to sell fuel oil at a discount to the neediest communities. CITGO was the only company that responded to the initiative.

The White House, often befuddled when dealing with the Chávez phenomenon, decided to take action in 2005, when Bush declared the Venezuelan president "a threat to regional stability," "decertified" Venezuela in the fight against the drug trade,[19] and blocked the sale of Brazilian and Spanish planes—the manufacture of which required U.S. parts—to the Venezuelan armed forces.

Though the tension between the two countries frequently approaches the breaking point, both presidents have taken care to back away from an official rift. Two episodes from 2005 illustrate this well: at one point Chávez threatened to break off relations if the U.S. judicial authorities did not approve the extradition of the anti-Castro activist Luis Posada Carriles, but when the Venezuelan request was rejected, no further action was taken. And in the middle of the year, the Venezuelan president ordered the suspension of the country's agreement with the DEA claiming that certain agents had been involved in "intelligence infiltration that threatened the security and defense of the country." But by January 2006 the two countries had worked out a new bilateral agreement.

One month later, relations froze over when the Venezuelan government had John Correa, the naval attaché at the U.S. Embassy in Caracas, expelled from Venezuela under accusations of espionage. In response, the U.S. government ordered Jenny Figueredo, the general secretary of the Venezuelan Embassy in Washington, to leave the United States.

Chávez's most memorable anti-imperialist moment, however, came when he took the stage at the U.N. General Assembly in September 2006. "The Devil came here yesterday. It still smells like sulfur today," declared the Venezuelan president in reference to U.S. President George Bush, whom, later on in Harlem, Chávez described as an "alcoholic" with "a lot of hang-ups."

His thundering words caused a fair amount of disgruntlement in the United States, but they did not affect business in any real way. According to an estimate that the U.S. Embassy in Caracas released a month after the incident, the Venezuela-U.S. trade balance for 2006 may well have topped $50 billion, which would be a 25 percent increase over the previous year and the highest dollar amount in recent years. The lion's share of their deals these days revolve around Venezuela's export of oil and oil-derivative products to the U.S. market. In 2005, bilateral trade between the two countries reached $40 billion, with Venezuelan exports accounting for $32 billion and U.S. exports for only $8 billion of this colossal pie.

In the Venezuelan daily *El Nacional,* U.S. Ambassador William Brownfield underscored the importance of accepting the fact that Venezuela and the United States were bound to have ideological and philosophical differences. He also observed that these differences would not go away and instead focused on the fact that there are plenty of other things both nations agree upon—such as economics.[20]

The effect of the Bush-Chávez dynamic can be felt all across Latin America. The Venezuelan leader has had serious run-ins with government leaders he considers to be allies of Washington (Mexico's Vicente Fox, Peru's Alejandro Toledo, Colombia's Alvaro Uribe) and has cultivated alliances with the leftist governments that have emerged up and down the continent. Though he may have been something of an inconvenience to certain leaders in the beginning, Chávez has conquered more and more territory, and nowadays there are few who can resist the generous offers of his "petrodiplomacy."

THE TURMOIL THAT CHARACTERIZED the early years of the Chávez administration has worn off a bit. The everyday mood in Venezuela during 2006 was less contentious. Some believe that while the government may have made its presence felt in every corner of the Venezuelan experience, the oil bonanza has also managed to reach every corner, as well. The restaurants and malls of Caracas are bustling, Venezuela is once again one of the world's number one importers of scotch, and the sale of luxury automobiles has gone through the roof. The atmosphere is once again redolent of "sweet cash" and the spirit of the "Saudi Venezuela" that Carlos Andrés Pérez governed in the 1970s.

The dance of dollar signs also continues to obey the dictates of the revolution, as Chávez maintains his adversarial discourse. The government has purchased a hundred thousand rifles from Russia for the defense of the country in the event of a United States invasion, which it considers a serious possibility. In 2005, more than $2 billion went to the acquisition of military equipment, and Chávez appointed himself the direct military chief of a reserve corps that, he hopes, will grow to 2 million members. He has also expressed his desire to create popular defense units out of the social organizations that support his revolution.

The Venezuelan president has also decided to postpone the date of his retirement. In mid-August 2005, during an official event at the National Pantheon, he made an announcement that thrilled his followers and infuriated his opponents: "Yes, I said that I would retire in 2021. But no! I have changed the date, I have to continue until 2030."[21]

To this end he is counting on the new parliament, made up entirely of congressmen loyal to his "process," to reform the Constitution (which his own movement designed in 1999) and allow for the immediate reelection of the president, without term limits. To remove any lingering doubts, the president of the National Assembly, Nicolás Maduro, a former worker in the Caracas metro, said, "The contribution of this new Assembly will be to strengthen the revolution, to legislate so that Chávez governs not until 2021 but until 2030." He said this on December 6, 2005. Maduro was appointed foreign minister in 2006. His wife, Cilia Flores, is now the president of the parliament.

One year later, on December 3, 2006, the Chávez dream continued to shine brightly, intact. "The Bolivarian victory is indisputable, unquestionable, and overwhelming," the Venezuelan president proclaimed to the multitudes that had gathered around Miraflores Palace minutes after his reelection, with 62.84 percent[22] of the votes, was made official. More than 7 million Venezuelans had decided that he should remain in power for another six years. The opposition, having wagered on a center-left platform, quickly conceded its defeat—a significant gesture that confirmed the legitimacy of the elections. "We acknowledge that today we were defeated," stated opposition candidate Manuel Rosales, who obtained 36.9 percent of the vote.

Surrounded by his children and closest aides, Hugo Chávez heralded the end of the transition period and the start of a new era, the basis of which "will be to deepen, broaden and expand the Bolivarian Revolution. . . . More than 60 percent of the Venezuelan people voted not for Chávez but for a project that has a name: Bolivarian socialism." Aware of the deep reservations that exist in Venezuela regarding this particular issue, he appealed to followers and detractors alike with the following exhortation: "Let none of us fear socialism!"

Despite the head of state's broad support base, few people seem to have a clear picture of what Chávez means, exactly, when he speaks of twenty-first-century socialism. An interview conducted by the firm Datanálisis, published by *El Nacional* the last week of December 2006, revealed that 80 percent of those polled rejected the Cuban model, and 51.6 percent preferred socialism to capitalism, but in the sense of "a moderate, Chilean- or European-style socialism."

Hugo Chávez keeps the rhythm of his revolution on tenterhooks. Even now, eight years after he became president for the first time, nobody seems able to make any predictions about him. And on the rainy night of December 3, 2006, only one thing was certain: Venezuela would most certainly continue to hang on his every word. For how long? Nobody knows. Though the Constitution states that this will be his last term of office, Hugo Chávez has a faithful parliament ready to help overcome that obstacle. In "the kingdom of socialism" that he has promised for Venezuela—that is, his kingdom—his popularity and power seem to know no end. The revolution still needs a quarter century to achieve its dreams. That, it seems, is its new destiny—*for now.*

	1999	2000	2001	2002	2003	2004	2005
POVERTY POOR HOUSEHOLDS							
Official statistics (INE) %	42.38	40.98	39.25	45.02	54	53.1	37.9
Unofficial statistics (UCAB)[1]	49.9	49.5	48.2	41.5	60.2	59.6	57.9
Population (million inhabitants)	23.8	24.3	24.7	25.2	25.6	26.3	27.0
Unemployment (%)	14.9	13.9	13.25	15.85	18.05	13.9	11.4
Life expectancy (years)	72.94	73.34	73.53	73.72	72.98	73.18	73.18
Infant mortality rate (%)	18.52	18.18	17.84	17.5	17.16	17.1	15.85
Literacy rate (%)	90.9	90	93.6	93.6	93.6	95	95
Human Development Index (UNDP)	0.74	0.75	0.77	0.69	0.76	0.79	0.72
Corruption Perceptions Index (TI) (rank/total)	78/99	72/90	70/91	86/102	104/133	120/146	138/159

Sources: National Statistics Institute, Venezuela (INE); Central Bank of Venezuela; United Nations Development Program (UNDP); and Transparency International (TI).

1. Poverty Project, Andrés Bello Catholic University.
2. Estimated.

	1999	2000	2001	2002	2003	2004	2005
Foreign debt (billions)	$22.7	$21.9	$22.9	$22.5	$22.5	$24.8	$31.0
National debt (billions)	$5.4	$10.0	$13.8	$11.2	$14.5	$13.5	$15.5
International reserves (billions)	$15.1	$15.8	$12.2	$12.0	$21.3	$21.1	$30.3
Gross National Product (annual variation in %)	−6	3.7	3.4	−8.9	−7.6	17.3	9.3
Per capita income	$3,282	$3,477	$3,734	$2,335	$3,338	$4,020	$4,810
Exchange rate (bolivars per dollar)	648.25	699.75	763	1,401.25	1,600	1,920	2,150
Inflation (%)	20	13.4	12.3	31.2	27.1	23	14.4

Sources: National Statistics Institute, Venezuela; Venezuelan Finance Ministry; Central Bank of Venezuela; World Bank.

CHAPTER 1: THE REVOLUTION HAS ARRIVED

1. Hugo Chávez, personal diary (unpublished).
2. Mempo Giardinelli, "Yo garantizo hasta el abuso en la libertad de expresión," *El Nacional,* October 10, 1999.
3. Chávez, diary.
4. L. Lucía Lacurcia, "Entrevista con la madre del presidente," *Primicia,* May 18, 1999.
5. Rosa Miriam Elizalde and Luis Báez, "Chávez nuestro," an interview with Hugo Chávez, from a pamphlet published by the Venezuelan government, 2004.
6. Frontline/World, "Venezuela—A Nation on Edge," June 2003, www.pbs.org/frontlineworld/stories/venezuela/chirinos.html. Rangel was replaced as vice president in January 2007.
7. After the government of dictator General Marcos Pérez Jiménez was overthrown, he was succeeded by the following presidents: Rómulo Betancourt (Acción Democrática [AD], 1959–64), Raúl Leoni (1964–69), Rafael Caldera (COPEI, 1969–74), Carlos Andrés Pérez (AD, 1974–79), Luis Herrera Campins (COPEI, 1979–84), Jaime Lusinchi (AD, 1984–89), Carlos Andrés Pérez (1989–93), Ramón J. Velásquez (independent, transition, 1993–94), Rafael Caldera (Convergencia, 1994–99), Hugo Chávez (1999–   ).
8. Editorial, *El Nacional,* December 7, 1998.
9. Luis Ugalde et al., *Detrás de la pobreza* (Caracas: Civil Association for the Promotion of Social Studies and the Andrés Bello Catholic University, 2004).
10. "La boina imagen de Chávez," *Revista Producto* 184 (February 1999).
11. *El Nacional,* June 8, 1998.
12. Petkoff ended his activism with MAS when the party decided to support the candidacy of Hugo Chávez.
13. *El Nacional,* July 24, 1998.
14. William Izarra, *En busca de la revolución* (Caracas: unpublished manuscript, 2001), 134.

CHAPTER 2: "ME, A COMMUNIST?"

1. Agustín Blanco Muñoz, *Habla el comandante,* 2nd ed. (Caracas: Fundación Cátedra Pío Tamayo, Central University of Venezuela, 2003), 332.
2. Ibid., 83.
3. Elizalde and Báez, "Chávez nuestro."
4. A book by the Chilean journalist Marta Harnecker.
5. Marta Harnecker, *Un hombre, un pueblo* (Caracas: n.p., 2002), 24.

6. Elizalde and Báez, "Chávez nuestro."
7. Venezolana de Televisión documentary, August 13, 2004.
8. Blanco Muñoz, *Habla el comandante,* 562.
9. Harnecker, *Un hombre, un pueblo,* 15–16.
10. Institute for Economic and Social Research, University of the Andes.
11. Blanco Muñoz, *Habla el comandante,* 40.

CHAPTER 3: AN EXISTENTIAL CONFLICT

1. Elizalde and Báez, "Chávez nuestro."
2. Ibid.
3. Venezolana de Televisión documentary, August 13, 2004.
4. Hugo Chávez, unpublished letters.
5. Venezolana de Televisión documentary, August 13, 2004.
6. Elizalde and Báez, "Chávez nuestro."
7. See Blanco Muñoz, *Habla el comandante,* and Harnecker, *Un hombre, un pueblo.*
8. Though he stepped down in 1978, Torrijos continued to control the political machine in Panama until his death in a 1981 airplane crash.
9. Blanco Muñoz, *Habla el comandante,* 44.
10. Harnecker, *Un hombre, un pueblo,* 20.
11. Ibid., 21.
12. Ramón Piñango, "Muerte de la armonía," in *En esta Venezuela, realidades y nuevos caminos* (Caracas: Ediciones IESA, 2003), 17.
13. Ibid., 56.
14. Gabriel García Márquez, "El enigma de los dos Chávez," *Cambio,* February 1999, www.voltairenet.org/article120084.html.
15. Blanco Muñoz, *Habla el comandante,* 57.
16. Ibid.
17. Harnecker, *Un hombre, un pueblo,* 24.

CHAPTER 4: THE MAN, THE CONSPIRATOR

1. Alberto Garrido, *Guerrilla y conspiración militar en Venezuela* (Caracas: Fondo Editorial Nacional, 1999), 53.
2. The Venezuelan Communist Party (PCV), founded in 1931 and banned until 1969; the Movement of the Revolutionary Left (MIR), founded in 1960 as a Marxist-Leninist offshoot of the governmental Democratic Action party, banned in 1962 and legalized in 1969.
3. The Betancourt government reported the case to the Organization of American States, invoking the Inter-American Treaty of Reciprocal Assistance. An investigative commission sent by the OAS concluded that the weapons had come from Cuba, and to this end in July of 1964 a group of foreign ministers held a meeting at which they decided (14 votes in favor, 4 against, and 1 abstention) to sever diplomatic, consular, and economic ties with Havana, which had already been excluded from the Inter-American system in 1962.

4. Elizalde and Báez, "Chávez nuestro."
5. Blanco Muñoz, *Habla el comandante*, 45.
6. Carúpano, on May 4, 1962, and Puerto Cabello, on June 2, 1962.
7. Izarra, *En busca de la revolución*, 67.
8. Garrido, *Guerrilla y conspiración militar en Venezuela*, 56.
9. The officer David López Rivas, brother of Samuel López, a member of the Party for the Venezuelan Revolution.
10. Alberto Garrido, *Testimonios de la revolución bolivariana*, (Mérida: privately published, 2002), 123.
11. The president was probably confusing the MIR with the Party for the Venezuelan Revolution.
12. Elizalde and Báez, "Chávez nuestro."
13. Garrido, *Testimonios de la revolución bolivariana*, 11.
14. Ibid., 12.
15. Iván Jiménez, *Los golpes de estado desde Castro hasta Caldera* (Caracas: Centralca, 1996).
16. Marta Harnecker, *Venezuela, militares junto al pueblo* (Madrid: El Viejo Topo, 2003), 194.
17. Alberto Garrido, *El otro Chávez, testimonio de Herma Marksman* (Mérida: author's edition, 2002), 107–8.
18. Carlos Croes, "El Ejército Bolivariano lo fundamos en el año del viernes negro," *Quinto Día* (February 2, 1999): 4.
19. Garrido, *Testimonios de la revolución bolivariana*, 17.

CHAPTER 5: PREPARING THE UPRISING

1. M. Socorro, "Hugo Chávez," *Venezuela Analítica* (www.analitica.com).
2. Blanco Muñoz, *Habla el comandante*, 158, 466.
3. Ibid., 416.
4. Jiménez, *Los golpes de estado desde Castro hasta Caldera*, 134.
5. Blanco Muñoz, *Habla el comandante*, 133–34.
6. Poll conducted by Gaither published in *El Nacional*, January 26, 1992.
7. Blanco Muñoz, *Habla el comandante*, 135.

CHAPTER 6: STROKE OF LUCK

1. According to the report submitted by Vice Admiral Elías Daniels, inspector of the armed forces at the time, Hugo Chávez left Maracay with 2 superior officers, 13 subordinates, 3 noncommissioned officers, 3 professional soldiers, and 440 enlisted men. For more detail, see Daniels, *Militares y Democracia* (Caracas: José Agustín Catalá Editor, 1992), 188–89.
2. Harnecker, *Un hombre, un pueblo*, 32.
3. Blanco Muñoz, *Habla el comandante*, 479.
4. The rebel operative was headed up by Miguel Rodríguez Torres, at the time a captain and now the director of the Scientific Police (CIPCJ).

5. Blanco Muñoz, *Habla el comandante,* 473.
6. General Eutimio Fuguet Borregales.
7. Blanco Muñoz, *Habla el comandante,* 143.
8. The men in question were Captain Ronald Blanco La Cruz, governor of the state of Táchira, and Captain Antonio Rojas Suárez, governor of the state of Bolívar, who has since abandoned the ranks of the pro-Chávez party.
9. According to the testimony of Chávez and the other commanders, this was Captain René Gimón Alvarez.
10. Elías Daniels, *Militares y democracia* (Caracas: José Agustín Catalá Editor, 1992), 179–80.
11. Blanco Muñoz, *Habla el comandante,* 147–48.
12. Ibid., 148.
13. Ibid., 491.
14. Ibid.
15. Daniels, *Militares y democracia,* 194.
16. Blanco Muñoz, *Habla el comandante,* 473.
17. Jiménez, *Los golpes de estado desde Castro hasta Caldera,* 133.
18. The register kept by Vice Admiral Elías Daniels, inspector of the armed forces at the time, spoke of 2,668 troops involved.
19. Blanco Muñoz, *Habla el comandante,* 476.
20. Ibid., 261.
21. According to the detailed account offered by the journalist Angela Zago in her book *La rebelión de los ángeles,* one captain, two second lieutenants, two corporals, nine soldiers, four policemen, one sergeant, and one civilian died in the operation.
22. Blanco Muñoz, *Habla el comandante,* 550.
23. Ibid., 226.

CHAPTER 7: A MODEL OFFICER

1. "La noche de las boinas rojas," *Revista Zeta* 885 (February 6, 1992): 56–62.
2. Judith Martorelli, "Interview with Hugo Chávez," *El Globo,* February 29, 1992.
3. *Golpes militares en Venezuela* (Caracas: José Agustín Catalá Editor, 1998), 132.
4. Ibid., 124.
5. Alberto Arvelo Ramos, *El dilema del chavismo, una incógnita en el poder* (Caracas: José Agustín Catalá Editor, 1998), 56.
6. *Golpes militares,* 148.
7. Arvelo Ramos, *El dilema del chavismo,* 71.
8. Y. Delgado, "Chávez admitió existencia de los decretos del 4F," *El Nacional,* September 18, 1998.
9. Kléber Ramírez, *Historia documental del 4 de febrero* (Caracas: n.p., 1998).
10. Arvelo Ramos, *El dilema del chavismo,* 56.
11. Blanco Muñoz, *Habla el comandante,* 149–50.
12. He said the following to Marta Harnecker: "Even I remember that I brought a truck full of weapons from Maracay to Caracas, and nobody ever came to pick

them up. We had agreed to arm those popular combat groups. . . . There was no popular mobilization, nothing. So we were left alone in the rebellion, without people, as if in a void, like a fish without water." This quote is taken from Harnecker, *Un hombre, un pueblo,* 32.

13. Blanco Muñoz, *Habla el comandante,* 153–54.
14. Garrido, *Testimonios de la revolución bolivariana,* 23–24.
15. Ibid.
16. Reproduced by the newspaper *El Globo,* May 8, 1992.
17. Alfredo Meza, "Cuestionario Proust a Hugo Chávez," *Estampas, El Universal,* August 9, 1998.

CHAPTER 8: "BOLÍVAR AND I"

1. Luis Bilbao, "Chávez por Chávez," Brazilian Workers' Party, www.pdt.org.br /internacional/hugochavez_4.htm.
2. Laura Sánchez, "Ya comienzan a oírse las cacerolas," *El Nacional,* March 2, 1992.
3. "Hugo Chávez Frías: En vez de Superman mi héroe era Bolívar," Revista *Qué Pasa* (Chile), August 16, 1999.
4. Luis Castro Leiva, *De la patria boba a la teología bolivariana* (Caracas: Monte Avila Editores, 1987).
5. Germán Carrera Damas, *El culto a Bolívar,* 2nd ed. (Caracas: Alfadil Ediciones, 2003), 375.
6. Elías Pino Iturrieta, *El divino Bolívar, ensayo sobre una religión republicana* (Madrid: Los Libros de la Catarata, 2003), 28.
7. Jiménez, *Los golpes de estado desde Castro hasta Caldera,* 238.
8. The leaders of the insurrection were Rear Admirals Hernán Gruber Odreman and Luis Enrique Cabrera, Air Force general Francisco Visconti, Army colonel Higinio Castro, and National Guard major Carlos Salima.
9. Blanco Muñoz, *Habla el comandante,* 331.
10. Izarra, *En busca de la revolución bolivariana,* 97.
11. Blanco Muñoz, *Habla el comandante,* 355.
12. Pino Iturrieta, *El divino Bolívar,* 187–96.
13. Néstor Francia, *Qué piensa Chávez* (Caracas: privately published, 2003), 31.
14. Hugo Chávez, *Un brazalete tricolor* (Valencia: Vadell Hermanos Editores, 1992).
15. Blanco Muñoz, *Habla el comandante,* 59.
16. José León Tapia, *Maisanta, el último hombre a caballo,* 6th ed. (Caracas: José Agustín Catalá/El Centauro, 2000), 22.
17. The admiration and gratitude Hugo Chávez felt for Tapia led the doctor-writer to ally himself with the government in 1999, when he participated in the process of drafting the country's new constitution. The president mentions him frequently, every time he makes any sort of allusion to Maisanta, and his name has been connected to the Chávez movement, something that has recently been a source of irritation for Tapia. He now refuses to grant interviews in which political topics are to be discussed.

18. Interview with José León Tapia, *El Globo,* February 19, 1992.
19. Gustavo Wanloxten, "Maisanta regresó con tanques," *El Globo,* February 21, 1992.
20. Sánchez, "Ya comienzan a oírse las cacerolas."
21. Pino Iturrieta, *El divino Bolívar,* 182.
22. Bilbao, "Chávez por Chávez."

CHAPTER 9: THE SKINNY GUY IN THE *LIQUI-LIQUI*

1. According to a Datanalysis poll carried out in 1996, Irene Sáez had a 49.2 percent popularity rating; Chávez had 7.3 percent.
2. The *liqui-liqui,* also known as a *liquilique,* is worn in Venezuela and Colombia.
3. Blanco Muñoz, *Habla el comandante,* 512.
4. After the 1992 coup attempts, the political pressure on Pérez continued to mount and it was suggested he resign from the presidency. In March 1993, the attorney general of the Republic initiated proceedings against Pérez for embezzlement of public funds. The money in question was $17 million worth of aid to the Nicaraguan president, Violeta Barrios de Chamorro, which had come from the secret accounts of the presidency. On May 20, the Supreme Court of Justice ruled that there was sufficient cause to try him, and the Congress resolved to replace him so that the trial could continue. Pérez was removed from the presidency and placed under house arrest while he awaited sentencing. Finally, on May 30, 1993, the court gave him a sentence of two years and four months of incarceration, which he completed at home.
5. In the parliamentary session that was intended to condemn the uprising, Caldera, a senator at the time, had this to say: "It is difficult to ask the people to sacrifice themselves for freedom and democracy when they think that freedom and democracy are incapable of giving them food to eat, of preventing the astronomical rise in the cost of subsistence, or of placing a definitive end to the terrible scourge of corruption that, in the eyes of the entire world, is eating away at the institutions of Venezuela with each passing day."
6. Harnecker, *Un hombre, un pueblo,* 41.
7. National Opinion Poll.
8. Harnecker, *Un hombre, un pueblo,* 44.
9. *El Nacional,* February 4, 1996.
10. *El Nacional,* March 27, 1996.
11. Izarra, *En busca de la revolución bolivariana,* 95.
12. Harnecker, *Un hombre, un pueblo,* 46.
13. Izarra, *En busca de la revolución bolivariana,* 97.
14. Blanco Muñoz, *Habla el comandante,* 512–13.

CHAPTER 10: STATE OF GRACE

1. Poverty Project, Andrés Bello Catholic University. According to official statistics, it was 42.3 percent.
2. Harnecker, *Un hombre, un pueblo,* 54.

3. President Chávez's proposal received 87.75 percent of the vote of 37.65 percent of the total electorate. The abstention rate was over 60 percent. In all, 11,022,031 Venezuelans were registered to vote, yet only 4,129,547 cast votes, according to data from the National Electoral Council.
4. Three other seats had previously been allotted to indigenous representatives.
5. Given the type of system in place—plurinominal with a single, open list—it was a very unfavorable situation for the opposition. With 66 percent of the vote, the Chávez party ended up with 95 percent of the 122 seats, whereas the opposition, with 34 percent of the votes, obtained only 5 percent of the seats—that is, 6. Had the principle of proportional representation for minorities been applied, the opposition would have secured 44 seats. Voter abstention hovered around 53.8 percent, according to the statistics of the National Electoral Council.
6. Marisol Decarli and Alicia La Rotta, "Chávez instó a venezolanos a acudir masivamente a votar," *El Universal,* December 15, 1999.
7. Alicia La Rotta, "Chávez aseguró que no hará campaña por la presidencia," *El Universal,* February 3, 2000.
8. There was a record-breaking abstention rate: 43 percent.
9. Harnecker, *Un hombre, un pueblo,* 57.
10. "Chávez: ¿le quitamos el subsidio a los colegios privados?" *El Nacional,* February 8, 2001.
11. Ibid.
12. *Aló, Presidente,* Sunday, June 17, 2001.
13. The initiative was in direct violation of two articles of the 1999 Constitution. The first article, 67, states that "the use of government funds to finance organizations of a political nature is prohibited"; the second article, 145, stipulates, "Public employees are at the service of the State and not of any particular partiality."
14. Heinz Dieterich, interview with Hugo Chávez, Venezuela Analítica (www.analitica.com), December 5, 2001.
15. Ibid.
16. The agriculture and livestock sector also questioned the fact that the adjudication of these properties to the small farmers would be limited: they could use them and transfer them to their heirs, but the plots could not be "the object of any legal sale." Their properties could be only "object of a credit guarantee under the modality of guarantee pending the harvest," which would effectively halt any financing. Fourteen percent of the Venezuelan population is rural.
17. Dieterich, interview with Hugo Chávez.
18. Tulio Hernández, "No es un adiós sino un hasta luego," *El Universal,* January 26, 2002.

CHAPTER 11: AROUND THE WORLD IN AN AIRBUS

1. "Chávez advierte a Bush sobre nuevos Vietnam," *El Universal,* November 6, 2004.

2. The reader should bear in mind that this manuscript was completed on August 31, 2004.
3. A. Morán, "Le tengo el ojo puesto a La Casona," *El Universal*, February 10, 1999.
4. Ibid.
5. Y. Delgado, "Gran fondo social," *El Nacional*, February 10, 1999.
6. Elizabeth Araujo, "Los gastos del oficio," *Gatopardo*, June 20, 2003.
7. A. Jiménez, "Presupuesto de la presidencia aumentó a Bs. 115,7 millardos," *El Nacional*, May 11, 2004.
8. Abdelaziz Bouteflika, president of Algeria; Abdurrahman Wahid, president of Indonesia; Sayed Mohammad Khatami, president of Iran; Olusegun Obasanjo, president of Nigeria; Sheik Hamad ben-Khalifa ben-Hamed al-Thani, emir of Qatar; Hammad ben-Mohamed al Sharqui, member of the Supreme Council of the United Arab Emirates; Abdullah bin Abdulaziz al Saud, crown prince of Saudi Arabia; Tami Ramada, vice president of Iraq; Mustafa al-Kharrubi, member of the Revolutionary Council of Libya; Saud Nasser al-Sabah, oil minister of Kuwait; and Rilwanu Lukman, secretary-general of OPEC.
9. Statistics from the Central Bank of Venezuela.
10. As of February 1999, the total number of people on the PDVSA payroll was 50,000, of whom 32,000 were on the per-day payroll, 16,000 were in the superior payroll, and 2,000 were in the executive payroll, according to information published in the newspaper *El Nacional*, March 19, 2004.

CHAPTER 12: ENTANGLED APRIL

1. Miguel Bonasso, "Anatomía íntima de un golpe contada por Chávez," *Página 12* (Argentina), June 12, 2003.
2. Ibid.
3. Ibid.
4. Marta Harnecker, *Venezuela, militares junto al pueblo* (Barcelona: El Viejo Topo, 2003), 208.
5. Sandra La Fuente and Alfredo Meza, *El acertijo de abril* (Caracas: Random House Mondadori, 2004), 80.
6. Cristina Marcano, "En Venezuela hubo un 'pinochetazo light,' " *Milenio Semanal*, May 27, 2002.
7. La Fuente and Meza, *El acertijo de abril*, 23.
8. Television interview with the journalist María Cristina Uribe, Colombia's Channel One, May 18, 2002.
9. Fragment of a conversation with Chávez while he was being held at Turiamo; see Venezuela Analítica, www.analitica.com/bitblioteca/hchavez/cautiverio.asp.
10. Bonasso, "Anatomía íntima de un golpe contada por Chávez."
11. Harnecker, *Un hombre, un pueblo*, 117.
12. *El Nacional*, April 15, 2002. Press conference.
13. Bonasso, "Anatomía íntima."

14. Pedro Carmona, *Mi testimonio ante la historia* (Caracas: Editorial Actum, 2004), 124.
15. Marcano, "En Venezuela hubo un 'pinochetazo light.' "
16. Harnecker, *Un hombre, un pueblo*, 230.
17. Bonasso, "Anatomía íntima."
18. Carmona, *Mi testimonio ante la historia*, 103.
19. Bonasso, "Anatomía íntima."
20. www.analitica.com/bitblioteca/hchavez/cautiverio.asp.
21. "4 días de historia," *El Nacional*, April 11, 2004.
22. La Fuente and Meza, *El acertijo de abril*, 175.
23. Néstor Francia, *Puente llaguno, hablan las víctimas* (Venezuela: privately published, 2002), 7.

CHAPTER 13: THE SHOWMAN OF MIRAFLORES

1. "Hugo Chávez Frías: En vez de Superman mi héroe era Bolívar," Revista *Qué Pasa* (Chile), August 16, 1999.
2. Elizalde and Báez, "Chávez nuestro."
3. Chávez, diary.
4. Angela Zago, *La rebelión de los ángeles* (Caracas: Warp Ediciones, 1998).
5. Izarra, *En busca de la revolución*, 104.
6. "Chávez, el *publisher*," *Producto* (Caracas: Grupo Editorial Producto, June 1999).
7. Harnecker, *Un hombre, un pueblo*, 186.
8. Ibid., 189.
9. Ibid., 57.
10. Rafael Poleo, "Los medios de comunicación como factor de poder en el proceso venezolano," *Chávez y los medios* (Caracas: Alfadil Ediciones, 2002), 42.
11. Vladimir Villegas, "Medios vs. Chávez: la lucha continúa," *Chávez y los medios*, 50.
12. Cristina Marcano, "Venezuela: ¿esquizofrenia mediática?," *Milenio Semanal*, July 14, 2002.
13. Villegas, "Medios vs. Chávez," 53.
14. "Chávez, el *publisher*."

CHAPTER 14: BUSH THE *PENDEJO* AND FIDEL THE BROTHER

1. Judith Martorelli, "Un golpe de suerte salvó a CAP," *El Globo*, February 29, 1992.
2. Ibid.
3. Editorial, *The New York Times*, November 6, 2000.
4. Otto Reich was the ambassador in Venezuela from 1986 to 1989. In January 2002, President Bush named him assistant secretary of state for Western Hemisphere affairs, but the Senate never approved the appointment. Ten months later, the White House named him special envoy for Latin American

initiatives, a position that did not require congressional approval. In May of 2004, he resigned for "personal, financial reasons." On that occasion he said that as he left his post he felt frustrated by the fact that he had been unable to find a solution to the situations in Venezuela and Cuba. Of the Venezuelan situation he said, "Venezuela is not yet under a dictatorship, but it is important to be very careful there."

5. Roger Noriega was a member of the Senate Foreign Relations Committee in the United States and was OAS ambassador from 2001 to 2003. In 2003, he was appointed assistant secretary of state for Western Hemisphere affairs and was confirmed in July of that year by the U.S. Senate.

6. *El Nacional,* April 23, 2001.

7. In 2003, Venezuela exported 2.25 million barrels of oil per day, of which 1.63 million barrels per day went to the United States—in other words, 72.44 percent, according to statistics from the Energy Information Administration of the U.S. Department of Energy.

8. Joint radio and television broadcast, October 29, 2001.

9. *El Nacional,* November 3, 2001.

10. *El Nacional,* February 6, 2002.

11. *El Nacional,* April 18, 2002.

12. *El Nacional,* April 20, 2002.

13. Among those involved in the U.S.-Venezuela controversy: Colin Powell, secretary of state; Condoleezza Rice, national security adviser; Ari Fleischer, White House press secretary; Richard Boucher and Philip Reeker, State Department spokespeople; Otto Reich, special envoy for Latin America; Roger Noriega, assistant secretary of state for Western Hemisphere affairs; George Tenet, director of the CIA; John Maisto, then U.S. ambassador to the OAS; and Charles Shapiro, the U.S. ambassador in Caracas until August 2004.

14. Speech given February 29, 2004.

15. Orlando Ochoa, "Influencias alquiladas," *El Universal,* May 9, 2004.

16. Ramón López Martínez, *Un seguimiento a los viajes internacionales de Hugo Chávez Frías* (Caracas: privately published, 2000), 211–15.

17. *El Nacional,* November 19, 1999.

18. *El Nacional,* May 8, 1999.

19. $912 million for the year 2000.

20. *El Nacional,* December 1, 1999.

21. *El Nacional,* October 27, 2000.

22. *El Nacional,* October 29, 2000.

23. Program 49, October 30, 2000.

24. The Cooperation Agreement, based on the Caracas Energy Pact, signed in 2000 by ten Caribbean and Central American countries, provided for the sale of 53,000 barrels of oil per day to Cuba under most preferential conditions: 80 percent at market prices and 20 percent to be paid in fifteen years, with a two-year grace period, a 2 percent interest rate, and a price between $15 and $30 per barrel. It was stipulated that Cuba might barter goods and/or services as a form of payment.

25. *El Nacional,* January 18, 2001.
26. *El Nacional,* January 11, 2006.

CHAPTER 15: THE UGLY DUCKLING

1. Luis Pineda Castellanos, *El diablo paga con traición a quien le sirve con lealtad, anécdotas de mi vida como amigo de Hugo Chávez Frías* (Mérida: Producciones Farol, 2003), 118.
2. Agustín Blanco Muñoz, *Habla Herma Marksman: Chávez me utilizó* (Caracas: Fundación Cátedra Pío Tamayo, UCV, 2004), 174.
3. Ibid., 119.
4. Alfredo Meza, "Hugo Chávez a golpe de batazos, disparos y piropos," *Estampas/El Universal,* August 9, 1998.
5. Ibid.
6. Faitha Marina Nahmens, "Marisabel de Chávez a régimen," *Exceso* 139, March 2001.
7. Sebastián de la Nuez, *Marisabel, la historia te absolverá* (Caracas: Editorial Exceso, 2002), 51.
8. Ibid., 86.
9. Pineda Castellanos, *El diablo paga,* 129.
10. Nuez, *Marisabel, la historia te absolverá,* 69.
11. Cenovia Casas, "La Asamblea Nacional está desperdiciando el tiempo," *El Nacional,* January 2, 2001.
12. Carlos Hernández, "Después del golpe, el divorcio," *El Universal,* June 2, 2002.
13. Ibid.
14. Ibid.
15. Vanesa Davies and E. Delgado, "Marisabel no aceptó que Hugo Chávez estuviera casado con su pueblo," *El Nacional,* June 3, 2002.

CHAPTER 16: LA CHAVERA

1. A. Beroes, *La corrupción en los tiempos de Chávez;* see http://es.geocities.com/malversacion/cap09_05.htm.
2. Alfredo Meza, "Los Chávez son acosados por el comandante Cazorla," *El Nacional,* November 28, 1999.
3. Ibid.
4. Elizalde and Báez, "Chávez nuestro."
5. Dimas Medina, "Mi hijo no se parece a Fidel Castro," *La Prensa* (Barinas), March 24, 2000.

CHAPTER 17: 2021: LOOKING AHEAD

1. Luis Alberto Butto Montes, "El nuevo profesionalismo militar de Seguridad Interna y Desarrollo Militar," *Militares y sociedad en Venezuela* (Caracas: Andrés Bello Catholic University, 2001), 129.

2. Fausto Masó, *Los amantes del tango* (Caracas: Random House Mondadori, 2004), 46.

3. According to the records kept by the Program for Education—Action in Human Rights, Provea.

4. Teodoro Petkoff, *Una segunda opinión, la Venezuela de Chávez. Libro hablado con Ibsen Martínez and Elías Pino Iturrieta* (Caracas: Grijalbo Mondadori, 2000), 77.

5. Olga Wornat, "De Chávez y algo más," *Poder,* October 5, 2001.

6. Luis Britto García, *La máscara del poder. I: Del gendarme necesario al demócrata necesario* (Caracas: Alfadil/Trópico, 1988), 200.

7. Patricia Márquez, "Vacas flacas y odios gordos: la polarización en Venezuela," *En esta Venezuela. Realidades y nuevos caminos* (Caracas: Ediciones IESA, 2003), 40.

8. According to the National Institute for Statistics, the number of families in poverty went from 42.3 percent in 1999 to 53.1 percent in 2004. According to the Poverty Project at the Andrés Bello Catholic University, poverty rose from 49.9 percent in 1999 to 60.2 percent in 2003. Please refer to the appendix for more socioeconomic indicators.

9. "Presidente Chávez anunció Misión Cristo para acabar con la pobreza," Venpres, official state news agency, December 6, 2003.

10. Alberto Garrido, *Mi amigo Chávez* (Caracas: self-published, 2001), 73.

11. Of a total of 14,037,900 voters, 5,619,954 voted in favor of the president, 3,872,951 against him, and the remaining 32 percent abstained.

12. Britto García, *La máscara del poder,* 13.

13. Ramos Jiménez, "Los límites del liderazgo plebiscitario," *La transición venezolana* (Caracas: Research Center for Comparative Politics, 2002), 26.

14. Armando Durán, *Venezuela en llamas* (Caracas: Random House Mondadori, 2004), 275.

15. Mark Lilla, "The New Age of Tyranny," *The New York Review of Books,* October 24, 2002.

EPILOGUE

1. *El Universal,* August 16, 2005.

2. www.aporrea.org, December 22, 2004.

3. December 2004 and March 2005, respectively.

4. Of a total of 14,469,027 registered voters, 3,659,216 cast votes and 10,809,810 abstained; 114 congressmen from Chávez's Fifth Republic Movement party were voted into the unicameral National Assembly. The rest of the seats were split among other progovernment politicians.

5. A speech given by the president of Venezuela during the closing act of the Twenty-ninth Mercosur summit in Montevideo, December 9, 2005.

6. *Aló, Presidente,* December 11, 2005.

7. *Tal Cual,* May 2, 2005.

8. Miguel Cabieses, "¿Hacia dónde va usted, presidente Chávez?" *Punto Final* (Chile) 2005; www.kaosenlared.net/noticia.php?id_noticia=14106.

9. Ibid.
10. *El Nacional,* August 15, 2005.
11. Unión Radio, September 27, 2005.
12. Unión Radio, April 14, 2005.
13. From 42.38 percent in 1999 to 60.1 percent in 2004.
14. *Aló, Presidente,* April 3, 2005.
15. In UNESCO's 2005 report, Venezuela is the fifth most literate country in Latin America, after Uruguay, Argentina, Cuba, and Chile.
16. An allusion to one of the characters in *Doña Bárbara,* by the writer and former Venezuelan president Rómulo Gallegos.
17. Chávez and Serrano negotiated an agreement to provide 8 million gallons of oil to properties belonging to three nonprofit corporations in the Bronx: the Mount Hope Housing Company, the Fordham Bedford Housing Corporation, and VIP Community Services.
18. With some 14,000 gas stations in U.S. territory, CITGO, a subsidiary of Petróleos de Venezuela, possesses more than 6 percent of the fuel-refining capacity in the United States.
19. There is, however, an exception that may be applied "in order to maintain U.S. programs that aid democratic institutions in Venezuela."
20. *El Nacional,* October 25, 2006.
21. Special session in honor of the commemoration of the bicentennial of the oath of Liberator Simón Bolívar at Monte Sacro, National Pantheon, August 15, 2005.
22. With 99 percent of the votes tabulated, Hugo Chávez Frías obtained 7,300,988 votes (62.84 percent) and Manuel Rosales obtained 4,287,467 votes (36.9 percent). Of 15,921,223 voters, there was an abstention rate of 25.94 percent.

Books

Arvelo Ramos, Alberto. *El dilema del chavismo, una incógnita en el poder.* Caracas: José Agustín Catalá Editor, 1998.

Avendaño, Jaime. *El militarismo en Venezuela.* Caracas: Ediciones Centauro, 1982.

Beroes, Agustín. *La corrupción en tiempo de Chávez.* http://es.geocities.com/malversacion/index.htm.

Blanco Muñoz, Agustín. *Habla el comandante,* 2nd ed. Caracas: Fundación Cátedra Pío Tamayo, Universidad Central de Venezuela, 2003.

———. *Habla Herma Marksman, Chávez me utilizó.* Caracas: Fundación Cátedra Pío Tamayo, Universidad Central de Venezuela, 2004.

———. *Habla Jesús Urdaneta Hernández, el comandante irreductible.* Caracas: Fundación Cátedra Pío Tamayo, Universidad Central de Venezuela, 2003.

Boersner, Demetrio. *Relaciones internacionales de América Latina.* Caracas: Editorial Nueva Sociedad, 2004.

Bolívar, Adriana, and Carlos Kohn (eds.). *El discurso político venezolano.* Caracas: Comisión de Estudios de Postgrado and Fondo Editorial Tropikos, Universidad Central de Venezuela, 1999.

Bolívar, Simòn. *Para nosotros la patria es América.* Caracas: Fundación Biblioteca Ayacucho, 1991.

Britto García, Luis. *La máscara del poder.* Vol. 1, *Del gendarme necesario al demócrata necesario.* Caracas: Alfadil Ediciones, 1988.

Caballero, Manuel. *La gestación de Hugo Chávez.* Madrid: Los Libros del Catarata, 2000.

———. *Revolución, reacción y falsificación.* Caracas: Alfadil Ediciones, 2002.

Cabrunas, José Ignacio, et al. "Heterodoxia y Estado, 5 respuestas," *Estado y Reforma, Revista de Ideas.* Caracas: Edición de la Comisión Presidencial para la Reforma del Estado, COPRE, 1987.

Carmona, Pedro. *Mi testimonio ante la historia.* Caracas: Editorial Actum, 2004.

Carrera Damas, Germán. *El culto a Bolívar,* 5th ed. Caracas: Alfadil Ediciones, 2003.

Castro Leiva, Luis. *De la patria boba a la teología bolivariana.* Caracas: Monte Avila Editores, 1987.

Chávez Frías, Hugo. *Un brazalete tricolor.* Valencia: Vadell Hermanos Editores, 1992.

Daniels, Elías. *Militares y democracia.* Caracas: José Agustín Catalá Editor, 1992.

Díaz Rangel, Eleazar, et al. *Chávez y los medios de comunicación social.* Caracas: Alfadil Ediciones, 2002.

Durán, Armando. *Venezuela en llamas.* Caracas: Random House Mondadori, 2004.

Francia, Néstor. *Hablan las víctimas.* Caracas: privately published, 2002.

———. *Qué piensa Chávez, aproximación a su discurso político.* Caracas: privately published, 2003.

Garrido, Alberto. *Guerrilla y conspiración militar en Venezuela.* Caracas: Fondo Editorial Nacional José Agustín Catalá, 1999.

———. *Mi amigo Chávez. Conversaciones con Norberto Ceresole.* Caracas: privately published, 2001.

———. *El otro Chávez. Testimonio de Herma Marksman.* Mérida: privately published, 2002.

———. *Testimonios de la revolución bolivariana.* Mérida: privately published, 2002.

Golpes militares en Venezuela, 1945–1992. Caracas: José Agustín Catalá Editor, 1998.

Gott, Richard. *In the Shadow of the Liberator.* London: Verso Books, 2000.

Harnecker, Marta. *Un hombre, un pueblo.* Caracas: n.p., 2002.

———. *Venezuela, militares junto al pueblo.* Madrid: El Viejo Topo, 2003.

Hernández, Carlos Raúl. *Agonía de la democracia. A dónde va Venezuela con la "revolución bolivariana."* Caracas: Editorial Panapo, 2001.

Irwin, Domingo, et al. *Militares y sociedad en Venezuela.* Caracas: Universidad Católica Andrés Bello, 2003.

Izarra, William. *En busca de la revolución.* Caracas: privately published, 2001.

Jiménez, Iván Darío. *Los golpes de estado desde Castro hasta Caldera.* Caracas: Centralca, 1996.

La Fuente, Sandra, and Alfredo Meza. *El acertijo de abril.* Caracas: Random House Mondadori, 2004.

López Martínez, Ramón. *Un seguimiento a los viajes internacionales de Hugo Chávez Frías.* Caracas: privately published, 2000.

López Maya, Margarita (coordinator). *Protesta y cultura en Venezuela: los marcos de la acción colectiva en 1999.* Buenos Aires: FLACSO, 2002.

Márquez, Patricia, and Ramón Piñango (eds.). *En esta Venezuela.* Caracas: Ediciones IESA, 2003.

Masó, Fausto. *Los amantes del tango.* Caracas: Random House Mondadori, 2004.

Mazzei, Pedro. *Sabaneta de Barinas.* Caracas: Editorial Nemesio Martínez, 1992.

Medina, Pablo. *Rebeliones.* Caracas: privately published, 1999.

Müller Rojas, Alberto. *Epoca de revolución en Venezuela.* Caracas: Solar Ediciones, 2001.

Nuez, Sebastián de la. *Marisabel, la historia te absolverá.* Caracas: Editorial Exceso, 2002.

Petkoff, Teodoro. *La Venezuela de Chávez, una segunda opinión. Un libro hablado con Ibsen Martínez y Elías Pino Iturrieta.* Caracas: Grijalbo-Mondadori, 2000.

Pineda Castellanos, Luis. *El diablo paga con traición a quien le sirve con lealtad, anécdotas de mi vida como amigo de Hugo Chávez Frías.* Mérida: Producciones Farol, C.A., 2003.

Pino Iturrieta, Elías. *El divino Bolívar, ensayo sobre una religión republicana.* Madrid: Los Libros de Catarata, 2003.

Ramírez Rojas, Kléber. *Historia documental del 4 de febrero.* Caracas: n.p., 1998.

Ramos Jiménez, Alfredo, et al. *La transición venezolana.* Mérida: Centro de Investigación de Política Comparada, Universidad de los Andes, 2002.

Rangel, Domingo Alberto. *¿Quién paga los muertos del 11 de abril?* Mérida: Mérida Editores, 2002.

Romero, Aníbal. *Decadencia y crisis de la democracia. ¿A dónde va la democracia venezolana?* Caracas: Editorial Panapo, 1999.

——, et al. *Chávez, la sociedad civil, y el estamento militar.* Caracas: Alfadil Ediciones, 2002.

Tapia, José León. *Maisanta, el último hombre a caballo,* 6th ed. Caracas: José Agustín Catalá Editor, 2000.

Ugalde, Luis, et al. *Detrás de la pobreza.* Caracas: Asociación Civil para la Promoción de Estudios Sociales, Universidad Católica Andrés Bello, 2004.

Uslar Pietri, Arturo. *Golpe y estado en Venezuela.* Bogotá: Grupo Editorial Norma, 1992.

Wilpert, Gregory. *Coup Against Chávez in Venezuela.* Caracas: Fundación por un Mundo Multipolar and Fundación Venezolana para la Justicia Global, 2003.

Zago, Angela. *La rebelión de los ángeles.* Caracas: Warp Ediciones, 1998.

Zapata, Juan Carlos. *Plomo más plomo es guerra, proceso a Chávez.* Caracas: Alfadil Ediciones, 2000.

Newspapers

El Globo (Venezuela)
El Nacional (Venezuela)
Notitarde (Venezuela)
La Prensa (Barinas, Venezuela)
La Razón (Venezuela)
Ultimas Noticias (Venezuela)
El Universal (Venezuela)
Clarín (Argentina)
La Nación (Argentina)
La Tercera (Chile)
El Espectador (Colombia)
El Tiempo (Colombia)
Granma (Cuba)
Liberazione (Italy)
La Jornada (México)
El Universal (México)
The Miami Herald (USA)
The New York Times (USA)
The Washington Post (USA)

Magazines

Comunicación (Venezuela)
Discurso y Sociedad (Venezuela)
Estampas (Venezuela)
Exceso (Venezuela)
Primicia (Venezuela)

Semanario Quinto Día (Venezuela)
Qué Pasa (Chile)
Gatopardo (Colombia)
Semana (Colombia)
Cambio (México)
Caretas (Perú)
Foreign Affairs (USA)
The New Yorker (USA)

Electronic References

Bolivarian News Agency (ABN; formerly Venpres), www.abn.info.ve/index.php
Central Bank of Venezuela, www.bcv.org.ve
CNN, www.cnnenespanol.com
Dictionary of the History of Venezuela of the Fundación Polar, www.fpolar.org.ve
Energy Information Administration of the Department of Energy, U.S.A., www.eia
  .doe.gov
Latin Reporters, www.latinreporters.com
Ministry of Communication and Information, www.minci.gov.ve
National Electoral Council of Venezuela, www.cne.gov.ve
National Statistics Institute, www.ine.gov.ve
Program for Education–Action in Human Rights, www.derechos.org.ve
Rebelión, www.rebelion.org
Venezuela Analítica, www.analitica.com

CRISTINA MARCANO is a journalist with extensive experience in the Venezuelan media. She has worked as the chief of international information and the political subeditor for the newspaper *El Nacional* in Caracas. She currently works as a correspondent for the Mexican newspaper *Reforma* and as an independent collaborator for *El Nacional*.

ALBERTO BARRERA TYSZKA is a widely read Sunday editorial columnist for *El Nacional*. In 2006 he won the prestigious Herralde literary prize for his novel *La Enfermedad*. He is the author of several books, including the novel *También el corazón es un descuido*. He regularly publishes in *Letras Libres*. Barrera is also a scriptwriter for television soap operas, as well as a professor at the Universidad Central de Venezuela.

MOISÉS NAÍM is a former minister for trade and industry for Venezuela and is currently the editor in chief of *Foreign Policy* magazine, one of the world's leading publications on international politics and economics and winner of the 2003 National Magazine Award for general excellence. He has written extensively on international political economy, economic development, world politics, and globalization's unintended consequences. His introduction to *Hugo Chávez* will contextualize this biography for American audiences.

This book was set in Dante, a typeface designed by Giovanni Mardersteig (1892–1977). Conceived as a private type for the Officina Bodoni in Verona, Italy, Dante was originally cut only for hand composition by Charles Malin, the famous Parisian punch cutter, between 1946 and 1952. Its first use was in an edition of Boccaccio's *Trattatello in laude di Dante* that appeared in 1954. The Monotype Corporation's version of Dante followed in 1957. Though modeled on the Aldine type used for Pietro Cardinal Bembo's treatise *De Aetna* in 1495, Dante is a thoroughly modern interpretation of that venerable face.